JON FRANKLIN is the author of *Shocktrauma*, among other books. He is an associate professor of journalism at the University of Maryland and was previously a writer for the Baltimore *Evening Sun*. Mr. Franklin's awards include the James T. Grady Medal (1975) and the Helen Carringer Award (1984). He is the only writer in history to win two first-in-category Pulitzer Prizes: in 1979 he received the first Pulitzer ever given for feature writing, and in 1985 he won the inaugural Pulitzer for explanatory journalism. Jon Franklin lives in Glen Burnie, Maryland.

D1264115

WRITING FOR STORY

*Craft Secrets of
Dramatic Nonfiction
by a Two-Time
Pulitzer Prize Winner*

JON FRANKLIN

A MENTOR BOOK

NEW AMERICAN LIBRARY

NAL BOOKS ARE AVAILABLE AT QUANTITY DISCOUNTS WHEN USED
TO PROMOTE PRODUCTS OR SERVICES. FOR INFORMATION PLEASE
WRITE TO PREMIUM MARKETING DIVISION, NEW AMERICAN
LIBRARY, 1633 BROADWAY, NEW YORK, NEW YORK 10019.

This is an authorized reprint of a hardcover edition
published by Atheneum Publishers.

ACKNOWLEDGMENTS

YA GOT TROUBLE from "The Music Man"
by Meredith Willson
© 1957, 1958 FRANK MUSIC CORP. and
THE ESTATE OF MEREDITH WILLSON
© Renewed 1985, 1986 FRANK MUSIC CORP. and
THE ESTATE OF MEREDITH WILLSON
International Copyright Secured
All Rights Reserved   Used by Permission

Library of Congress Catalog Card Number: 86–063378

SIGNET, SIGNET CLASSIC, MENTOR, ONYX, PLUME, MERIDIAN
and NAL BOOKS are published *in the United States* by NAL PENGUIN INC.,
1633 Broadway, New York, New York 10019,
in Canada by The New American Library of Canada Limited,
81 Mack Avenue, Scarborough, Ontario M1L 1M8

First Mentor Printing, May, 1987

1 2 3 4 5 6 7 8 9

PRINTED IN THE UNITED STATES OF AMERICA

Acknowledgments

AN AUTHOR WHO writes a book such as this, drawing in the process on a lifetime of training and experience, owes a debt of gratitude to every person who has significantly influenced his life, his viewpoint, and his accumulation of skills and his professional growth.

My abiding love for words, and my respect for their power, came via the osmosis of childhood from my mother. Teachers played a big role, and particularly one principal in Lebanon, Missouri. So did a policeman in Sante Fe, New Mexico. So did hundreds of others who went before me, and never heard of me, but nonetheless shaped my mind: Asimov, Balzac, Hemingway, Salinger, Steinbeck, Wolfe . . . the list goes on and on and on.

These people all had an impact. But two times in my life, as I stood at crossroads and contemplated going in the wrong direction, I was saved from myself by men who took the time to care. They are the ones to whom this book is dedicated; my sorrow is that neither lived to read it.

The first was my father, Benjamin Franklin.

The time was 1957 and I was fourteen. As a gringo in a predominantly Mexican-American school in Santa Fe, New Mexico, I had become the victim of the kind of racial bullying and intimidation that, elsewhere, was the fate of nonwhites. We responded the same way minority adolescents always do, banding together in gangs, first for protection and then for revenge, which we carried out with switchblades, bicycle chains, and zip guns. Pretty soon, I was the ringleader of the whites.

My involvement came to my father's attention one night when I came home somewhat worse for wear after a dispute with another gang over something important I don't recall. I had expected my dad to be mad, and had steeled myself against his anger. Instead he seemed interested, curious, and concerned. He introduced me to the healing balm of a steak over a black eye, cleaned my scalp wounds, and satisfied himself that my right hand—which had been holding the zip gun when it blew up—still had all its fingers.

As he bandaged me up he encouraged me to talk, and he listened patiently and sympathetically as I explained my actions with words like "right" and "justice" and "equality" and "truth." Pretty soon I was sobbing out my feelings of helpless frustration and anger at the discrimination I had suffered.

The discrimination was real enough, of course, and I was too young, too innocent, too emotionally involved to draw perspective from the fact that in most places it was the whites who discriminated against the Mexicans. So my father, with a cagy self-restraint I would come to appreciate only when I became a father myself, didn't try to talk logic to me. Instead he agreed with me. Yeah. Damned right! The world was a rotten place, and it ought to be changed. And I might as well be the one who changed it—except that, being fourteen, I didn't know how.

Oh yeah? I didn't? Man, if that pipe gun had worked . . .

Nah, my father said. That was the wrong way—not because it was illegal, mind you, but because it didn't work. It would be a little difficult, even for me, to kill all the Mexicans in Santa Fe. Switchblades and zip guns were the tools of adolescents. True revolutionaries, the ones who actually DID change the world, used different instruments. They used words, typewriters, and paper.

I was, as you might imagine, dubious. But all night long we talked, and talked, and talked, and talked, and somehow he worked his magic on me. By dawn I had become a real, grown-up revolutionary, and later we went out together and he bought me a beat-up Underwood.

Rather quickly I drifted away from the gang. One of my best friends was later killed in a knife fight, and another went to jail for murder. But I wasn't at those rumbles, or any others. I was at home, with the Underwood, doing something More Important.

The stuff I wrote, of course, was adolescent drivel. My father could turn me in the direction of words, but as an electrician, he couldn't help me learn to use them. Instead, he talked about art. So for the next eight years, first as a high school student and then as a U.S. Navy journalist, I kept trying, and trying, and trying—and failing, and failing, and failing.

But in the early 1960s, shortly after my father's death, the Navy sent me to Washington, D.C., and into the clutches of one G. Vern Blasdell.

Vern, the news editor of *All Hands* magazine, was an expert, acerbic and ancient (perhaps fifty) old man with a bad stomach and a mobile face capable of showing ten thousand different grades of disgust. He told people he had narcolepsy, but the truth was he was so bored with his job he had great difficulty staying awake. To keep his circulation going he made a hobby of targeting the worst, most illiterate writer on his staff—and proving that he, G. Vern

Blasdell, could teach him how to write. So as soon as he saw my first piece of copy I became Vern's protégé.

His boredom was matched only by my desperation to learn, and for five years I suffered under him. I'd put my copy into his basket and watch out of the corner of my eye until he picked it up. He'd sometimes get to the second page before he blanched. Sometimes he'd cover his face with his hands and seem about to cry. Other times he'd turn around in his swivel chair to stare disgustedly out of his picture window at the Pentagon below. Sometimes he'd just go to sleep. I, of course, would die a thousand deaths.

Eventually he'd pull himself together, look at me sternly, and point his finger at the straight chair he kept beside his desk. I'd slink over to it and sit, bottom on the edge of the chair, while he proceeded to rip my copy to shreds. When he was done with me I'd crawl back to my typewriter and do it over again, and again, and again, until he pronounced it readable. Thus I learned to write without inspiration or ego, relying solely upon knowledge, and in the process became a professional.

Five years at the mercy of Vern left me with an ulcer, a discipline, a craft, and a love for the old man that was equal to what I once felt for my father. When the day finally came that he called me over and told me he could teach me no more, I was as sad as I was the day he died a decade later.

Since then there have been others who taught me, befriended me, defended me, and helped me along. I think, for instance, of Dr. E. Earl Newsom, the University of Maryland professor who got me a scholarship when it looked like I was going to go broke and have to drop out of college. I think of Kelly Gilbert, another *All Hands* veteran, who introduced me to Ernie Imhoff, then the city editor of the *Evening Sun*—and of Ernie himself, who bent the rules to hire me right out of college.

I think of Alan Doelp, my writing buddy and co-conspirator, who kept telling me I was good when I was beginning to have serious doubts. I think of George Rodgers, now assistant managing editor of the *Evening Sun*, who encouraged me and argued my case when I ran rough-shod over the style book, and who finally became my principal editor. I think of Jack Lemmon, my managing editor, who had the confidence to give me something newspaper reporters rarely got—the freedom to write what-ever I pleased.

The debt I owe these people, and particularly my father and Vern, could only be repaid by passing along my skills to the next generation. That meant teaching, and eventu-ally Dr. Irene Shipman, chairman of the Department of Speech and Mass Communications at Towson State Uni-versity, gave me my chance. She hired me as a part-time instructor—and then stood behind me when I flunked half of my first class. Finally, after several years teaching part-time at Towson and then at the University of Mary-land in Baltimore County, Reese Cleghorn, dean of the University of Maryland College of Journalism, appointed me to a full-time associate professorship.

The narrative you are about to read evolved over the years as part of my teaching strategy. It was first a sylla-bus, and later a set of handouts and lectures. As time passed I began to receive requests for the material, and particularly for the annotated versions of ''Mrs. Kelly's Monster,'' and a number of teachers urged me to combine the material into a book. The first to do so was Jenny Killgallon, of the Baltimore County School System; a later and most persuasive advocate was Jo Elaine Harris, who teaches high school English in my home town of Enid, Oklahoma. My closest friends took up the call.

But writing about writing is close combat of the scariest sort, and there were many false starts. It was these friends, then, who kept my nose to the grindstone.

One of the worst naggers was Alan Doelp, whom I mentioned earlier. Another was Lynn Scheidhauer, who refuses to marry me on the grounds that she'd rather we remained in love. Finally there was my eldest daughter, Teresa, who fell into the ways of her father and now writes for the *Laurel Leader*. All three read my copy and made suggestions—virtually all of which were followed. So, with their help, the manuscript was completed.

But a manuscript is one thing and a book another. To make the transition required the work and faith of my indomitable agent, Dominick Abel, and the insight of my editor at Atheneum, Trish Lande. Her astute suggestions made this book a far better one than it would otherwise have been. Finally the book was befriended by Frank Kurtz, Patricia McEldon, and Barbara Campo, fine copy editors whose sharp eyes saved me from tripping over my own words more times than I am about to admit.

Without the help and friendship of these people, this book would never have been. I, as well as anyone who gains from the words herein, owe them a debt of gratitude.

Jon Franklin
BALTIMORE, 1985

Contents

Preface

As a young man desperately committed to literature, I restlessly searched my local libraries for a book that would reveal to me The Secret of Writing.

I looked especially hard for books by bona fide professional writers. Whenever I found one I always rushed right home with it and, with flushed face and pounding heart, read it through from cover to cover.

I loved such books. I was always delighted with the easy, swaggering way the writer took me into his confidence. I identified with him as he described his early rejection slips (Oh, I knew, I *knew*!), and chuckled as he described his agonies over writer's block and his exploits in the dark and dangerous jungle of publishing. Ah, yes, it is a writer's lot to suffer.

Yet as sincerely as I appreciated the writers who shared

their war stories with me, I somehow always reached the end of the book before they got around to revealing The Secret.

The really unnerving part was that the writes would often make a point of saying that while writing was a craft, it was also an art—and ultimately one either had it (whatever "it" was) or one didn't. The clear implication was that if you didn't understand what they were driving at, you didn't have it. By that measure, I sure didn't.

But that answer was unacceptable, so I kept looking. There had to be a Secret. There just had to be.

I swore then that if I ever found that Secret, if I ever "made it" as a writer, I would do better by my artistic heirs. I would lay out the craft, or as much of it as I could fathom, in a book that would dispense with mystique and focus in a systematic way on the laws of the literary universe.

Many years have passed since then, and in the interim I have indeed become a successful writer. I have books on my shelf, a gold medal on my dresser, two Pulitzers on my wall, and publishers' money in my bank account. But I still don't have "it."

"It," as I now understand, is simply a conglomeration of skills and laws that the writer follows but has never examined in any detail. Few writers are very analytical; most do what they do out of instinct and because it works, after a fashion at least, for them. If in their how-to-write books they don't explicitly address such issues as "focus" and the relativity of levels it's because while they obey the literary laws of the road, they haven't the faintest idea why those laws are there.

A gut writer may know that when his mind locks up, a glass of warm milk followed by two hours of vigorous exercise will get him back on track, but he doesn't know what writer's block is and he can't tell you what will work for you.

I operate differently. Not having "it," life has forced me to be analytical—I am what some call a "conscious" writer. Instead of instinct I have learned to rely on my knowledge of the patterns that exist, in one variation or another, in all effective stories.

Obviously, those patterns aren't simple. But neither are they too complex for the serious beginner to comprehend. For one thing there are principles, specific principles arranged in a clear heirarchy, to cling to. They can be taught, and they can be learned. And if you will follow me to the end of the yellow brick road, you will find that there is, indeed, a Secret.

The strategy in the coming chapters is to concentrate on one particular genre of modern writing, the nonfiction short story. I chose it because I believe it to represent the revival, in new form, of the old fiction short story—the traditional training ground for writers.

I've arranged the chapters to make your mind flow from the broadest aspects of story to the narrowest ones. The first chapter begins, for instance, with a discussion of the true story and its place in modern literature. That is followed by two examples of such stories. I believe they will entertain you and impress you with the power and creativity inherent in the form.

Those stories will also prepare you for the following chapter, which concentrates on how to find and recognize the stories around you.

With that chapter I adopt a step-by-step, cookbook approach to the subject. My intent is that you should eventually try to follow those steps as you ferret out and compose a true story of your own. But don't try it the first time through.

Instead, read the whole book from beginning to end as though it were a novel, because like a novel, it goes someplace. Notice only what interests you most, without attempting to penetrate below the surface. Enjoy it. If you love language and story, you won't be bored.

If you don't understand something, muddle through and go on. Don't feel stupid; it'll make sense later. The true meaning of structure won't crystallize until the final chapter, and only then will you be in a position to begin to appreciate its sweeping implications.

When you are finished with the initial reading you should have gained a perspective, an attitude, that will allow you to understand much more on your next read-through.

The second time through, read more slowly and look for subtleties. Notice what I've left out; what I dismiss by omission is often as important as what I emphasize by inclusion. One of the key things I'm trying to do is give you a sense of proportion, of what's critical and what's peripheral.

Try, as you reread, to apply the principles of story to your own experiences. Look at the people around you, and try to discern the stories in their lives. Try to understand those people in terms of the ancient dramatic form you will have learned.

Finally, choose a story and, beginning with Chapter 4, develop it as you read the "cookbook" chapters. Choose a story you don't much care about—on your first attempt, the odds are heavily against you.

If your first story doesn't turn out well, don't try to fix it. Throw it away, choose another, reread the pertinent chapters, and repeat the process. Stories are nothing. The process is everything.

How many attempts it takes to finally write a powerful story depends on two factors: your ability, and the difficulty of the stories you choose. Neither reflects your own worth. Your current ability is a starting point only; what counts isn't where you begin but where you finish.

If it's in your nature to choose complex stories, that speaks well of the potential depth of your insight. On the other hand, it will take you longer to master the form and you will succeed only if you have great patience.

If you don't yet have the confidence that underlies patience, then trim back on the magnitude of your ambition, at least until you learn the rudiments of craft. Choose simpler stories. Then, having gained confidence in your ability to control the process, you can attack more complicated projects.

Above all, be patient with yourself. When you get confused, don't panic. Professional writers are often confused. It goes with the territory.

It has taken me three long, painful, and often impoverished decades to develop the coherent approach to structure that is my definition of professionalism. I hope with this book to ease your labors and shorten your apprenticeship, but I can't make it easy. Be prepared to think, to wonder, to ponder, to experiment—to fail, to wallow in confusion, and to reread. This book is designed so that with each rereading you will discover new perspectives that escaped you before.

And be prepared, as well, to stop and smell the roses along the way. The craftsmanship of the writer is no less beautiful than that of the cabinetmaker or the builder of temples or of fine violins.

For me as for most of my colleagues, craftsmanship began as a means to an end. It was the vehicle with which I would express my feelings and make for myself a place in the world. But in the process of paying my dues, of working and learning, it metamorphosed into something else, into a compulsion, into an addiction, into a love. And it has rewarded me beyond my wildest hopes.

I owe it something. With this volume, I begin my repayment.

I

The New School for Writers

SAMUEL LANGHORNE CLEMENS, Jack London, F. Scott Fitzgerald, Ernest Hemingway, John Steinbeck and dozens of others whose flames burn only slightly less luminously in the history of literature had one thing in common: They learned their craft by writing short stories. Only when they had mastered that form did they undertake the long trek of the novel. The short story, in its heyday, was the universal school for writers.

It was an elegant form, and a sure one. The short story was constructed along the same classic lines that had characterized drama since the day of Shakespeare and before: There was a complication, a body of story (the development), and a resolution.

The shortness of the short story made it the most technically demanding form in all of literature. With only a few words the writer had to create a narrative hook to catch the reader's attention and thrust him full tilt into the story. There was no space for leisurely character sketches; the protagonist had to emerge from his own actions, actions that defined him while at the same time propelling him into some complicating situation that created tension and carried the reader into the story.

The plot, in its development, twisted and turned in strict accordance with the changing viewpoint of the character and the fluid logic of his situation. In every sentence the narrative had to plunge ahead, character and situation feeding back on one another in a fiendishly subtle, multilevel interaction that led inexorably to a critical insight in which the character, changed now by his experience, glimpsed the solution and moved to seize it. When he did, the story ended in a flash of clarity that left even the reader somehow . . . different.

It was a form that demanded the utmost of the writer, both technically and artistically. Yet the shortness of the short story—the same thing that made it so difficult—was also its saving grace. That kept it from being overwhelming despite its complexity.

The outline of a book, for instance, can be kept in one's mind only with difficulty, but the plot of a short story can be remembered easily—and tinkered with in one's head on the way to work. The shortness of the form helped the young writer learn to see his story as an integrated whole.

Also, because the short story involved a relatively minor expenditure of effort, the beginner had the freedom to fail. Though it was always heartbreaking to lose a brainchild, the young writer who got bogged down in a poorly conceived short story could throw it away and, after some initial anguish, forget about it.

So it was that the short story served as the great eliminator of mediocre talent, the test of a young writer's ambition, the measure of his courage to try and fail and try and fail and somehow try again.

The writer grew stronger with every story; like his protagonists, he learned something with every sentence.

He grew steadily more mature, strengthening his art and craft, perfecting the techniques and tempering the insight that he hoped and prayed would one day carry him into the highest reaches of literature.

This testing, this practicing, this experimenting, equipped the young Hemingway and the young Steinbeck for ever-larger literary tasks. Eventually the writer who stuck with it was able to graduate with reasonable safety to the world of books, where failure of a single project is a disaster that wipes out years of work and can lead to bankruptcy and/or divorce.

For all these reasons and more, the short story was the greatest training ground that literature has ever known. For a hundred years it provided both a livelihood and a classroom for almost every major American writer.

Then, after the Second World War, society changed and the market for short stories waned. *Collier's* died, as did *The Saturday Evening Post*. In a mere instant, as history is reckoned, the audience for quality short fiction all but vanished; the demand, instead, was for nonfiction and journalism.

Unfortunately, nonfiction wasn't as good a training ground as the short story had been. Nonfiction often emphasized subject over form and rewarded reporting skills at the expense of writing technique; the writer who chose that route spent his apprenticeship instructing his readers on the finer points of tuning pianos or applying makeup. In the process he got published, but he learned few if any dramatic skills.

Then, in the '60s, Truman Capote, a novelist, short-story writer, and playwright, performed a literary experiment that opened the way for a new kind of literature. Capote recognized and accepted the public's growing interest in nonfiction but objected to the genre's traditionally dry style. What would happen, he asked, if a true story were told in the form of a novel?

The result was the publication in 1965 of *In Cold Blood*, a meticulously researched, factual account of the rampage and ultimate execution of two sociopathic murderers. The book melded the accuracy of nonfiction with the dramatic force of fiction, and immediately became a best-seller.

The success of *In Cold Blood* and other such books that came later ushered in the new genre of nonfiction drama, but it was the next generation of writers, working on the foggy frontier between journalism and literature, that rejuvenated the short-story form.

At this juncture, history mingles with my own personal experience: That was my generation.

A few of us doggedly wrote short stories despite the fact that they were almost impossible to sell—and payment, when they *were* sold, was made as often as not in free copies of the publication. But, like most young writers, I couldn't afford that. I had a wife and children to support.

So like many other would-be fiction writers I ended up on a newspaper, hoping blindly that somehow I could translate the journalistic experience into a literary career. That meant, I assumed, fiction.

I wrote a novel. I sent it to New York. New York sent it back. I sent it to another publisher, and in the fullness of time it came back again. I sent it out again. It came back again. And so it went. In the meantime I wrote another; it escaped certain rejection because I didn't submit it. It just wasn't good enough, and I knew it.

The reason it wasn't good enough wasn't that I was incapable . . . at least, that's the attitude I tried to keep fixed in my mind. The reason I couldn't sell my novels was simply that I had no short-story experience.

I needed to learn dramatic skills and earn a living at the same time. But how?

By the mid-1970s, to abbreviate a long and agonizing story, I had solidified my position on my newspaper and honed my reporting skills to the point where my editors trusted me to experiment. Increasingly, following Capote's example, I began to incorporate fiction techniques into my news stories. I started asking different questions, so that my notebook would contain the facts I'd need later for characterization. I started looking more closely at human motivation. Hunched over a typewriter, I adapted stream-of-consciousness transition technique to nonfiction form.

My first breakthrough came in 1975, when a series of articles about Maryland geology won the James P. Grady medal, an award given by the American Chemical Society— one that in previous years had gone to Isaac Asimov and Loren Eiseley. This convinced me I was on the right track, somehow, and further solidified my position at the newspaper.

I went back and read how-to-write books from the '30s and '40s, and discovered complication-resolution form— the essential form of the short story of old. I vowed to use that form to give shape to my newspaper stories. Within two years I was writing true short stories, complete with complications and resolutions—stories, as one puzzled newspaper editor put it, with "beginnings, middles, and ends."

In the beginning the stories were simple and hackneyed. One of them, I remember, was based on the ancient "day with a dogcatcher" theme.

I chose to do such lackluster stories because I was acutely aware of my weaknesses, and was afraid to try anything more complex. My assumption was that if I kept my sights relatively low, I was more apt to pull off what I attempted. That would increase the likelihood of my stories' getting printed . . . and getting printed was my object. I didn't care much, in those days, whether my stories said anything or not. All I cared about was technique. Looking back, I can see this was my apprenticeship.

In time, I felt confident enough to try more complex stories. I did a short story about a retarded man who had mistaken pain for love—in the course of the story he learned, with the help of a kind nurse, that love was something quite different.

Another story, about a road crew building a median wall in the center of a busy highway, gave me my first experience with the overt use of stream-of-consciousness journalism.

The approach wasn't exactly new. I know for a fact that Hemingway did at least one such story, and Ernie Pyle did many. But in those days it was a secondary form; it did well enough, but there was no crying literary need for it. Now, there was.

By late 1978, having grown comfortable with the new nonfiction-short-story form, I felt confident enough to begin telling stories with real dramatic potential. One of the first (which you will read in the next chapter) involved a brain surgeon and a woman with a blood-vessel malformation in her brain. The next year this story won the first Pulitzer ever given in the feature-writing category.

As the establishment of a new Pulitzer category implies, I wasn't the only writer doing this kind of work. By the 1970s many writers of my generation had found themselves, as I had, compelled to go into journalism. There they had been faced with the same questions that had confronted me, and, each in his own way, many had arrived at similar conclusions. We didn't know what we had in common, though, and our efforts proceeded in the privacy that goes hand in hand with obscurity.

But by about 1980 we were beginning to hear about one another, and our stories were getting published in national magazines—the two of mine that you will read in coming chapters were eventually reprinted in *Reader's Digest*. In the years since 1979, virtually every Pulitzer prize for feature writing has gone to a story that used one version or another of the new nonfiction-short-story form.

Today such stories, varying greatly in quality and treating a wide range of human subjects, are appearing in almost every type of publication from weekly newspapers to national magazines.

The popularity of the new technique lies in the fact that it combines the appeal, excitement, and reading ease of fiction with the specific information content of nonfiction. In so doing, it recaptures a widely read, intelligent audience. Because the market is so large, it is available to the young writer seeking an arena in which to develop and test his dramatic writing skills.

In my mind, and in the minds of many other editors and writers, the advent of the nonfiction short story as a viable commercial form is destined to heal the wound inflicted by the demise of the short-fiction market.

The principal difference between the short story of old and the nonfiction short story of today is that in its modern form, the story is true. This means the young writer must learn basic journalistic techniques, such as interviewing and researching, in addition to the traditional ones. But, in writing terms, the two forms are identical.

Best of all, the new form, once mastered, translates easily into both fiction and nonfiction novels. Within five years of my brain-surgery story I had published two nonfiction novels and one book of nonfiction short stories.

For all of these reasons and more, the advent of the nonfiction short story is a profoundly important event in the history of modern literature. After three bitter and anguished decades, there is once again a suitable training ground for young writers of quality and integrity.

Perhaps some such writers will find in these pages the basic perception they need to write and publish nonfiction short stories. Perhaps a few of those will publish many.

Perhaps they will doggedly hone the skills discussed here, improving them with practice, building on them with experience, adapting them as their styles mature and their themes gain power. Perhaps they will serve out their apprenticeships and finally rise on the wings of the written word to help rejuvenate the spirit of American literature.

It is in this fond hope that I offer two nonfiction short stories and, following them, a detailed analysis of the form.

II

Mrs. Kelly's Monster

(Originally published in *The Evening Sun*
[Baltimore], December 1978; received the first
Pulitzer prize in feature writing, May 1979;
condensed in *Reader's Digest*, December 1983.
Used by permission of the A. S. Abell
Company.)

IN THE COLD HOURS of a winter morning Dr. Thomas Barbee Ducker, chief brain surgeon at the University of Maryland Hospital, rises before dawn. His wife serves him waffles but no coffee. Coffee makes his hands shake.

In downtown Baltimore, on the 12th floor of University Hospital, Edna Kelly's husband tells her goodbye. For 57 years Mrs. Kelly shared her skull with the monster: No more. Today she is frightened but determined.

It is 6:30 a.m.

"I'm not afraid to die," she said as this day approached. "I've lost part of my eyesight. I've gone through all the hemorrhages. A couple of years ago I lost my sense of smell, my taste. I started having seizures. I smell a strange odor and then I start strangling. It started affecting my legs, and I'm partially paralyzed.

"Three years ago a doctor told me all I had to look

forward to was blindness, paralysis and a remote chance of death. Now I have aneurysms; this monster is causing that. I'm scared to death . . . but there isn't a day that goes by that I'm not in pain, and I'm tired of it. I can't bear the pain. I wouldn't want to live like this much longer."

As Dr. Ducker leaves for work, Mrs. Ducker hands him a paper bag containing a peanut butter sandwich, a banana and two fig newtons.

Downtown, in Mrs. Kelly's brain, a sedative takes effect.

Mrs. Kelly was born with a tangled knot of abnormal blood vessels in the back of her brain. The malformation began small, but in time the vessels ballooned inside the confines of the skull, crowding the healthy brain tissue.

Finally, in 1942, the malformation announced its presence when one of the abnormal arteries, stretched beyond capacity, burst. Mrs. Kelly grabbed her head and collapsed. After that the agony never stopped.

Mrs. Kelly, at the time of her first intracranial bleed, was carrying her second child. Despite the pain, she raised her children and cared for her husband. The malformation continued to grow.

She began calling it "the monster."

Now, at 7:15 a.m. in operating room eleven, a technician checks the brain surgery microscope and the circulating nurse lays out bandages and instruments. Mrs. Kelly lies still on a stainless steel table.

A small sensor has been threaded through her veins and now hangs in the antechamber of her heart. The anesthesiologist connects the sensor to a 7-foot-high bank of electronic instruments. Oscilloscope waveforms begin to build and break. Dials swing. Lights flash. With each heartbeat a loud speaker produces an audible popping sound. The steady pop, pop, popping isn't loud, but it dominates the operating room.

Dr. Ducker enters the O.R. and pauses before the x-ray films that hang on a lighted panel. He carried those brain images to Europe, Canada and Florida in search of advice, and he knows them by heart. Still, he studies them again, eyes focused on the two fragile aneurysms that swell above the major arteries. Either may burst on contact.

The one directly behind Mrs. Kelly's eyes is the most likely to burst, but also the easiest to reach. That's first.

The surgeon-in-training who will assist Dr. Ducker places Mrs. Kelly's head in a clamp and shaves her hair. Dr. Ducker checks to make certain the three steel pins of the vice have pierced the skin and press directly against Mrs. Kelly's skull. "We can't have a millimeter slip," he says.

Mrs. Kelly, except for a six-inch crescent of scalp, is draped with green sheets. A rubber-gloved palm goes out and Doris Schwabland, the scrub nurse, lays a scalpel in it. Hemostats snap over the arteries of the scalp. Blood spatters onto Dr. Ducker's sterile paper booties.

It is 8:25 a.m. The heartbeat goes pop, pop, pop, 70 beats a minute, steady.

Today Dr. Ducker intends to remove the two aneurysms, which comprise the most immediate threat to Mrs. Kelly's life. Later, he will move directly on the monster.

It's a risky operation, designed to take him to the hazardous frontiers of neurosurgery. Several experts told him he shouldn't do it at all, that he should let Mrs. Kelly die. But the consensus was that he had no choice. The choice was Mrs. Kelly's.

"There's one chance out of three that we'll end up with a hell of a mess or a dead patient," Dr. Ducker says. "I reviewed it in my own heart and with other people, and I thought about the patient. You weigh what happens if you do it against what happens if you don't do it. I convinced myself it should be done."

Mrs. Kelly said yes. Now Dr. Ducker pulls back Mrs. Kelly's scalp to reveal the dull ivory of living bone. The chatter of the half-inch drill fills the room, drowning the rhythmic pop, pop, pop of the heart monitor. It is 9 o'clock when Dr. Ducker hands the two-by-four-inch triangle of skull to the scrub nurse.

The tough, rubbery covering of the brain is cut free, revealing the soft gray convolutions of the forebrain.

"There it is," says the circulating nurse in a hushed voice. "That's what keeps you working."

It is 9:20.

Eventually Dr. Ducker steps back, holding his gloved hands high to avoid contamination. While others move the microscope into place over the glistening brain the neuro-surgeon communes once more with the x-ray films. The heart beats strong, 70 beats a minute, 70 beats a minute. "Were going to have a hard time today," the surgeon says to the x-rays.

Dr. Ducker presses his face against the microscope. His hands go out for an electrified, tweezer-like instrument. The assistant moves in close, taking his position above the secondary eyepieces.

Dr. Ducker's view is shared by a video camera. Across the room a color television crackles, displaying a highly-magnified landscape of the brain. The polished tips of the tweezers move into view.

It is Dr. Ducker's intent to place tiny, spring-loaded alligator clips across the base of each aneurysm. But first he must navigate a tortured path from his incision, above Mrs. Kelly's right eye, to the deeply-buried Circle of Willis.

The journey will be immense. Under magnification, the landscape of the mind expands to the size of a room. Dr. Ducker's tiny, blunt-tipped instrument travels in millimeter leaps.

His strategy is to push between the forebrain, where conscious thought occurs, and the thumblike projection of the brain, called the temporal lobe, that extends beneath the temples.

Carefully, Dr. Ducker pulls these two structures apart to form a deep channel. The journey begins at the bottom of this crevasse. The time is 9:36 a.m.

The gray convolutions of the brain, wet with secretions, sparkle beneath the powerful operating theater spotlights. The microscopic landscape heaves and subsides in time to the pop, pop, pop of the heart monitor.

Gently, gently, the blunt probe teases apart the minute structures of gray matter, spreading a tiny tunnel, millimeter by gentle millimeter, into the glistening gray.

"We're having trouble just getting in," Dr. Ducker tells the operating room team.

As the neurosurgeon works, he refers to Mrs. Kelly's monster as "the AVM," or arterio-venous malformation. Normally, he says, arteries force high-pressure blood into muscle or organ tissue. After the living cells suck out the oxygen and nourishment the blood drains into low-pressure veins, which carry it back to the heart and lungs.

But in the back of Mrs. Kelly's brain one set of arteries pumps directly into veins, bypassing the tissue. The unnatural junction was not designed for such a rapid flow of blood and in 57 years is slowly swelled to the size of a fist. Periodically it leaked drops of blood and torrents of agony. Now the structures of the brain are welded together by scar tissue and, to make his tunnel, Dr. Ducker must tease them apart again. But the brain is delicate.

The screen of the television monitor fills with red.

Dr. Ducker responds quickly, snatching the broken end of the tiny artery with the tweezers. There is an electrical bzzzzzt as he burns the bleeder closed. Progress stops while the blood is suctioned out.

"It's nothing to worry about," he says. "It's not much, but when you're looking at one square centimeter, two ounces is a damned lake."

Carefully, gently, Dr. Ducker continues to make his way into the brain. Far down the tiny tunnel the white trunk of the optic nerve can be seen. It is 9:54.

Slowly, using the optic nerve as a guidepost, Dr. Ducker probes deeper and deeper into the gray. The heart monitor continues to pop, pop, pop, 70 beats a minute, 70 beats a minute.

The neurosurgeon guides the tweezers directly to the pulsing carotid artery, one of the three main blood channels into the brain. The carotid twists and dances to the electronic pop, pop popping. Gently, ever gently, nudging aside the scarred brain tissue, Dr. Ducker moves along the carotid toward the Circle of Willis, near the floor of the skull.

This loop of vessels is the staging area from which blood is distributed throughout the brain. Three major arteries feed it from below, one in the rear and the two carotids in the front.

The first aneurysm lies ahead, still buried in gray matter, where the carotid meets the Circle. The second aneurysm is deeper yet in the brain, where the hindmost artery rises along the spine and joins the circle.

Eyes pressed against the microscope, Dr. Ducker makes his tedious way along the carotid.

"She's so scarred I can't identify anything," he complains through the mask.

It is 10:01 a.m. The heart monitor pop, pop, pops with reassuring regularity.

The probing tweezers are gentle, firm, deliberate, probing, probing, probing, slower than the hands of the clock. Repeatedly, vessels bleed and Dr. Ducker cauterizes them. The blood loss is mounting, and now the anesthesiologist hangs a transfusion bag above Mrs. Kelly's shrouded form.

Ten minutes pass. Twenty. Blood flows, tbe tweezers buzz, the suction hose hisses. The tunnel is small, almost filled by the shank of the instrument.

The aneurysm finally appears at the end of the tunnel, throbbing, visibly thin, a lumpy, overstretched bag, the color of rich cream, swelling out from the once-strong arterial wall, a tire about to blow out, a balloon ready to burst, a time-bomb the size of a pea.

The aneurysm isn't the monster itself, only the work of the monster, which, growing malevolently, has disrupted the pressures and weakened arterial walls throughout the brain. But the monster itself, the x-rays say, lies far away.

The probe nudges the aneurysm, hesitantly, gently.

"Sometimes you touch one," a nurse says, "and blooey, the wolf's at the door."

Patiently, Dr. Ducker separates the aneurysm from the surrounding brain tissue. The tension is electric.

No surgeon would dare go after the monster itself until this swelling killer is defused.

Now.

A nurse hands Dr. Ducker a long, delicate pair of pliers. A little stainless steel clip, its jaws open wide, is positioned on the pliers' end. Presently the magnified clip moves into the field of view, light glinting from its polished surface.

It is 10:40.

For eleven minutes Dr. Ducker repeatedly attempts to work the clip over the neck of the balloon, but the device is too small. He calls for one with longer jaws. Soon that clip moves into the microscopic tunnel. With infinite slowness, Dr. Ducker maneuvers it over the neck of the aneurysm.

Then, in an instant, the jaws close and the balloon collapses.

"That's clipped," Dr. Ducker calls out. Smile wrinkles appear above his mask. The heart monitor goes pop, pop, pop, steady. It is 10:58.

Dr. Ducker now begins following the Circle of Willis back into the brain, toward the second, and more difficult, aneurysm that swells at the very rear of the Circle, tight against the most sensitive and primitive structure in the head, the brainstem. The brainstem controls vital processes, including breathing and heartbeat.

The going becomes steadily more difficult and bloody. Millimeter, millimeter after treacherous millimeter the tweezers burrow a tunnel through Mrs. Kelly's mind. Blood flows, the tweezers buzz, the suction slurps. Push and probe. Cauterize. Suction. Push and probe. More blood. Then the tweezers lie quiet.

"I don't recognize anything," the surgeon says. He pushes further and quickly finds a landmark.

Then, exhausted, Dr. Ducker disengages himself, backs away, sits down on a stool and stares straight ahead for a long moment. The brainstem is close, close.

"This is a frightening place to be," whispers the doctor.

In the background the heart monitor goes pop, pop, pop, 70 beats a minute, steady. The smell of ozone and burnt flesh hangs thick in the air. It is 11:05 a.m., the day of the monster.

The operating room door opens and Dr. Michael Salcman, the assistant chief neurosurgeon, enters. He confers with Dr. Ducker, who then returns to the microscope. Dr. Salcman moves to the front of the television monitor.

As he watches Dr. Ducker work, Dr. Salcman compares an aneurysm to a bump on a tire. The weakened wall of the artery balloons outward under the relentless pressure of the heartbeat and, eventually, it bursts. That's death.

So the fragile aneurysms must be removed before Dr. Ducker can tackle the AVM itself. Dr. Salcman crosses his arms and fixes his eyes on the television screen, preparing himself to relieve Dr. Ducker if he tires. One aneurism down, one to go.

The second, however, is the toughest. It pulses dangerously deep, hard against the bulb of nerves that sits atop the spinal cord.

"Technically, the brainstem," says Dr. Salcman. "I call it the 'pilot light.' That's because if it goes out . . . that's it."

On the television screen the tweezer instrument presses on, following the artery toward the brainstem. Gently, gently, gently, gently it pushes aside the gray coils. For a moment the optic nerve appears in the background, then vanishes.

The going is even slower now. Dr. Ducker is reaching all the way into the center of the brain and his instruments are the length of chopsticks. The danger mounts because, here, many of the vessels feed the pilot light.

The heartbeat goes pop, pop, pop, 70 beats a minute.

The instrument moves across the topography of torture, scars everywhere, remnants of pain past, of agonies Mrs. Kelly would rather die than further endure. Dr. Ducker is lost again.

Dr. Salcman joins him at the microscope, peering through the assistant's eyepieces. They debate the options in low tones and technical terms. A decision is made and again the polished tweezers probe along the vessel.

Back on course, Dr. Ducker works his tunnel ever deeper, gentle, gentle, gentle as the touch of sterile cotton. Finally the gray matter parts.

The neurosurgeon freezes.

Dead ahead the field is crossed by many huge, distended ropelike veins.

The neurosurgeon stares intently at the veins, surprised, chagrined, betrayed by the x-rays.

The monster.

The monster, by microscopic standards, lies far away, above and back, in the rear of the head. Dr. Ducker was to face the monster itself on another day, not now. Not here.

But clearly these tangled veins, absent on the x-ray films but very real in Mrs. Kelly's brain, are tentacles of the monster.

Gingerly, the tweezers attempt to push around them.

Pop, pop, pop . . pop . . . pop . . . . pop . . . . pop.

"It's slowing!" warns the anesthesiologist, alarmed.

The tweezers pull away like fingers touching fire.

. . . . pop . . . pop . . pop . pop, pop, pop.

"It's coming back," says the anesthesiologist.

The vessels control bloodflow to the brainstem, the pilot light.

Dr. Ducker tries to go around them a different way.

Pop, pop, pop . pop . . pop . . . pop . . . .

And withdraws.

Dr. Salcman stands before the television monitor, arms crossed, frowning.

"She can't take much of that," the anesthesiologist says. "The heart will go into arrhythmia and that'll lead to a . . . call it a heart attack."

Dr. Ducker tries a still different route, pulling clear of the area and returning at a new angle. Eventually, at the end of a long, throbbing tunnel of brain tissue, the sought-after aneurysm appears.

Pop, pop, pop . pop . . pop . . . pop . . . .

The instruments retract.

"Damn," say the neurosurgeon. "I can only work here for a few minutes without the bottom falling out."

The clock says 12:29.

Already the gray tissue swells visibly from the repeated attempts to burrow past the tentacles.

Again the tweezers move forward in a different approach and the aneurysm reappears. Dr. Ducker tries to reach it by inserting the aneurysm clip through a long, narrow tunnel. But the pliers that hold the clip obscure the view.

Pop, pop . pop . . pop . . . pop . . . .

The pliers retract.

"We're on it and we know where we are," complains the neurosurgeon, frustration adding a metallic edge to his voice. "But we're going to have an awful time getting a clip in there. We're so close, but . . ."

A resident who has been assisting Dr. Ducker collapses on a stool. He stares straight ahead, eyes unfocused, glazed.

"Michael, scrub," Dr. Ducker says to Dr. Salcman. "See what you can do. I'm too cramped."

While the circulating nurse massages Dr. Ducker's shoulders, Dr. Salcman attempts to reach the aneurysm with the clip.

Pop, pop, pop . pop . . pop . . . pop . . . .

The clip withdraws.

"That should be the aneurysm right there," says Dr. Ducker, taking his place at the microscope again. "Why the hell can't we get to it? We've tried, ten times."

At 12:53, another approach.

Pop, pop, pop . pop . . pop . . . pop . . . .

Again.

It is 1:06.

And again, and again, and again.

Pop . . . pop . . . pop, pop, pop . . . pop . . . pop-pop-
pop . . .

The anesthesiologist's hands move rapidly across a panel
of switches. A nurse catches her breath and holds it.

"Damn, damn, damn."

Dr. Ducker backs away from the microscope, his gloved
hands held before him. For a full minute, he's silent.

"There's an old dictum in medicine," he finally says.
"If you can't help, don't do any harm. Let nature take its
course. We may have already hurt her. We've slowed
down her heart. Too many times." The words carry defeat, exhaustion, anger.

Dr. Ducker stands again before the x-rays. His eyes
focus on the rear aneurysm, the second one, the one that
thwarted him. He examines the film for signs, unseen
before, of the monster's descending tentacles. He finds no
such indications.

Pop, pop, pop, goes the monitor, steady now, 70 beats a
minute.

"Mother nature," a resident growls, "is a mother."

The retreat begins. Under Dr. Salcman's command, the
team prepares to wire the chunk of skull back into place
and close the incision.

It ends quickly, without ceremony. Dr. Ducker's gloves
snap sharply as a nurse pulls them off. It is 1:30.

Dr. Ducker walks, alone, down the hall, brown paper
bag in his hand. In the lounge he sits down on the edge of
a hard orange couch and unwraps the peanut butter sandwich. His eyes focus on the opposite wall.

Back in the operating room the anesthesiologist shines a
light into each of Mrs. Kelly's eyes. The right pupil, the
one under the incision, is dilated and does not respond to
the probing beam. It is a grim omen.

If Mrs. Kelly recovers, says Dr. Ducker, he'll go ahead
and try to deal with the monster itself, despite the remaining aneurysm. He'll try to block the arteries to it, maybe
even take it out. That would be a tough operation, he says
without enthusiasm.

"And it's providing that she's in good shape after this."
If she survives. If. If.

"I'm not afraid to die," Mrs. Kelly had said. "I'm scared to death . . . but . . . I can't bear the pain. I wouldn't want to live like this much longer."

Her brain was too scarred. Tbe operation, tolerable in a younger person, was too much. Already, where the monster's tentacles hang before the brainstem, the tissue swells, pinching off the source of oxygen.

Mrs. Kelly is dying.

The clock on the wall, near where Dr. Ducker sits, says 1:40.

"It's hard to tell what to do. We've been thinking about it for six weeks. But, you know, there are certain things . . . that's just as far as you can go. I just don't know . . ."

He lays the sandwich, the banana and the fig newtons on the table before him, neatly, the way the scrub nurse laid out the instruments.

"It was triple jeopardy," he says finally, staring at his peanut butter sandwich the same way he stared at the x-rays. "It was triple jeopardy."

It is 1:43, and it's over.

Dr. Ducker bites, grimly, into the sandwich.

The monster won.

III

The Ballad of Old Man Peters

(Originally published in *The Evening Sun* [Baltimore], January 1983; reprinted in *Reader's Digest*, January 1984. Used by permission of the A. S. Abell Company.)

VERSE ONE

TIME IS PRECIOUS as it runs out, and Old Man Peters spends long hours at his desk, writing and studying, fighting for a little more knowledge. Death is near, but he brushes away the comprehension. There has never been time for fear, and there is none now.

Prudence, though . . . prudence is another matter.

Outside, beyond the double-locked doors, poor teenagers traverse the alley on the way to nowhere, casting occasional glances at the old man's rowhouse.

For a lifetime Wilk Peters traveled the world in search of its people and its wisdom, and he brought his knowledge back to black universities to share with the students there—but the children who pass in the alley know nothing of that.

Their minds are filled with the hormones of youth, and to them the old man is . . . an old man, that's all, an incomprehensibly ancient old man, 82 years old. Spent. Finished.

To some of them, he is prey. For those Mr. Peters has locks on the doors, locks on the garage, steel screens on the windows . . . but he doesn't consider moving. Moving would take precious time.

He sits at his desk, a book of Italian grammar open in front of him. He stares at it. The mind behind the eyes is old, years beyond the average life expectancy of, as the actuaries so succinctly put it, a black male.

Outside, a truck thunders down The Alameda.

He reads a line, loses it, reads it again.

The scientists say that there are two kinds of memory, short-term and long-term. It is as though life writes its current experiences upon some blackboard in the mind and, as the days pass, the brain copies the information into a permanent library.

But at 82 the blackboard often goes blank prematurely. Then what Mr. Peters learned today, a moment ago, is lost. When that happens, he stubbornly begins again. In recent years he has learned to make notes to himself, lest he forget an appointment, or an important fact.

But he needs no notes to remember his childhood, and the romantic, impossible dream that saw him safely through decades of racism, poverty, and ignorance . . . the dream that guides him still.

The dream began in Trinity County, Texas, in the southern forest east of the great prairie, the part of Texas that had enough rainfall for cotton to grow; Klan country, where the nights were ruled by racial paranoia.

Wilk's father John had once owned his own farm, but that was a violation of the racial code. After a series of night attacks by anonymous riflemen he abandoned the land and fled for his life.

Wilk was born a few years later, in 1900, in a share-cropper's cabin. His mother, Martha, carried him with her when she went to work in the fields, and soon he was joined by another baby, and then another.

With each season the family changed farms, hoping for a better life but finding hard labor instead. Wilk learned to supervise his younger brothers and sisters, then to hoe.

At the age of eight he was an American serf walking behind a plow mule.

But even then there was some special, indefinable thing about Wilk Peters. Somehow he sensed that the world stretched far beyond the Texas horizon.

Though he had never seen them, he knew from school that the earth included seas and mountains, and was home to people who were hues of brown, red and yellow. To the north was Oklahoma, somewhere to the southwest a place called Mexico.

Mexico . . . he liked the way the word slid along the tongue.

It was a foreign country—exotic in the poor boy's mind, yet near enough that he occasionally heard Spanish spoken by travelers. It had a romantic sound, rich with rhythm and vowels, and to hear the incomprehensible words filled him with a restless, inarticulate lust to . . . to . . . *to go*.

His parents had attended grammar school, and though they had never learned to read without effort they understood enough to know that education was the path to emancipation. And they recognized that Wilk's . . . specialness . . . if it was to flourish, required tangible aspirations.

Considering his son's future, father John groped far beyond his own experience.

He had never seen a library or a college campus. He knew nothing of engineers and scientists, of economists or accountants. There was only one educated man in his humble experience, an awesome figure in a tall black hat—the doctor.

Wilk would be . . . a doctor.

A doctor.

The word was a gift from father to son, and it settled in

the boy's mind and lodged there, a kernel of reality around which his inchoate yearnings could coalesce. The word gave definition to his life and focus to his mind, and it led him to an instinctive understanding of the enemy.

The doctor represented knowledge. The antithesis, the enemy, was ignorance.

The dream gave school a special urgency, and while his classmates daydreamed Wilk diligently pursued the art of penmanship and the abstract rhythms of mathematics.

He learned that there was a country called France, beyond the Atlantic Ocean, and another called Russia. Switzerland was a place of mountains. In Spain, matadors challenged enraged bulls. Armies marched in Germany. Boatmen poled gondolas through the canals of Venice.

The boll weevil was by virtue of its six legs an insect, and separate from the eight-legged family of spiders.

Wilk was wary of spiders, snakes and white men, but he wasn't afraid of them. In his nightmares he recoiled from a far more horrible evil, ignorance, and with his entire being he concentrated on the desperate need to beat it back. Step by encouraging step, he saw himself succeeding.

Another sister was born, then a brother, then another sister, finally seven in all. Mother and father slept in the main room of the cabin, the children in the side room.

John Peters was a good and provident farmer, and though there was little cash there was no hunger. The family raised its own poultry, grew its own garden, smoked its own hams and kept range cattle.

The seasons changed and Wilk grew. With the approach of Christmas and Thanksgiving the cabin began to smell of baking cookies and cakes. The holiday table was laden with turkey, stuffing, bowls of home-grown vegetables and woman's most wonderful contribution to man, sweet potato pie. If there was no Christmas tree with gifts beneath it, no one felt the lack.

They were years of innocent hope, of family laughter and poverty lightly borne, when life stretched on toward infinity and dreams were indistinguishable from reality. Of course Wilk would be a doctor. Why not?

Then, in the spring of 1913, his father returned from an errand and collapsed heavily on the bed, disoriented. The next day he couldn't move his left side.

Somehow the family got through the summer. From his bed John gave orders, advice and encouragement to his wife and eldest son. Leaning on one another, Wilk and his mother hoed the corn, tended the livestock, and struggled to keep the farm and equipment in good repair. In late summer the whole family helped pick the cotton and Wilk drove it to market.

Then, in the autumn, as the days began to grow short, Wilk's father died. They buried him in a small cemetery not far from the farm he'd been forced to abandon. There was no money for a tombstone.

Wilk stood, numb, by the grave. Without his father's strength and knowledge, the poverty was suddenly crushing.

When school began a few days later, Wilk's brothers and sisters went but Wilk stayed home. He was needed to take his father's place on the farm.

As the boundaries of Trinity County closed in around him, the 13-year-old clung desperately, hopelessly, to the only thing he had left: his dream.

VERSE TWO

In the early years of the 20th century, the dream that a black sharecropper's son could become a doctor was an audacious one. But while Wilk had his father to encourage and instruct him, it had somehow seemed possible.

With the approach of the winter of 1913, however, his father lay in an unmarked grave and Wilk, as the eldest of seven children, inherited adult responsibilities. For him, there could be no more school.

His father had taught him the fundamentals of farming,

and Wilk could plow, hoe, chop, pick, milk and do most of the other chores. But the boy's best efforts had gone into books, and he lacked the practical savvy that had allowed his father to support the large family.

The winter passed, followed by a summer of hard work, followed by a poor harvest, followed by a desperate winter. The next year was no better. Nor the next. Wilk yearned passionately for the sound of his father's voice, a voice that knew all things, a voice . . .

A voice that spoke clearly in his the boy's memory, a voice that still said, with proud love: "I want you to be a doctor."

A *doctor*.

The dream had no place behind a plow, no application to the process of butchering a hog, no meaning at all for a boy who had dropped out of school so early. And yet . . . somehow . . . without it he would perish.

The dream sustained him as he fought for the family's survival, and it comforted him when he failed.

He worked hard, but hard work didn't suffice when the rains didn't come, or when they came too early and beat down the tiny cotton seedlings. Hard work didn't stop the boll weevil or the worms that burrowed into the ears of corn, and hard work couldn't help his little sister.

Wilk's youngest sister had always been sickly, but now she grew increasingly thin and weak. A doctor was called.

Wilk watched with awe as the man examined his sister, but the outcome wasn't any comfort. The girl was very weak, the doctor said. But he didn't know why, and he had no medicine that would help.

Harvest brought still another failure. The family needed money for food and Wilk and his mother looked around for something to sell.

There was nothing left but the mules. They brought very little.

It was then that the Reverend Eva Johnson entered their lives.

The Reverend Johnson was part black and part American Indian, a man with a bible, a bible and a job, a real job in the turpentine forests . . . and a man with an eye for Wilk's mother.

Wilk instinctively disliked the preacher. He watched suspiciously as the courtship developed, but was helpless to prevent the marriage. Then, when the family moved to the turpentine camp, the boy's worst fears were confirmed.

Soon he and his brothers and sisters were at labor in the long-leaf pine forests, scarring the trees to bring the resin out, collecting the sap and pouring it into barrels, hauling it to the distillery for conversion into turpentine.

As for the preacher . . . sometimes he read a few words from the bible, but he wasn't a *real* preacher after all. Sometimes he worked in the turpentine forests, but he usually had something more important to do, like hunting and fishing.

The turpentine work was difficult, menial labor, from dawn to dusk, and the days blended into one another. With the passage of time Wilk's image of himself as a doctor deteriorated into fantasy, a fantasy that grew increasingly difficult to capture.

Wilk was in the forests, scarring trees, when word came that his youngest sister was dead.

Then he stood, at age 16, in another anonymous free cemetery, miles from where his father was buried, watching them lower his sister's wooden coffin into the ground.

For two years he worked, taking orders from his stepfather. But he balked when the man decreed that the family would move again, to work for a new turpentine company.

Wilk, for his part, suspected that one turpentine forest was much like another, and, anyway, he wasn't going anywhere . . . nowhere, at least, with the preacher.

He stayed and the family moved on. For the first time in his life, Wilk was alone. He was 18.

Confused and unsure of himself, he hung around the turpentine forest and grappled with the future. The dream was all but gone now, and it offered no inspiration.

Finally, hearing of work in the lumbermill town of

Diboll, and having no reason to stay where he was, he took his few belongings and headed down the dirt road, one foot in front of another.

Diboll was a small town of perhaps 2,500, a collection of greenwood shacks, dirt roads, and a company store . . . and it was always in need of another strong back. Within a few days of his arrival Wilk was pushing slabs of lumber toward a howling planer.

It was a tiny, humble place, lost in the hot south Texas forest, a transient town that would vanish as soon as the timber was gone.

But to the young farmboy it was a wonder. Model A Fords, used by the lumber company, frightened horses on the street. There was electricity, a boardwalk in front of the store, and a bewildering number of faces.

And some of those faces, he found as he settled into the first of a long line of cheap rooming houses, had intelligence behind them.

Almost all the residents of Diboll could read and write, and most had at one time or another journeyed down to Tyler, 125 miles away . . . Tyler, the place of dreams, home of the black place of learning, the Methodist-owned Texas College.

Wilk found that some of the other young men at the lumbermill had also dreamed of getting an education, and that some of them had actually gone to Tyler and enrolled. They had failed, however, and had returned to the mill in Diboll.

This intelligence had a dramatic impact on young Wilk. If they could go, so could he! The gossamer fantasy instantly solidified in his mind, from possibility to dream to goal to necessity.

Yet . . . the men he talked to had failed.

In Tyler they had somehow lost the dream, forgotten their priorities, mismanaged their money, failed to apply themselves to their studies, flunked out . . .

It was said in Diboll that an illiterate, once he became

an adult, was done for. The mind was set, firm, impossible to teach.

The thought filled Wilk with cold terror. He couldn't believe it was too late; he refused to believe it. If he ever got the chance, he promised himself, *he* would not drop out.

If he got the chance?

Wilk looked around him, at the automobiles, at the sawmill, at the goods in the company store, at the simple machinery he operated at the sawmill. To make those things, somebody, somewhere, had to know something. To make the trains run, somebody had to know something.

Desperately, he wanted to be one of those people.

So it wasn't *if* he went to college, not if.

When.

He would have to save money, and in the meantime he would have to study, to make up for lost time.

The resolution made, his ignorance became suddenly intolerable, and he couldn't wait. He borrowed some primers and, when he wasn't working, he reviewed arithmetic and grammar. Then he found a book on mathematics. It was incomprehensible, but he refused to put it down.

By day he worked at the sawmill, by night he studied, on Sundays he went to the local church, on payday . . .

On payday, every two weeks, he carefully divided his money into three small stacks. One stack was for home—for shoes for his sisters, a dress for his mother, for whatever was needed. The second stack was for his own modest requirements.

The third stack was the smallest, by far, but by far the most precious. It was for the dream.

A dollar became, with the addition of another, two dollars. Five dollars grew into ten, ten became twelve, twelve became thirteen.

Wilk began to worry about security. There weren't any banks in Diboll, and he didn't dare leave the money in his room.

The solution was to fold it and knot it into a handkerchief. Before he went to work he put the handkerchief into his right pants pocket, then tied a string around the bottom of the pocket so that the handkerchief couldn't possibly fall out. At night, he slept with the handkerchief pinned into his pajama pocket.

A year passed in work and study, then two. The more he learned, the more voracious his appetite for knowledge became. Slowly the puzzle of mathematics yielded to his stubborn attack, and he was captivated by the sweet logic of it.

As he learned, the idea of learning itself broadened. When some of the townspeople talked of forming a band, for instance, he was mesmerized by the idea.

Back in the turpentine forests some people had played a guitar, but . . . a band! All those different instruments!

Music was still another thing for a young, hungry mind to learn, and Wilk spent precious money on a used clarinet. After that he worked, he studied, and he played.

The handkerchief got too full to carry with him. He walked to a nearby town, located a trusted aunt, and gave her $50 to hide for him.

And another year passed, and another. He sent off to Tyler for a college catalog. He pored over it, neglecting the clarinet.

Soon, now.

One Sunday a note appeared on the church bulletin board, announcing an educational meeting. Dr. W. R. Banks, the president of Texas College, would give a lecture and be available afterward to answer questions.

Wilk returned to his room and re-counted his savings. The total, including the money that had been left in the care of his aunt, amounted to almost $300.

That evening Wilk was at the church early, and when the program began he listened spellbound to the tall, unbelievably erudite gentleman who seemed to know every word in the dictionary and could make ideas dance in the air like notes on a page of music.

Afterwards, Wilk overcame his intimidation, went up to the man, and demanded his attention.

Wilk confessed that he was 23, and had only a sixth-grade education. But he'd saved some money. And he could work hard.

Was it possible?

The college president studied the intent young man. Experience told him Wilk was too old, but he hadn't the heart to say so.

Nothing, he equivocated, was impossible.

It was all Wilk needed to hear.

That autumn, almost precisely ten years after his father had died, Wilk packed up his belongings, bought a ticket on the lumber train, and headed for Tyler.

VERSE THREE

Intimidated, but firm in his resolve, Wilk Peters demonstrated his knowledge to the admissions officials at Texas College. He could do sums, and he could do take-aways. He knew nouns and verbs . . .

The officials shook their heads, sadly. The fellow knew a little, but too little, and he spoke in the condemning, ignorant slur of the field hand. A pity.

The illiterate adult who showed up on campus, hat in his hands and life savings in his pocket, was a familiar story to black educators. The eagerness to learn had somehow survived in such men as Wilk, but the youthful plasticity was gone from their minds. They tried, but they failed.

Wilk was too old . . . but who would tell him so?

No one. He would have to learn that himself.

They gave him a job shoveling coal in the furnace room of the girls' dormitory, showed him a tiny cubbyhole where he could sleep, and explained to him where the path to knowledge began.

And so Wilk found himself, at age 23, a full-grown man with callused hands and hardened muscles, sitting with his knees jammed under a tiny desk, wrestling with long division, surrounded by prepubescent sixth-graders.

The effect was not what the admission officials had predicted.

Wilk viewed his place in class as opportunity, not insult. If the children laughed at him he didn't notice, preoccupied as he was with the serious business of fractions, with the parsing of sentences and the memorization of poetry.

The college maintained a secondary school on campus, so that the student teachers could get experience teaching neighborhood children. If Wilk could survive sixth grade, he was sure that next fall he would be allowed to enroll there. If he survived secondary school, then . . .

Wilk had never known security, but neither had he ever had anything to lose. Now, he had opportunity. At night, scooping coal into the big dormitory furnace, he was sometimes overwhelmed with fear.

What if something happened?

What if he got sick? What if one of his family got sick, and he had to drop out and support them? What if . . . what if, now that he stood on the threshold of a world which he wanted desperately . . . but which he didn't understand . . . *what if he lost his courage?*

If there might be no tomorrow, he would have to study harder today. In that way, the sixth grader progressed. The following summer he went to Dallas to work and save money.

When he'd left in the spring the Texas College faculty had assumed they'd seen the last of him. Their surprise showed on their faces when he returned in the fall and asked to enroll in secondary school.

That year he met Shakespeare. Shakespeare seemed to speak directly to him, over a span of four centuries, from beyond an ocean, across the immense chasm of race.

He read the famous words, ''To be or not to be: that is the question,'' and then he read them again, and again. At night, as he shoveled coal, he thought about the English bard, he considered the symbols of elementary algebra, and he memorized Latin.

He also discovered the library.

It was a sacred place, as hushed as a church, and it occupied the entire top floor of one of the college buildings. The library had books on every subject Wilk had ever heard of . . . and many he hadn't . . . and there were more titles than he'd ever imagined could exist. They were all neatly arranged by some scheme that he didn't immediately grasp.

The young man walked the aisles in wonder, looking at the words on the spines and touching the bindings.

The librarian was Govina Banks, the president's wife, and she, as much as her husband, was responsible for the careful nurturing of the black community's meager intellectual resources. Thoughtfully, she watched the young man.

A year passed, another. Sometimes on Saturday and Sunday Wilk found odd jobs in Tyler, a thriving metropolis of perhaps 11,000 souls. One Christmas a package arrived from Wilk's mother. It contained a blanket.

He found his support and courage in books. When he discovered something he considered particularly valuable, he transferred the words to memory:

"The stones are sharp, and cut my hands. But I must build . . . and build . . . and build . . . until this temple stands."

In a volume of obscure quotations he discovered the motto, "Keep on keeping on." He soon forgot who said it, but he would never forget the words.

Slowly, so slowly that he would not perceive it for many years yet, Wilk began to change.

In part it was knowledge that changed him, the simple accumulation of historical dates and geometric theorems, of Shakespeare and the exotic sound of Latin. But he also responded, on a more fundamental level, to his own success.

He had been a dreamer. Now, in beating back the ignorance, he was turning his dream into reality.

He had always respected knowledge.

Now, he began to respect himself.

If he could survive the junior year of high school, what else might he do? Might he . . .

What, he wondered, was Shakespeare's England like? What was it like in Hamlet's Denmark? What was a place called "France"? And what would it be like to walk the streets of Italy?

His thoughts moved in another direction, as well. One of his student teachers was a young lady named Geneva Crouch . . . and . . . and she was one of the prettiest women he had ever seen.

Sometimes, as he listened to her, his mind wandered far off the subject of English . . .

He said nothing to her, of course. It was against the rules for students to date teachers, and he didn't dare risk the anger of the administration.

When he graduated from high school in the spring of 1928 there was a small ceremony, but Wilk missed it because he had to work. He didn't feel sorry for himself, though. It wouldn't be the last time he graduated from something; of that he was certain.

His fear of failure had vanished. If he had made it this far then he could keep on keeping on all the way to . . . where?

It didn't matter. Somewhere. Medical school.

That fall, the year he turned 28, he enrolled as a freshman in Texas College.

Though his education was still far from complete, life was different now. As a laborer in grammar school he'd been nothing, a nobody, an inevitable failure who would probably be back in the fields by next year.

But a college student . . . now, *that* was different. In the black community in South Texas at the close of the Roaring Twenties, a college student merited respect.

The next two years were consumed by work and study. Wilk traded Latin for French. He wrestled with higher algebra, and won. Analytical geometry followed, and history, and sociology, and biology. Such were the threads of fantasy, that went into the fabric of dreams.

As he grew, the little Methodist campus seemed to shrink. There were, after all, only 300 students—and the college lost substantially in appeal when Dr. Banks, the president, quit to take over as president of the state's Prairie View A & M College some 150 miles distant.

Worse, the pretty teacher, Geneva, left for Prairie View too.

Then in the autumn of 1929 the stock market crashed, and there was talk that the menial jobs formerly reserved for black people should go, instead, to out-of-work whites.

As the economic situation deteriorated Wilk understood that he might not be able to go directly to medical school, as his father would have wished, but he wasn't alarmed.

He would have to go to work for a while, that was all, until he could save enough money for medical school. He could teach mathematics, a subject in which he was quickly becoming an expert.

And anyway, he felt as though he had shed the cloak of ignorance. He was a student, a good one, smart enough to get high marks, good enough to write away to Prairie View and get accepted immediately.

At Prairie View, Mrs. Banks helped him find a job waiting tables in the student cafeteria.

During the next two years at the larger college, Wilk continued his intellectual and emotional growth. He concentrated on mathematics and took up German on the side. There was even enough time, occasionally, for conversations with Geneva.

He said nothing personal, of course, because he was still a student and she a teacher, but in subtle ways he expressed his interest. He couldn't tell by her reserved manner whether she reciprocated his feelings or not.

As the winter of 1930–31 tapered into spring, and Wilk's graduation approached, he faced the world with high hopes. He had become fascinated with languages, and a few years spent teaching math would give him time to get deeply into German.

He sent off applications to every black Texas high school he could think of, and sat back to await the replies.

A week passed. He got a rejection, then another. But mostly there was . . . nothing.

He couldn't understand what was wrong.

As graduation approached, Wilk borrowed enough money to rent a cap and gown. His family didn't come, but Geneva did.

The commencement speaker was a woman who was president of another black college in Texas, and Wilk listened, along with 150 other graduating seniors, as she counseled them not to be disheartened by the economic situation.

"It's not dusk," she insisted. "It's dawn."

Afterwards Wilk approached her, as he had approached Dr. Banks ten years earlier in that Diboll church. But now, as he inquired about teaching jobs, he was not nearly so humble.

"What can you do?" she inquired.

"Well," he said proudly, "I can teach math."

She waited for a moment, as though expecting him to continue. When she realized he had finished, a frown settled on her face.

"Our schools need more than that," she snapped. "They're poor. The windows are broken out. The water is cut off. The roof leaks . . . It's not enough to just teach math! What I'm asking is what *else* can you do."

Wilk was taken aback. The *cum laude* on his new college degree notwithstanding, he had to stammer an admission that, beyond mathematics, he had almost no skills at all.

The woman shifted her attention to another graduate and Wilk, wounded, withdrew.

Not since he had been a 23-year-old grammar school student, memorizing multiplication tables with children, had he been so acutely aware of his ignorance.

VERSE FOUR

After graduation in 1933 Wilk Peters hung around the Prairie View campus, hoping that some high school, somewhere, would hire him as a mathematics teacher. But as the depression deepened, no acceptance letter came.

There was no work in town, either, so Wilk volunteered to help file and cross-reference material at the college library.

He liked library work, and thought it was good for him. There was peace there, in that temple-like place, handling the precious books, indexing the valuable knowledge so that it could be found by other hungry minds. The library freed his mind for thought.

He looked at the shelves of books that he'd never read, and he asked himself, again and again, what he knew of the world. The answer was not reassuring.

As he worked, the chief librarian watched him and noted the reverence with which he handled each volume. She discussed him with Mrs. Govina Banks, the wife of the college president.

Mrs. Banks thought back to the old days at Texas College, when she had been in charge of the library there. She remembered the ignorant young laborer who had gazed with such wonder at her mere 6,000 volumes. Obviously, a college degree had not changed him.

She approached Wilk.

Had he ever thought, she inquired, of becoming a librarian?

Wilk stared at her in shock. The idea was so perfect . . . and he'd never even thought of it, so firmly had he fixed his mind on his father's edict to become a doctor.

But "becoming a doctor," Wilk knew, had been no more than a symbol in his father's mind. The doctor was the persona of the educated man.

It wasn't an M.D. that his father had really wanted for him, it was *knowledge*. And what was a librarian after all but a custodian of knowledge? Mrs. Banks was right; his father would have approved.

The decision made, Wilk's floundering ended. At Mrs. Banks's urging he applied for a scholarship to the Hampton Institute's college of library science in Virginia, and was accepted. Then he proposed marriage to Geneva Crouch, and she accepted him too.

It was a wonderful summer, almost as though life were beginning anew.

That autumn Wilk, who at 33 had never been beyond the borders of Texas, left his bride, hitched a ride to Kentucky and traveled the rest of the way to school in Virginia by train.

He made the trip wide-eyed, his overflowing brain absorbing new sights, sounds and cultures faster than he could process them. He felt himself becoming wiser with each mile.

For years he had fantasized about traveling, but the idea had seemed frivolous and he'd repressed it. But by the time his trip to Virginia ended he understood that travel wasn't frivolous at all—it was another way of beating back the ignorance.

Finally, in Virginia, he stood one cold day on a beach, looking out over the famous Atlantic Ocean. Standing there, the wind in his face and the crashing of the waves in his ears, he found himself trying to visualize the exotic places that lay on the other shore.

Suddenly, he was consumed by the lust to see them all.

It was an awakening, and though Wilk would return to Texas College the following spring, there to serve as librarian for four years, he would never be the same.

Back in Texas, as soon as his finances would allow he purchased an automobile, and that spring he and his wife drove to New York and spent the summer studying at Columbia. Afterwards they drove to Quebec.

It was like being in fairyland. Wilk was surrounded by foreigners speaking strange sounds . . . *and he understood them.*

On the way back to Texas he thought about the many kinds of peoples in the world, and all the different languages, and how the people were barred from talking with one another.

The language barrier, he decided, was a kind of ignorance . . . an impediment to knowledge.

He was chagrined that he could speak only French . . . French, and a little German. He would have to do something about that.

There wasn't much time or energy for the new dream, though. At Texas College, and later at Langston University in Oklahoma, Wilk was brought face-to-face with hundreds of young black people, ignorant as he had been ignorant, desperate to learn.

He was all but consumed in the task of teaching them to thread their way through the encyclopedias, the histories, the periodicals.

But at night there was always some time, if only a few minutes, to study German.

In 1944 Wilk received an invitation to join the staff of the Cleveland Public Library, which at the time was widely considered to be among the top three city library systems in the country. He jumped at the chance.

Mrs. Banks had indeed been right. Wilk's profession was perfectly matched to his dream of learning. Everything he did in library science brought him into contact with more information, and every job he had taught him something new.

In Cleveland, for instance, he was one of several people who were required to read the new books that came in and report on each one's approach and its value to the library.

Because the other book review librarians worked an earlier shift, Wilk had to read whatever they left . . . dull stuff. And, because it was the mid-1940s, a lot of that dull stuff was contained in arcane, analytical tomes about Russia and communism.

It fascinated Wilk that the Russian people, as far as he could determine, were not much different from Americans.

They apparently had the same aspirations, the same dreams, the same need to understand and cope with the world around them. But for the Russians it had somehow gone tragically wrong.

Wilk wished he could speak Russian . . .

Well, why not?

And so Russian became language number three. It allowed him to read books by Russian Jews and, as the son of a black American serf, Wilk identified with their travails.

It would be wonderful, he thought, to visit Russia. He couldn't of course . . . he had neither the money nor the time.

In 1948 Wilk moved on to the Tuskegee Institute, where he landed a good job as an assistant reference librarian. As usual it was hard work and long hours, but also as usual there were many new things to learn.

In addition to language, he now sought the humble skills he lacked.

He became fascinated, for instance, with small engines. He knew from his farming and gardening experiences that plants, when intelligently cared for, rewarded the gardener far beyond the measure of his effort. Might not small engines respond the same way?

He ordered an engine repair manual and, when he wasn't working or studying languages, he tinkered with his lawnmower. When he had it running perfectly, he started working on his neighbors'.

He also found interesting and profitable relationships with people. One of his coworkers was a native of Haiti, and when the man went home for a visit he invited Wilk and Geneva to come along. They leaped at the chance.

It was Wilk's first truly foreign country, and he was repelled by the poverty . . . but fascinated by the people. The common folk spoke a mysterious language called Creole, but the professionals could all speak French.

They treated Wilk like royalty, and his ability to converse with them made him feel like a citizen of the world.

The visit was far too short, and coming back felt like a return to prison.

Wilk turn 50 at Tuskegee. The students, he couldn't help but notice, called him "sir" with increasing frequency.

He shrugged it off. Certainly he didn't *feel* any older and he still had plenty of . . . of . . . of whatever it was that made young men chase dreams.

He sat in the Tuskegee Library, helping students, filing books, organizing material, contributing, working . . .

God, but he wanted to go to Germany.

Or Australia. Australia would do nicely.

Anywhere.

The months passed, one after another, but the yearning didn't go away.

Then one day he got a letter from a friend he'd made long ago in Oklahoma, a man who was now chairman of the English department at Morgan State College in Baltimore. Morgan was expanding into library sciences, and needed a good teacher. Was Wilk interested?

For the first time in his life, Wilk hesitated. After all, he explained via return mail, Tuskegee had a good retirement plan—a better plan than Morgan State.

Wilk's friend in Baltimore thought about it, thought about Wilk, and pondered what he knew about what made Wilk tick. Finally he wrote back.

Morgan State, he pointed out, with the brilliance of a psychological matador going in over the horns with a sharp sword . . . Morgan teachers worked on a nine-month contract, with summers off.

If Wilk took the job he would have time to do, well, to do . . . whatever he wanted.

Wilk stared at the letter. Tbe idea was pure nitroglycerin.

Whatever . . . he . . . wanted.

Whatever . . . or *wherever*!

France.

Germany.

Australia.

The moon.

He forced himself to think logically.

France would be first. In fact, he had a little savings . . . why not go to France the summer *before* moving to Baltimore? Yes. Of course. Adrenaline pumped through his brain. That was a wonderful idea.

Life would never be the same.

At Morgan State, Wilk Peters became the ageless, friendly librarian who seemed to have a personal grudge against ignorance.

He was the one who was always helping out the foreign students . . . the absent-minded fellow who was always ready to assist an American student with a French translation, or to help with an essay that had to be written in German, or to decipher the meaning of an obscure Russian, Italian or Spanish phrase . . . the man who studied languages at night and disappeared every summer.

He traveled inexpensively, on reduced-rate steamships and bargain airlines, tramping through kingdoms his father had never heard of, eating local food, staying in student dormitories or private homes, studying, observing, absorbing, learning.

In the summertime Wilk was a student, not a teacher. He spent three months at the University of Barcelona, studying Spanish, geography, music, literature and art. At the Sorbonne in Paris he studied French and French civilization. He studied in Quebec, in Berlin, in Vienna. As he grew more proficient, he began studying more on his own.

Each autumn he returned to Morgan State, bearing gifts of the mind . . . tales from Denmark, Switzerland, Portugal, Norway, England, Ireland . . . so many countries that, when he was asked to list them by a fascinated student or a campus newspaper reporter, he couldn't name them all from memory. Finally, he started keeping a list.

In the summer he traveled and studied, in the winter he taught library sciences. In 1961 Wilk was appointed the college's official advisor for foreign students.

The years passed.

And then, on the 30th of June in 1966, the timeclock

ran out and the professional résumé ended. At 66, Wilk applied for his pension.

He was retired.

In the terms of a youth-oriented culture he was finished, washed-up, farmed-out and pumped-dry, and it was all over.

The world, as usual, was wrong.

Wilk Peters emptied his desk into a cardboard box and drove home . . . gleeful as a teenager on the first day of summer vacation.

VERSE FIVE

At the innocent age of 42 William Shakespeare proclaimed that all the world's a stage. But by the time Wilk Peters retired he was 66, 24 years wiser than a man of 42, and he knew better.

The world wasn't a stage at all.

It was a campus.

And the idea that 66 was old was a wives' tale, a fraud perpetuated by the young. Wilk felt fine; never better. And he was free!

As a free man he could choose what to do with his life. He could study more languages. He could travel in the winter, when the fares were low. He could go to bed when he liked and get up when he liked.

So, on the morning after his retirement, he got up at 7 a.m., dressed, ate breakfast, sat down at his desk and began to study. When he needed to rest his mind, he went downstairs and tinkered with the lawnmower.

Wilk took special pleasure in caring for the 1955 Chevy he'd purchased new—and which now, finally, he had time to maintain properly.

By his retirement in 1966 there were still plenty of 1955 Chevys running around, most of them rusted-out hulks that were followed wherever they went by billowing clouds of smoke. But not Wilk's.

In Wilk's view, 1955 was a vintage year for Chevys, and his was a standard-transmission model with no extras to conk out. He had kept it in a garage and cared for it intelligently, and it had no rust.

The old car was much like the old man, in many respects, and he drove it with pride. Every winter, before he went overseas, he put it up on blocks.

Spanish . . . now there was another thing, as elegant in its own way as the Chevy . . . a mechanism of beautiful, feminine vowels and romantically-twirled R's. If he knew Spanish well enough he could travel independently in Latin America, spending little, learning much.

When he wasn't working on the Chevy, tending his garden (or someone else's), when he wasn't fixing a lawnmower, he was at his desk studying—or was listening intently to foreign broadcasts on his short-wave radio.

As the retirement years passed, Wilk's front lawn received lavish care and it grew lush and thick, without a weed in it.

Flowers bloomed, the holly grew, and the hedges that surrounded the little yard took on topiary shapes, green bowls and hoops and breaking ocean waves. While Geneva stood by, proudly, the Mayor of Baltimore awarded Wilk the "Order of the Red Rose" as part of the city's beautification program.

The Chevy ran, if anything, better than ever before. That was true of Wilk, too. His mind stayed sharp and his body, while somewhat slower to respond, remained sound.

In the winter he studied at the University of Madrid, in Tenerife, in Switzerland, in Puerto Rico, in Peru, and he traveled throughout South America and Europe. Sometimes Geneva went with him, and sometimes she preferred to stay home.

For the first time in Wilk's life he felt truly satisfied, a student of the world, just what he'd always wanted to be. Year by year, he could see the hated ignorance retreat.

When he wasn't traveling and studying, when there were no more weeds in his yard and when his neighbors' lawnmowers were all running perfectly, he did volunteer work for the Girl Scouts, the Red Cross, the United Fund and other charities.

Several days a week he worked as an unpaid multilingual receptionist at the Spanish Apostolate in the 200 block of East 25th Street. It made him feel good to help others.

They were wonderful years, the best of his life, but sometimes he heard an unsettling reminder of passing time. Sometimes now he thought the teenagers looked at him strangely, even speculatively, and he overheard one say to another something about . . . about that "pitiful old man and that pitiful old car . . ."

The words didn't make sense to Wilk. He was fine. He was young . . . younger than they, and not nearly so ignorant. He felt fine, perfect, and the car started every time without an instant's hesitation.

The year he turned 70 he got a letter from the Gerontology Research Center at City Hospitals. The GRC, the letterhead explained, was an arm of the National Institutes of Health located at City Hospitals in Baltimore.

The scientists at the center were looking for healthy old men they could study. They were trying to find out, they explained to Wilk, why old age was a misery for some people and a pleasure for others.

In terms of basic science they were also trying to determine the biochemical basis of the aging process—something that might, in theory, be isolated and identified in people like Wilk.

Wilk agreed to cooperate and spent several days in the hospital while the scientists examined him in painstaking detail. He no longer had the physique of a laborer but, for a man of 70, he was physically perfect. The doctors were astonished.

Wilk wasn't though; sure, he was in perfect health. He could have told them that.

There was an awkward moment, however, when the psychiatrist asked him where he'd been in his lifetime.

Wilk couldn't remember all the places . . . Argentina, Austria, Belgium, Brazil . . . Ghana, Gibraltar, Greece . . . Panama, Paraguay, Peru, Poland . . . and finally Uruguay, Venezuela and the Virgin Islands. There were 56 in all.

His memory?

Well, he admitted to being a little absent-minded, always had been. And sometimes he forgot some perfectly obvious Russian phrase, or some word in one of his other languages . . . The psychiatrist stared at Wilk.

Six languages and still learning more at age 70?

Obviously, the old man's brain was fine.

The news from the gerontology center was nothing but good, but the doctors' interest in his combination of good health and old age bore an unmistakable message. And, when he was working outside, the stares of passing children sent a cold wind blowing through Wilk's mind.

He was getting old.

No, he wasn't.

He couldn't be.

He felt just like he always had. He was just as bright, just as curious, just as filled with the lust to learn. And yet what it all meant was that he was going to . . .

He didn't like the word "die." "Passed," was far preferable. But "passed . . ."

Wilk had always gone to church, and hoped that there was an afterlife. He hoped, but it didn't seem very likely. Still the concept of "God" was helpful here. At 70, anytime . . .

The words that came were, "At 70, the man upstairs might pull your ticket anytime."

And he left it at that, in favor of Spanish, German . . . Italian.

Italian was a new love. Italian was springtime and romantic youth, the youth the old man felt in his bones when he was supposed to be feeling the icy presence of death.

Year followed year, and the Chevy grew older. The

people at the Motor Vehicle Administration told him he could buy historic tags for it, if he liked. It was an antique.

An antique! That was fascinating.

Wilk looked at the car and yes, it was old, but it was well cared for. It'd carry him many a mile yet.

Sometimes, in his late 70s, Wilk's memory started to slip.

His wife Geneva thought he was getting a little deaf, but he denied it. He could hear the roar of a climbing airplane, hear the sounds of Peruvian children, hear the perfectly-timed engine of the antique Chevy.

But the teenagers, now, began to seriously concern Wilk.

They seemed like a new group of people, alien almost, heads full of judgment but empty of wisdom. He saw them pointing at him and the old car, and heard their laughter. It made him uneasy.

He installed heavier locks on all the doors.

Finally one year the doctors at the gerontology center found a break in the armor of health. Wilk had diabetes, and it was serious enough to treat. It could be controlled, but he had to be careful about what he ate.

It was a small thing, but sobering.

If he had to eat special food, that severely circumscribed his ability to live off the land, restricted him to relatively civilized countries. Still, there were plenty of modernized countries to choose from, and there was no use worrying about it.

A joint condition, which he'd had since he was a young man, flared up.

It was ironic. Each day he knew still more about Russian and small engines, more about Germany, Uruguay, Senegal . . . real knowledge sometimes seemed almost within his grasp . . .

But each day that he grew less ignorant he also grew weaker.

With advancing age he was increasingly vulnerable to influenza, common cold, and dietary imbalances.

He turned 80, 81, 82 . . . He lived on, as did his Geneva, in the little house on The Alameda.

It was too late now, in 1982, for the dreamed-of trip around the world, too late to safely explore disease-ridden India.

But it was not yet over. It was not too late for . . . where? It was a big decision.

Italy.

So 1982 was the year he took out the Italian books, and started studying.

Learning was definitely more difficult now . . . the words kept slipping away, getting wiped off the blackboard before they could be committed to long-term memory. He sat at his desk, forcing his mind to concentrate, to digest.

There was a break in the routine when one day a letter arrived from Prairie View A & M College in Texas, his alma mater. The college leadership wanted Wilk to be the convocation speaker during homecoming in November.

It was a singular honor, and Wilk laid aside his Italian books to write his speech. He wanted to do it justice.

It was difficult going. He knew many languages, but they were just words, all equally useless when it came time to speak from the heart.

You had to keep on keeping on, that was all.

But how could he tell that to an audience of young students who would never know what it was like to walk behind a mule, to sit in the back of the bus? He thought of the teenagers, who knew too little to comprehend their own ignorance.

Wilk still didn't feel old, not even at 82, but writing the speech dredged up memories and made him think of all the years of learning that came after graduation. And he found, as he searched for honest words, an anger he hadn't known was there.

He was tired, sick and tired, of the complaining he heard around him.

Finally, in November, he stood before the audience.

He told them his story and then, searching for a way to make the lesson real, he told them a parable about a black couple. The couple lost everything they had because of drinking and poor management, but they complained all the time that "whitey" was to blame.

Racism is a fact, he said.

But so is courage.

And then, borrowing the words of James Ephraim McGirt, he read them an old poem:

> Success is a light upon the farther shore,
>   That shines in dazzling splendor to the eye,
> The waters leap, the surging billows roar,
>   And he who seeks the prize must leap and try.
>
> A mighty host stand trembling on the brink,
>   With anxious eyes they yearn to reach the goal.
> I see them leap, and, ah! I see them sink—
>   As gazing on dread horror fills my soul.
>
> Yet to despair I can but droop and die,
>   'Tis better far to try the lashing deep.
> I much prefer beneath the surge to lie,
>   Than death to find me on this bank asleep.

After the clapping and the handshaking was over, Old Man Peters went home to Baltimore, to his red brick rowhouse with steel mesh on the windows, behind the double-locked doors, and he sent off letters inquiring about a small apartment in Rome. When they were written he opened his Italian book.

Late into the autumn he sat at his desk, studying the language of Dante, absorbing the words with the undiminished intensity of a desperate black boy, born in the year 1900, angrily beating back the ignorance.

Each day Wilk forced a few more words into his mind, adding them to the tens of thousands already there, accumulated through a life of study. Each day the new words fitted in with the old, and he felt a little more comfortable with Italian, and with the world.

The man upstairs might have pulled Wilk's card at any time, but He stayed His hand.

On December 1, the Chevy safely up on blocks, Old Man Peters kissed his wife goodbye and flew to Rome.

IV

Stalking the True Short Story

HAVING JUST READ "Mrs. Kelly's Monster" and "The Ballad of Old Man Peters," you may make the envious observation that I was incredibly lucky to find such wonderful stories to tell. That brings us neatly around to our first lesson: stalking the true short story.

At a certain level, of course, your envy is appropriate—what were the odds that any given human would bump into Tom Ducker or Wilk Peters in the course of a normal lifetime? What are the odds that I would discover both? I have to admit they aren't very good.

But while granting that there are statistics at work, I do not concede that there was any luck involved. Not for an instant. If I did, I'd lose my nerve and, as a result, my livelihood.

To pluck an analogy from science, have you ever wondered why it is that some researchers consistently make

major discoveries while others fail, again and again, to
find anything new and worthwhile?

The answer is that the successful scientist is the one who
invests a maximum amount of time exploring the branch of
nature he's studying—he's out there, looking. Beyond
that, he actually cares, in a human sense, about nature;
because he cares he keeps his eyes open and does his best
to understand what he sees and fit it into some kind of
conceptual framework. His framework may be totally wrong,
but in creating and using it he sharpens his ability to
recognize and classify what he sees.

Because he's out there looking, the odds are that he'll
eventually stumble over an important clue of one sort or
another. Because he's been thinking as well as looking,
he's apt to recognize that clue for what it is.

Chance, as the historians of science sum it up, favors
the prepared mind. The odds are overwhelmingly against
the prepared scientist making any particular discovery . . .
but it's a foregone conclusion that he'll discover *something*.

The same process is at work when a skilled writer stalks the
true short story. The odds were vastly against my discover-
ing the specific stories that became "Mrs. Kelly's Monster"
and "The Ballad of Old Man Peters," but the chances that
I would discover some story of roughly the same quality
were strongly in my favor. I knew what I was looking for.

I know, in short, what a story is . . . and equally
important, I know what a story *isn't*. As a result I can
readily put my finger on a good yarn while my students
undergo the tortures of the damned to find mediocre ones.

The straightforward definition of a story is as follows:

> *A story consists of a sequence of actions that occur
> when a sympathetic character encounters a
> complicating situation that he confronts and solves.*

That looks simple enough, doesn't it? As you will discover, everything about writing is simple. But as you will
also discover, simplicity is deceptive.

To again dip into science for an analogy, one of the simplest statements in all of nature is Albert Einstein's observation that energy is equal to mass times the speed of light squared. Simplicity, carried to an extreme, becomes elegance; the implications of elegance can take a lifetime to absorb. To know that E equals MC squared is *not* to know physics.

Similarly, memorizing the formula for stories does not make you a writer. To become a writer of nonfiction short stories, and later of more complex works, you must learn the key implications of the formula.

For openers, the formula implies that while there are many types of stories, about many varieties of people who do all sorts of different things, all stories have some critical, universal similarities.

It also implies that stories have specific anatomies. Just as all uniquely individual human beings have brains, hearts, stomachs and pancreases, all stories have a common set of attributes that are arranged in a certain specific way. A story, any story, involves a special relationship between character, situation, and action. If all the parts are not present, and if their necessary relationships are not in order, then the story, like the human, cannot live.

The nonfiction dramatist on the prowl for material rarely sees the whole story, altogether, in one glance. In the vast majority of instances he will see just one identifying part of its anatomy as it momentarily boils to the top of the witches' brew of human existence.

If what he sees whets his interest he grabs it and proceeds to ascertain whether or not it has the other requisite parts attached. If it does, he may make it his own. If it doesn't, he will toss it back.

Most often, the piece of story anatomy that will catch your attention is the *complication*.

A complication is simply any problem encountered by any human being; it's an event that triggers a situation that complicates our lives, which is where it got its name.

Say, for instance, that a fly lights on my nose. It doesn't

do much for my image, strolling around there on my schnozolla, and besides—it tickles. I don't like that. My aversion to the situation is critical; if I didn't care, one way or another, then the fly wouldn't embody a complication.

Look around you, at the fabric of life, at the landscape of the vale of tears. You will see, once you start looking for them, that there are complications in copious excess.

It's a complication when a bully threatens someone. If your bills exceed your salary, that's a complication. If your car won't start, or your boss hates you, or your doctor tells you that you have cancer . . . all those are complications.

Complications aren't complications unless they pose problems, but that doesn't mean that they have to be palpably awful to qualify.

Falling in love, for instance, is a gloriously wonderful thing—but it poses the enigma of how to get that sexy other person to fall equally in love with you, too. Accomplishing that presents you with the problem of how to make a relationship endure. Winning a million dollars in the lottery poses a problem of how to spend it and how it will change your life . . . a problem that has destroyed the lives of many lottery winners.

The complications I've just described so far have one thing in common: They're all primarily external. That is, they might involve internal feelings but those feelings are triggered by outside forces such as a bully, a bill collector, a mysterious cancer agent, a lover, or a lottery commission. Some of the best complications, though, involve internal forces.

Consider, for instance, the person who suddenly perceives that the world around him is insane. This is a complication of the first order, but it exists only because the person perceives that it does.

Likewise, if you don't worry about nuclear war then the arms race is not a complicating factor in your life; if once you sit down and think about it, though, and frighten yourself into paying attention . . . eureka! you have a complication.

By that principle, a complication emerges each time a person perceives a threat or realizes that he wants something that he doesn't have. Every time he changes his mind about the world around him, a complication arises from the fact that he now needs to adjust his life to suit the new reality.

Most complications involve both internal and external forces, and can be defined in either way or in combination.

As you can see, how the complication is defined may depend in large measure not only on how the character perceives it but also on how you the writer perceive the character perceiving it. We will explore this aspect of story analysis in the next chapter.

In any event the complication, by raising a problem that will hang there until it's solved, introduces the element of *tension*, which is sometimes called "suspense." It raises a question in the reader's mind as to how the problem will be solved, and what the outcome will mean to (and tell about) the character.

The world is chock full of complications and, as a writer, you must learn to spot them, instantly and without effort. You must be constantly on the lookout for them, keeping your mind's eye peeled as you sit in class, ride the bus, stand in cafeteria lines and otherwise proceed through life. Seeing stories is like any other marketable skill: It requires effort and practice. If it didn't, people wouldn't pay you for doing it.

The ability to spot complications comes easy to some; if you're one of them, you're already on your way. If not, I offer you an additional trick: Look for action.

Whenever you see someone do something, anything, ask yourself: *Why did he do that? What was his motive?* Your answer will lead you to a complication. That's because human action is taken for one purpose and one purpose only, which is to solve a complication. Without complications we would all be as inert as stop signs.

Once you have polished your ability to spot complications in the world around you, it's time to consider the question of value. From a writer's point of view, some complications are better, which is to say more dramatic, than others.

> *To be of literary value a complication must, first of all, be basic.*

If a person wants to mail a letter, well, yes . . . that is a complication. But the act of dropping it in the mailbox doesn't involve basic human forces.

A mathematical enigma may certainly complicate the lives of computer programmers. But under normal circumstances (if our story isn't destined for publication in a computer programmer's trade magazine) it'd be a weak complication for a drama story. It's too obscure. It just doesn't touch us where we live.

Complications that are more fundamental to the human condition, involving love, hate, pain, death and such, are very basic to the human dilemma and thus are fair game for the professional storyteller.

But something more than basic forces is required to make a strong complication. The fly on my nose, after all, involves fundamental human forces. We've all had the experience, and few if any of us has enjoyed it. So it qualifies as basic.

The fly, though, doesn't meet the second criterion for a good complication. It may be basic, but it isn't significant.

> *To be of literary value a complication must be not only basic but also significant to the human condition.*

To be dramatic, the complication has got to matter deeply to the character involved. The fly on my nose is but a passing inconvenience, and the situation can be resolved very easily. A wave of the hand will do it; the fly will then buzz off and land on *your* nose.

Or assume the complication involves a stolen car. If the character who owns the car is so wealthy he can walk down to the dealership and buy another without thinking about it, then you don't have much of a complication.

It would be quite different, though, if the stolen car was a collector's item that the character spent six years finding and restoring, or if the character needed it to get his pregnant wife to the hospital, fast. In either of those cases, you've got a story.

There are lots of permutations in which the interplay of character and situation determines whether or not a complication is weak or strong.

Say, for instance, that the character is a woman and the complication is that she can't conceive children. If she's a career woman and has much else in her life, and doesn't particularly want children anyway, then it's not a very dramatic situation.

But if she happens to be married to a crown prince who desperately needs an heir, well, that's a whole different kettle of fish.

Or if the marriage was a forced one, arranged by the bride's father for political convenience, and the crown prince bears a strong resemblance to a frog, tortures beagle puppies for a hobby and has breath that smells like a cesspool . . . well, then the inability to have babies may not be a complication at all.

That brings us to the next important part of the anatomy of a story, the *resolution*. A resolution is simply any change in the character or situation that resolves the complication.

When the fly leaves my nose, that complication is resolved, at least for me. If you get a substantial raise, your problems with the bill collectors are resolved. If the lottery winner decides to give all his money to the American Society for Homes for Homeless Homing Pigeons, then he has found a solution to his problem of how to spend his money.

A resolution, like a complication, can be either physical

or psychological, external or internal. The cancer patient's problem can be solved externally, by the surgeon who cuts out the tumor and the radiologist who kills the remaining malignant cells. Or it can be solved internally, as the character makes peace with himself and accepts the approach of death. Either solution reduces anxiety, which is to say tension, and is therefore a resolution.

A resolution, by definition, destroys tension.

As you scrutinize your daily life for complications, you will find that most of them really don't have resolutions.

Most people are confused, and they stay confused. Most want more money, and don't get it. Most people want to win lotteries, but don't. Many people never even manage to clearly recognize the complications that face them, so they don't have a prayer of dealing with them.

These complications without resolutions are worse than useless to the writer. Not only do they make poor stories, they often have the ability to mesmerize; the apprentice writer may expend copious amounts of mental energy trying to make them into stories. In fact, most of the stories I get from beginners consist of complications that are never resolved.

I reject them. So do editors. In fact, editors reject unresolved stories with such emphatic unanimity that the writer, not knowing the basis of that unanimity, often begins to feel paranoid.

It is your job as a writer to sort through the complications you see around you and winnow out such chaff before you waste your time and the editors'.

Most stories are uncovered in just the sequence I have described: The writer spots a complication, goes after it, and identifies a resolution. Then, in theory at least, he has the makings of a story.

But a substantial minority of stories, and many of the best, present themselves in reverse order: The writer sees the resolution and tracks it backward to discover a complication.

One of the best ways to find such resolutions is to read local newspapers, the smaller the better. Resolutions, because they so often involve accomplishment or highlight change, lend themselves to the quick and dirty, one- to five-inch news stories that can be printed around tire ads.

Local police crack a stolen-home-computer ring. A politician gets elected. A handicapped person forces the city to install a ramp into city hall. Someone wins a prize, receives an award, is honored at a banquet, gets a promotion, earns a degree, paints a mural, or otherwise makes a mark on the world. Those are all resolutions to some unknown complication or complications, and the newspaper serves them up to you for almost nothing.

From the dramatic point of view, of course, the local reporter misses the point when, in typical news fashion, he concentrates on the culminating event—the awarding of a certificate or the arrest of a petty crook—while ignoring the actions that led up to that event. *Most news stories are endings without beginnings attached.*

The feature writer approaches such news items differently. They are not, in and of themselves, stories. They are, instead, tip-offs . . . clues to stories.

What makes resolutions so valuable is that while a majority of complications don't have resolutions, resolutions almost always have complications. People may destroy by accident, but they build only with careful forethought. And anything people do on purpose they do with motivation, and their motivation is invariaby linked to a complication.

One of my favorite illustrations of how *not* to approach a resolution story has to do with "The Ballad of Old Man Peters."

I didn't get that story first. A national newspaper reporter got to Wilk long before I did. Mr. Peters received a certificate of appreciation from a local church organization, where he served as a volunteer translator for down-

and-out foreign travelers. The reporter heard about it and went out for an interview.

But the reporter made a fatal error: Having been attracted by the certificate, he assumed the certificate was the story. He produced a long, static piece about what a great translator Wilk was, and how much good he did for the travelers. It was, well . . . a nice story.

I was also fascinated with Wilk's good works, but I approached the problem differently. What, I asked, motivated this black sharecropper's son to learn six languages? Why did he expend so much effort to learn them?

Well, shucks, Wilk said. He was just interested in languages.

The earlier reporter had been satisfied with that answer. I wasn't. Mere interest is simply not sufficient to explain heroic effort. So I sat Wilk down for an in-depth interview about his life; he held me off for better than an hour with his modesty routine before he finally got tired and told me what *really* happened.

The story, as I suspected would be the case, was not about the certificate at all, or even about Wilk's volunteer work. The story was about a young man, born in a shack in Texas, who was smart enough to be terrified of his own ignorance and who was driven to overcome it. "The Ballad of Old Man Peters" is a powerful saga of human aspirations, of man against both himself and the world, and of the stubborn will of the species to survive and prosper.

The national news reporter's story was soon forgotten; mine made me a tidy bundle of cash, was read by millions of people, and is still being reprinted.

The difference? The other reporter didn't look for the complication, and I did.

Why didn't he, and why did I? I had thought more about the concept of story than he had, and I was aware that the story, as Wilk told it, was missing a critical element that *had* to be there.

The moral? Never fixate on just one part of a story. A

story with only a complication and no resolution won't ever get printed. A story with a resolution and no complication may, but it will be dramatically weaker for the lack. When the writer finds a resolution, he should singlemindedly pursue the complication and not stop until he's found it. He should make it his business to thoroughly understand his story, the nature of the basic deed, and the source of the motivation that lies behind it.

It is also important to understand that resolutions, like complications, embody literary values. Some are a whole lot better than others.

First and foremost, the resolution must specifically resolve the complication. If the complication is that the character was in danger of going bankrupt, for instance, he does not resolve it by becoming a born-again Christian. He may resolve his *fear* of bankruptcy in that fashion, but not the bankruptcy itself.

It's important to check complication-resolution pairs for such near misses. For one thing, they can often be redefined; the complication, in the above case, might be changed to focus on the fear, not on the bankruptcy. Such adjustments, always assuming they conform to reality, strengthen the story and crystallize it in the writer's mind.

The resolution of greatest value is also one that is constructive: To the eternal chagrin of angry adolescents who yearn to pen indictments against a world they do not yet understand, successful stories generally have happy endings.

There are a number of reasons for this and, yes, one of them is the public's maudlin craving to believe everything is quite all right when the world is obviously going to hell in a handbasket. But there is a certain legitimacy in this attitude, in the sense that the average reader can't do anything about the hell-in-a-handbasket problem anyway.

Besides, the reader's world has a surplus of sad endings as it is, and the most maddening thing about them is that they're not even very instructive. A tornado flattens a schoolhouse. A truck runs over an old man. Cancer strikes a popular schoolteacher.

Why? Short of metaphysics, there *is* no reason. Sad endings all too frequently leave us shaking our heads, none the wiser for the tragedy.

Even when there is a lesson in unhappiness, it's a negative one. When a compact car gets squashed by a truck, for instance, it teaches us to respect trucks.

Negative lessons are helpful, up to a point, and they're part and parcel of the trial-and-error learning process. But there are, after all, millions of potential errors for every wise, insightful choice; a citizen can easily stumble through life accumulating long lists of things not to do and still not get a clear grasp of what he *should* do. Negative lessons are painful and inefficient, and the intelligent reader has learned to put a rather small value on them.

What the reader really wants is to be shown some insightful choices that have positive results. He wants to learn something the easy way for a change. It's an eminently reasonable desire, and the writer who fulfills it is destined for fame and fortune.

One of the best ways to teach positive lessons while entertaining at the same time is to write stories about how people successfully cope with the world, endure, and even sometimes win. This is teaching by example in the finest sense, and both "Mrs. Kelly's Monster" and "The Ballad of Old Man Peters" are specifically crafted to do so.

But you may object, "Mrs. Kelly's Monster" is a sad story! The heroine dies at the hand of the hero!

I first perceived the story in that fashion myself, but if you analyze the piece carefully you'll discover I didn't write it that way. If I had, it would have been soon forgotten.

Most stories, and especially the good ones, have more than one complication. Mrs. Kelly's complication was the monster in her skull, and it was resolved with death. Sad, sad story. But I chose to organize my drama not around Mrs. Kelly's complication and resolution but around Tom Ducker's.

Dr. Ducker made Mrs. Kelly's complication his own, of course, but when she died under his knife he didn't fade into oblivion with her. He had to go on, to continue, to live—to do another operation, to help someone he *could* help. With dogged endurance, *he accepted his failure but refused to hate himself for it*. That is a lesson that the world sorely needs to learn.

So there were two stories in "Mrs. Kelly's Monster," one about death and one about life. Though both were told, I made the craftsman's decision to focus on the one about life. I was lavishly rewarded for that choice.

Still, to remain on the point of happy endings versus sad ones for one moment longer, there are examples in the literature of great stories with truly sad endings. I concede this fact. But most if not all of them were written by people who had many stories under their belts, and who were real pros. Amateurs rarely if ever write them.

This leads to a final, practical reason for the happy-ending rule: Sad endings are tricky, tricky, tricky. It takes an experienced writer to make a reader sit still, and read on, when the story in front of him begins to take on the unmistakable grimness of all-too-familiar reality. For this reason the unhappy ending, when it is written at all, is the preserve of the master craftsman.

So serve your apprenticeship first and *then* you can stick it to the world—assuming you still want to.

The final important point about the literary quality of resolutions is that they must, absolutely and without exception *must*, be products of the character's own efforts.

Fiction writers sometimes call this the "Mack truck principle," which stipulates that the lazy writer isn't allowed to solve his complication by having all his characters get run over by Mack trucks. Lightning strikes are also taboo, and a pauper can't be rescued from his plight by finding a winning lottery ticket. Acts of God make excellent complications, but the resolution must grow out of the main character's own efforts.

This doesn't mean the writer can't write stories with

act-of-God endings, of course. What it means is that the resulting stories won't show character progression, and therefore they are not likely to get into print—and if by some miracle they do get into print, they won't be remembered.

So the resolution, to be valid, must result from the character's own effort; for the story to be powerful, that effort must be significant. This brings us to another fundamentally important characteristic of a good story, which is *action*.

Complications and resolutions are absolutely necessary to identify and define the story, but beyond this a good story depends on action.

Literary action involves both physical and psychological movement, usually in combination. When I realize that a fly has landed on the tip of my nose, that's psychological action. When I respond by shooing it away with my hand, that's physical action.

It's not terribly interesting action, though, because it's easy. Chances are my thoughts about the fly are barely even conscious. To be of much value to the writer, action has to require expenditure of significant psychological and/or physical energy. The more energy expended, the more powerful the story.

In "Mrs. Kelly's Monster," for instance, the action involves a heroic effort on the part of the surgeon. In "The Ballad of Old Man Peters," the effort is a slow and steady one that consumes a lifetime.

In both cases, the significance of the character's effort played a major role in the success of the story. Consider how it would blunt the dramatic impact of "Monster" if the operation, dangerous or not, had been quick and easy. And what would have been the effect if Wilk Peters had been naturally gifted in languages, and hadn't had to labor over his books?

Once we have isolated a significant and basic complication, and discovered a resolution to match, we can begin the process of assembling the component parts of our story. This is the action step, and if you don't have a computer (they're valuable for shuffling ideas), I suggest you get out a pencil and a packet of 3x5 cards.

As a first step write the complication on one card and the resolution on another. Cast these two statements in terms of action, such as "Cancer strikes Joe," and "Joe overcomes cancer."

The practice of using a noun-verb-noun form for outline statements is pivotal. Using three words forces you to reduce your story to its essentials. If you understand the bare bones of your story, you will have little trouble adding flesh later; if you don't, you will almost always end up with a shapeless blob of literary protoplasm.

Let me emphasize here, lest you brush over it lightly, that the verbs in such statements must, absolutely and without exception *must*, be "action" verbs: "Cancer strikes Joe"; "Joe overcomes cancer." "Strikes" and "overcomes" are action verbs, strong verbs that describe concrete, specific actions. Avoid static verbs. In "Joe has cancer" or "Joe is sad" "has" and "is" describe not action but states of being, and this makes them more abstract, less vital.

If your statements don't describe actions, don't proceed to the next step until you make them do so. If you can't make them do so, you've got serious problems; either you don't yet understand your story, or you don't have a story at all. Either way, you can't write it.

Once you've stated your complications and resolution in terms of clear action, identify the actions your character takes in his attempts to overcome the complication. If you've chosen a complication of significance, he will certainly take a series of actions.

Using three-word active statements, you should be able to form a chronological chain of actions that lead either directly or indirectly from the complication to the resolution. This composes the development of your story.

The complication, the action events that flow from it,

and finally the resolution compose the backbone of the true story. A fiction writer would say you now have your plot.

These action events, including those that mark the complication and resolution, should all involve your character directly; either he does something, or something is done to him. Nothing else is relevant at this stage.

It is not, however, necessary that the actions lead directly to the resolution in a logical fashion. They must get there eventually, but few human beings are able to go straight from problem to resolution.

Usually they try this and that, run up some blind alleys, have some failures. . . . Many people reach their resolution more as a result of diligence, stubbornness or tenacity than by wise planning. In this respect, stories do reflect reality.

Once you've identified the complication and resolution, and constructed an action chronology to connect them, it's time to move on to the element of *character*.

The fact that I put off the discussion of character for so long is no accident, and it calls for an explanation. I do believe firmly, as I suspect every good writer does, that character is the central element of any short story, be it real-life drama or the sheerest fiction.

At the same time, definition of character is extremely difficult for the obvious reason that human beings are multifaceted and, to put it mildly, inconsistent. Character is a labyrinth in which a writer can wander without direction for weeks, months and even years. Though it's still embarrassing to admit it, I once spent ten years of off-and-on musing trying to define a character in a novel—and then gave up in failure.

Today I avoid this by means of the "black box" theory of psychology. That theory holds that it's irrelevant to consider what a person thinks; *look instead at what he does*. Actions, in literature as in life, speak far louder than words.

So the practical writer looks first at the character's actions. Unlike vague elements of "personality," action can be defined specifically. But at the same time you must remember that actions are outgrowths of character; once defined, a character's actions can lead us to the character himself. Character is the most important element of the story, and the one on which all else depends; because it's so important, and also so complex, we approach it last.

End of digression.

"Character" has a literary definition. He or she is the human being whose life the complication complicates. It is he who acts, and is acted upon. It is he who reaches equilibrium when the resolution finally occurs.

The most important thing to remember about your character, whoever he is, is that he is a real, live human being. In fiction he must seem so; in the true story he *is*. Expect him to be idiosyncratic, unique, unlike any other. This is absolutely critical; since your complication is the most basic and universal you could use to describe your character's dilemma, you are relying on the uniqueness of your character to make your story unique as well.

This leads to a stern warning: Woe be unto the poor writer who transforms his character into a stereotype, for his story shall be boring and he shall be known as a hack.

Actually, when it comes to character development, the dramatic feature writer has life much easier than his fiction-writing counterpart. Making up a character out of whole cloth is one of the most difficult tasks fiction writers face; most of them ultimately resort to plagiarizing reality. The feature writer doesn't have to cheat. He copies from life without blushing.

The shaping of character involves asking, and answering, a series of questions based on your previous observations.

You know, for instance, that your character faced his complication and, in response, performed a series of actions. That means he took the complication seriously—it was significant to him, or he wouldn't have acted.

Now, ask yourself: What sort of person would take such a complication seriously?

The answer to this question is rich with literary meaning. The fact that Wilk Peters saw his own ignorance as an abiding complication in his life, for instance, speaks eloquently about Wilk—the vast majority of men and women find ignorance relatively easy to live with.

The case of a wealthy man's stolen car, mentioned above, is not much of a complication on the surface. But if the man is a miser the loss is quite a different matter.

The diagnosis of cancer seems like a very obvious and straightforward complication, since the fear of death is universal. Even so, the situation has different shades depending on character.

If the victim is deeply religious and looks forward to the afterlife, for instance, he will have resources to deal with the specter of impending death and may remain relatively calm. But if he's a hard-driven executive who has expended his years in the pursuit of money and power, and has never taken time to enjoy life or consider its spiritual aspects, the response is apt to be much more anguished. The situation presents a complication to both, but the executive will have fewer resources and, thus, more to learn—and to endure.

Finally, consider once more that hypothetical fly on my nose; think of how much stronger that complication becomes if I also happen to be paralyzed from the neck down.

The point is that how your character views the complication tells you something very important about the character. *What's more, what it tells you is relevant to the story*.

This is important, as we will see later, because characterization doesn't involve laying out the whole person; even in a novel, that would be wildly overambitious. The writer concentrates, instead, on probing those facets of character that are directly relevant to the story.

Having determined how your character views the complication, ask yourself *why* he views it that way. Almost inevitably, this is going to take you into the past.

If your complication involves a dog-shy woman whose neighbor buys a kill-trained Doberman, for instance, you need to know precisely what previous role dogs played in her life.

Is she afraid because she was bitten as a child? If so, write that down, complete with date and some detail, on another 3x5 card. Though it happened before the complication arose, it's relevant to the importance that the complication assumes in her mind. Therefore, it's part of your chronology and will eventually go in a flashback.

Ask yourself as many questions as you can to allow you to identify the action events in the person's past life that make him relate as he does to the complication.

Once you have run out of questions, turn your attention to the first of the actions your character takes in response to the complication, and ask the same questions again.

Why, faced with the complication, does this person respond the way he does? Does the woman punch her dog-loving neighbor in the nose? Does she get a lawyer? Does she cower in her house, doing nothing? Does she quietly plot to kill the dog?

Whatever she does, you need to know precisely what events in her past conditioned her into that approach. Those events, complete with dates, go on the 3x5 cards. Continue this process until you reach the resolution.

Now, having done that, proceed to the first action event—that is, to the person's first step in trying to resolve the complication. How does the world respond to that attempt? If she punches the neighbor in the mouth, does he punch her back? Does he get a lawyer?

These events, too, go on 3x5 cards.

When this is finished, lay the cards aside for a moment and ask yourself a few more questions, just to make certain you understand your story so far and to prepare yourself to analyze the significance of the resolution to the character.

First, did the character fully *understand* the complication he faced?

Most characters don't; they refine their understanding of the problem as they work their way through it, and firmly grasp its dimensions only in hindsight.

An alcoholic's complication, for instance, would probably involve his drinking—but by the very nature of his disease he would deny this even though it was clear to the reader. The alcoholic character would see his problem as arising because life is tough, or because others are picking on him. Only as he resolves his problems by going on the wagon does he realize that his battle was really with the bottle.

So ask yourself, finally, how the events of your story changed your character. What conclusions did he draw from each event? If presented with a similar complication today, would he respond in the same fashion or has he learned something from his struggles?

In the best stories, the odyssey from complication to resolution changes the character profoundly. In fact, the resolution often results not directly from the action but from a growing enlightenment—often a sudden flash of insight—as the character finally realizes what he has to do to solve his problem.

Screenwriters often call this flash of insight, or self-realization, a "plot point." Screenwriters talk about two plot points, the first being the complication and the second coming near the end of the story, where the character finally fully perceives the nature of his problem and, as a result, sees how to solve it. But since we are discussing complication and resolution form, we have the need to refer to only one plot point, the second, or point of insight.

Does your story have such a plot point? If it's a good story, full of action and character, it probably does—though you may have trouble putting your finger on it. If you do have trouble, the confusion may indicate that you have not defined your complication and resolution clearly enough.

Once you identify the plot point, you know you have found a story in which the character's struggle leaves him a better, more mature individual. You have thus tied character irrevocably to plot, and you have a viable story.

In the old days, when fiction was king, that was the hallmark of the superior short story. Today, in the era of the true story, it remains the ultimate test of quality.

If your story does not meet that final test, even though it meets all others, pitch it. It is many times more difficult to salvage a bad story than it is to keep looking, and looking, and looking, until you find the right one. When you finally do, you'll be glad you were patient.

If your story meets all the criteria it will, in the language of editors, "work." That means it will consist of a real person who is confronted with a significant problem, who struggles diligently to solve that problem, and who ultimately succeeds—and in doing so becomes a different character.

The "structure," as a nonfiction plot is called, will consist of a sequence of action events. Some of those action events will take place before the complication and will be related in flashback, in which you will establish the roots of character and motivation. The rest of the story will be the sequential actions that follow the complication and carry the story through to the resolution.

The reader will read the story because he identifies with the character and is caught up in the action . . . the plot. When he is finished he will be glad he took the time to read the story, and he will remember your byline.

The thing that will make him a satisfied customer is partly the fact that he was entertained. But the deeper satisfaction comes when the reader *learns with the character*. The reader, like the character, thus becomes a better and wiser person; the story, in the final analysis, is an artificial experience. It doesn't moralize but, like all experience, it teaches.

V

Structure

THE MOST FUNDAMENTAL TRUTH about the cosmos is that big things are composed of little ones. Quarks combine to form intermediate particles; intermediate particles fuse into protons, neutrons and electrons, which become atoms, which snap together into molecules, which combine into rocks and clouds and so on, and so on, and so on, until we have planets, stars, nebulae, galaxies, galactic clusters, clusters of clusters, and ultimately the universe.

This is not just a matter of physics. Stones and bricks form buttresses and walls, which enclose rooms and chambers, and so on unto Winchester Cathedral. Likewise atoms make molecules, which compose organelles, which form cells, which become organs, which combine into men and women, who organize themselves into societies. Everywhere you look big things are constructed from littler ones, and those from littler ones yet.

The principle applies equally in what we call the arts. Plays are composed of acts, which, in turn, are conglomerations of scenes. Great symphonies are amalgams of movements, poems are composed of stanzas, and stories are structures of . . . well, that's what this chapter is about.

That structure is pivotal to storycraft is obvious, or at least it should be, but if you've been steeped in the mysteriousness of art (as most of us have) it's difficult to think about writing in those terms. They seem too abstract and reductionistic to have any emotional relevance, too alien to have any appeal. So there is a natural tendency to turn away.

Don't. For it is here, in the coldly logical prefrontal realm of the mind and not in the heart, that the secrets of the masters are kept. He who would comprehend stories, no less than he who would understand universes or temples, must first grasp the nature of their component parts.

As we look closely at structures, whether they be physical or artistic, natural or manmade, we soon notice something rather odd and very important. The big things often don't relate to one another the way the little ones do.

The forces that allow mortar to stick bricks together, for instance, are different from those that keep arches and flying buttresses stable; the laws of psychology that cement a family are not quite the same as those that solidify nations.

In noticing this, we have raised the important structural concept of "scale" and "levels." Here there are strikingly important parallels between the physical universe and the artistic one.

The physical universe is governed by four forces: gravity, electromagnetism, the strong force, and the weak force. Those forces are all around us, yet they have their effects on different scales.

Within the atom the forces of electromagnetism and gravity are negligible; interactions between the substructural units of the atom are almost entirely determined by the strong and weak forces. But on the scale of everyday life, at which we can meaningfully speak of apples and oranges and mice and elephants and even mosquitoes and planets, the laws of gravity and electromagnetism dominate. The weak and strong forces are there, but they cancel one another out and almost nowhere we look (except at the stars) can we see evidence of their existence.

As a writer you will encounter similar shifts as you move from one structural level to another. When you deal with sentences, for instance, where relatively simple thoughts interact, the cliché is poison. But when large-scale structures are interacting that is no longer the case; at the conceptual levels, the cliché undergoes a strange metamorphosis: It becomes an eternal truth.

The apprentice who has not yet discovered this literary principle of relativity will be totally mystified by the contradictions it produces. It is this, more than any other single factor, that gives a mistaken legitimacy to the widespread impression that literary principles are arbitrary. They are not. What they are is tricky.

As heretical as it seems, for instance, words are not, repeat *not*, the basic unit of literary structure.

I'm certainly not saying they're irrelevant. And I'm not contradicting Mark Twain's admonition that the difference between the right word and the almost right word is the difference between the lightning and the lightning bug. A phrase like "ode on a Grecian urn" can carry a whole lot more information than "poem about a Greek jug," even though, according to the thesaurus, they say exactly the same thing.

But as you've surely noticed, very few people are capable of choosing the right word; they make do with almost-right words and in spite of their sloppiness they manage to live, love, run businesses, fight wars, and even write books. Sometimes they write very good books, with solid heart-pounding structures. We routinely forgive writers for sloppiness in word usage.

The reason we're so charitable is that what we most want is story—which is to say, structure. *That's* what's important to us, as readers. And words, as wonderful as they truly are, play a role analogous to that of the atom in biology.

Atoms are necessary to living things, insofar as they make up the molecules of life. Without them there's nothing. But it's the interaction of molecules, and not of individual atoms, that gives rise to the complexity of biology. Likewise in literature it's "molecules" of words, and not the individual words themselves, that impart life and vitality.

We call this literary molecule the *image*.

The image to which I refer, though, is probably quite different from the sort of image you studied in Composition 100.

To understand that difference, and its critical nature, we must take a roundabout route so that I can introduce the concept of *focus*.

"Focus" as a word has several meanings, all of them related but all slightly different, depending on the context. In its first and most common usage, "focus" is a verb. You "focus" your mind on a subject, for instance.

In another, more technical sense, it is a noun. As a noun it describes a particular chunk of copy that focuses on a single idea, action, or event.

In its third meaning, and the one we will discuss first, it is a principle.

The principle of focus was first explained to me by novelist J. T. Salamanca, who teaches creative writing at the University of Maryland. Salamanca was also interested in filmmaking, and so it was from that art form that he drew his analogy.

The scene was his office. I had just handed him a perfectly shapeless piece of copy.

He read it politely, though I could tell his stomach hurt. He thought about it, shifted around in his chair, and peered at me for a long time.

Imagine, he finally said, that I was a cameraman.

Imagine that I was standing, camera in hand, before a

huge crowd of people, and that I wanted to record the essence of that crowd on film.

As an amateur it would be my first reaction to pan the camera smoothly across the assembled faces. By doing so I would record a sea of people, all of them moving rapidly from one side of the frame to the other.

In one sense I would have fulfilled my assignment: The film would indeed show the crowd. But would it do so effectively?

The answer was no, it would not. It wouldn't be effective because the individual human beings would be a blur; the film would present a confusion of images and stimuli, without emphasis, to the audience—and it's the audience, not the film, that counts.

A professional filmmaker would do it differently. He would focus on a single representative face and zoom in on it until it filled the frame. He would linger there, for a moment—long enough for the viewer to perceive the emotional state of the person, to see if he's screaming in anger, or cheering, or crying. In that way the film captures the humanness of the face, a single face, a unique face, with which the audience can identify.

Then the filmmaker would zoom back, and the person who had filled the frame an instant ago would recede to become, once again, a face lost in the crowd.

Then, having panned back, the cameraman would move the camera—just far enough to find another face, and then he would zoom in on that and record whether that face was laughing, or crying, or shouting in anger.

The filmmaker would repeat the process several times, zooming in on individuals, giving the viewer a moment to make an identification, then zoom back, pan across the crowd for an instant, then find another face to zoom in on.

The resulting impression in the viewer's mind would be of an amalgam of children and old people, men and women, tall and short, fat and thin. The crowd, in the hands of an expert filmmaker, would become a *human* thing, and therefore meaningful.

Salamanca's example illustrated two closely related points. The first was that the audience, or in my case the reader, had to have something for the mind to focus on—*something specific*—in order to make an identification.

The other point was that there are two fundamentally different phases of communication. In the first, the audience was being invited to focus down. In the second, illustrated by the act of panning the camera, the audience was carried from one focus to another. (Note that, in this usage, "focus" becomes a noun.)

All of literature, in short, can be divided into two parts. Focuses are one thing. Transitions are quite another.

Salamanca gave me a moment to absorb the lesson, then handed my manuscript back to me. I had panned across my story as the amateur pans a crowd, and the result was a meaningless blur, without emphasis; having no emphasis, it had no drama. Having no drama, it had little interest.

Go back, he said, and rewrite it. Only this time tell the story in discrete chunks. I did so, and the difference in my copy was nothing less than astonishing.

Now, the concept of focus clearly in mind, we return to the subject of the "image" and "imagery." The image is the molecule of literature, the smallest possible subunit of story, the tiniest of all possible focuses.

But if you visualize "image" as static, something like "the ancient oak tree with its overhanging branches," you are dead wrong and you're going to have to unlearn everything you think you know about images.

In the context of story, "the ancient oak tree with its overhanging branches" just won't do as an image—it's as useless as a hemoglobin molecule without any carbon atoms. "The ancient oak tree with its overhanging branches" lacks a critical element.

That element is the verb.

It wasn't enough for the camera to focus on a face in the crowd; for the focus to be effective *that face had to be expressing emotion*.

Salamanca didn't point that out to me, because action is

such a fundamental part of life that filmmakers take it for granted . . . unless, of course, it isn't there. The fact is that faces in the crowd are always *doing* something, always laughing, shouting, crying, or otherwise expressing emotion. That's what crowds are about. That's what life is about.

The writer, unlike the filmmaker, works in a potentially static medium. Most of what the writer reads, in fact, is static—and therefore boring. So the writer has to think about action, about verbs, and he's got to think about them hard.

The fact that action is basic to life is grounded in the human brain.

We habitually think of the brain, ours and the reader's as being the organ of thought and emotion. But when neuroanatomists examine its wiring it turns out that it's at least 95 percent or more devoted to movement, and the remainder is there to allow us to figure out what that movement should or did accomplish. Human thoughts, all but the tiny minority of philosophical thoughts, are centered on action.

To be more prosaic, consider how we commonly judge one another. As children, perhaps, we judge people by what they say or who they are, but we are soon disabused of the usefulness of that strategy. As grownups we pay much more careful attention to what people do than to what they say. Actions, as the cliché instructs us, really do speak louder than words.

And that is why images, to function adequately, must be based on verbs. If they aren't, they can't transmit much in the way of meaningful information.

There are two kinds of verbs and, as a result, there are two kinds of images.

An image can be passive or active depending on the verb you use in its construction. Images built on static verbs—those that describe states of being—I call passive, because they convey almost no activity. Avoid the following static verbs in building images: have, has, had, be, am, is, do, does, did, being, been, are, was, and were. These are much weaker and less effective than action verbs. But *most* important, they lack the force necessary for effective outlining.

"The big oak tree *has* spreading branches" is a passive image built on the static verb "has." Make the verb stronger and more direct—use an action verb—and the image springs to life: "The oak tree *spreads* its branches." This is an active image.

This second type of image is so central to the writing process that henceforth in this book when I use the word "image" I will mean "active image" unless otherwise specified.

Active images, built on action verbs, are focuses of action. Here are a few examples:

The teenager kicked the dog.
The woman glowered at her accuser.
The judge slammed down his gavel.
The limb fell on the girl.
The car slammed into the abutment.

In theory, focuses are always separated by transitions. In practice, though, elemental focuses—which is to say images—often don't need explicit transitions. Because one action logically follows another, the transitions are understood.

For instance:

> *The bartender looked sternly at David and told him pointedly that homosexuals were not welcome in Joe's Tavern. David hesitated, slid off the bar stool and stomped away. As the door swung shut the bartender threw back his head and laughed.*

Until now no transitions have been needed because the focus stays steady, unwavering, on the scene. But now, to proceed further we need a transition:

Outside, on the street . . .

That transition carries us to the next set of images:

> *. . . David's shoulders slumped as his outrage shaded into the realization that he'd done it again. He'd walked out, angrily . . . but angrily or not, all the same, he'd walked out. What he should have done was punch the son-of-a-bitch in the mouth. . . .*

What we have there, in aggregate, is a series of active images, or focuses, that combine to form two larger focuses. The two larger focuses are joined by a simple transition ("Outside, on the street"). The transition is simple because we don't change anything but place, and we don't change that by more than a few feet.

A story is constructed in this fashion. Clusters of simple images form focuses, which in turn are joined by simple transitions to form larger focuses. Those larger focuses then combine to form still larger focuses that are glued together with increasingly complex transitions that guide the reader through changing times, moods, subjects and characters.

Ultimately the focuses combine to form several "major" focuses that compose the principle structural subunits of stories like "Mrs. Kelly's Monster."

To get a clearer idea of how the process works, let's take a look at the first major focus of "Mrs. Kelly's Monster."

In that story, the first subfocus describes Dr. Ducker eating his breakfast. The second switches to downtown Baltimore and introduces Mrs. Kelly and her pain. The third focus switches back to Dr. Ducker. The fourth returns to Mrs. Kelly, flashes back to her birth and quickly reveals what the reader must know about her past life in order for the story to make sense. The major focus ends as the reader discovers she calls her malformation "the monster."

The division of subfocus in this case is largely arbitrary;

subfocuses blend into one another, and where I see one you may discern two. That's all right.

But major focuses are quite distinct, and there isn't much room for personal interpretation. Where the first major focus ends is, somehow, distinct to all thoughtful observers.

This is because a whole new set of forces, which exerted no detectable influence at the level of image and subfocuses, come into play as we approach the highest level of all—the level at which "story" exists.

At first, as we dealt with images and the smaller range of focuses, their size and order seemed to depend on the individual circumstances of the story. But as the focuses grow larger they naturally conglomerate into several major structural units. In the short story, whether it is fiction or nonfiction, there are typically five.

The shape of *these* units, unlike the smaller one, is determined by a very specific set of laws that are more or less independent of the story's individuality. Where major focuses begin and end is not at all open to interpretation. What's more, each of the major focuses has a very specific and universal function.

The first focus in any story, for instance, is the "complicating" focus. This is the one in which the writer sets the stage for, and finally reveals, the event that complicates the character's life.

This is accomplished by a progression of "subfocuses" that hook the reader, reveal the character or characters, and finally show the nature of the dilemma the story will illustrate.

The number of aggregations of focuses between the level of the image and that of the story depends, generally, on the length and complexity of the story. Jokes are typically very short, and there the image may double as major focus, while a psychological novel may consist of aggregations on a dozen scales.

Regardless of how many organizational steps there are in the hierarchy between image and major focus, however, the practicing writer is most concerned with three levels; these are the levels between which the laws of literary nature seem to change.

The finest level, that of image, is called the *polish level*. The process of polish is concerned with grammar, word usage, the subcraft of imagery, and the various principles of sentence and paragraph structure.

Since this is the only level of composition that the reader ever sees directly, most people are of the grievously mistaken impression that it's the alpha and omega of writing. As a result, most of what you've been taught, and have figured out on your own, probably applies only to the polish level.

The intermediate level, which is concerned with the internal makeup of major focuses, is called the *structural level*.

This level is concerned with the internal organization of each major focus. It deals with sequence of action, as well as emphasis, pacing and orientation. When a writer is writing and rewriting he's working on the structural level and must be aware, on a moment-to-moment basis, of the laws peculiar to that level.

The *outline level* is by far the most abstract of the three and yet, in a certain sense, the most straightforward.

When he is working at the outline level the writer is concerned with the conceptual relationships between the character and the action, which boils down to the interrelationships between the five major focuses. It is at this level that the craftsman creates the foundation of his story.

All work at the outline level is based on the principle that dramatic stories invariably consist of three major parts. The first and the last part consist of a single major focus; the middle part generally consists of three major focuses.

The first major focus, without exception, is the complication.

The complication is usually a rather "busy" focus, since it must begin with a lead or "narrative hook," introduce the character and his time and place, and finally present him with the complication.

The next three focuses constitute the body of the story, or the "development," which describes the character's actions as he attempts to resolve the complication. Individually and collectively the developmental focuses tend to be long, compared to the first and last focuses, but they are also the least complex and the easiest to write.

(I say, by the way, that the development of the story consists of three focuses. That precise number is empirical; I have never seen a good story that could be conceptualized clearly in two developmental focuses; and I have rarely seen those that required four.)

The last focus is, of course, the resolution. It begins as the character sets off on the series of actions that will culminate in the achievement of the resolution, and it ends when that resolution is accomplished.

Given that overview, let's examine the five focuses again, this time including some of the salient principles and peculiarities associated with each.

The Complicating Focus

The complicating focus, as I have said, is . . . well, complicated. It's complicated because it serves an introductory function as well as a strictly narrative one, but at the same time it's imperative that it be kept short.

Any dramatic piece draws its energy from the reader's curiosity, both intellectual and emotional, about how the complication is going to be solved. In a whodunit, the reader wants to know, you guessed it, whodunit. In a dramatic short story, be it fiction or nonfiction, the reader wants to know how the character is going to make out . . . is he gonna get the girl, or isn't he? This is "dramatic tension."

And it doesn't exist until you get to the complicating event, which doesn't come until the *end* of the complicating focus. It is the climax of that focus; all that comes before is preamble, introducing the character and setting the scene for the confrontation of character and problem.

This embodies the dilemma that the writer faces in the complication. The writer doesn't really have the reader by the scruff of his neck until the complication is ended. Until then the writer has to keep the reader interested by sheer craftsmanship and wit, by breathing life into the character, by skillful use of language and, most of all, by fore-shadowing.

For example, consider "Mrs. Kelly's Monster." When I remark in the first paragraph that Dr. Ducker doesn't drink coffee because coffee makes his hands shake, I imply to the reader that Dr. Ducker is going to do some-thing very important with his hands. This is in effect a dramatic promise; on my honor, I promise the reader, I'm not telling him all this stuff for nothing.

Even so, a promise is not substance. It is therefore important for the narrative to proceed from the lead, or hook, as rapidly as possible to the complication.

The complicating event, the climax of the complication, delivers the reader finally into the writer's clutches. From that moment on the rules change; the writer now has some leeway. He has made a promise and fulfilled it, and having done so, he has won the reader's trust.

In the case of "Mrs. Kelly's Monster" that moment arrives when Mrs. Kelly is in the operating room and it becomes clear that Dr. Ducker is about to embark on a life-or-death combat with the monster.

At that point the complicating focus has served its purpose, and is done.

The Developmental Focuses

The development, or body, of your story will generally consist of three separate, interlinked substories that may or may not have internal structures in common.

The first developmental focus may show your reader muddling through his past, the second may show him muddling through the present, and the third may show him grasping the nature of the problem and, for the first time, taking logical and positive steps toward the resolution.

Or he may try one thing in the first developmental focus, fail at it, and try another tack in the second focus. He may fail at that, too, and go on to try still a third thing in the last developmental focus.

In either of those cases the developmental focuses are not strongly and logically linked to one another. But if the complication provides the character with three separate subproblems, then each of the developmental focuses will be reduced to a story-within-a-story.

Let us say, for instance, that the complication involves a knight who vows to kill a dragon. To do so he may have to travel to the land of Ku, cross a shallow sea to the isle of Ort, where the dragon dwells. Once there, he must find the dragon.

In this case your first developmental focus would describe his adventures on the road to Ku, the second would tell how he crossed the sea, and the third would show his search for the dragon.

Whatever overall form the three developmental focuses assume, though, they will have some internal similarities. Each will have, for instance, a specific beginning, middle, and end.

Explanatory material will come at the beginning; often there will be a minor complication there as well. The dramatic high point, your punch line, will always, always, *always* come at the end.

For example, in the story of the would-be dragonslayer, the focus in which he crosses the sea might have three subfocuses. The first might begin with him searching for a boat (a subcomplication) and then finally finding one (which resolves the subcomplication). Then he might have to sail the boat across a stormy sea (a second subcomplication) until he finds the island (resolving the second subcomplication). Finally he may have to navigate his way to the beach through rocks and shoals (a third subcomplication). When he sets foot on the island, the third subcomplication is resolved. He has also resolved the major complication of the focus, which is to cross the sea; therefore the focus ends.

Often the subfocuses will be much less linear. Let's assume for instance that the complication presents the character with a problem, such as impending bankruptcy, that admits to many different approaches.

The first subfocus of the first developmental focus might flash back to the general events of the character's poverty-stricken childhood. The second subfocus might dwell on his desire for a wagon. The third might show how he got the wagon by dint of hard work. This would lead the reader to suspect that the character will approach his present complication, the major complication of the story, in the same tenacious fashion. Once this message is communicated the flashback would end, along with the focus, and the narrative would emerge into "real time."

The subject of flashbacks brings us to a structural peculiarity of the first developmental focus. If there is to be a major flashback in a story, it will usually be there.

To begin with, a flashback is the most potentially disorienting technique in all of the writing craft. The reader's mind normally runs in a forward fashion, as life is lived, and a flashback forces it to flow in the opposite direction. It's work for the reader to flash back, and he won't do it unless he's really on your side. He will never be on your side so solidly as immediately following an exciting, tension-producing complication.

That's when you hit him with a flashback. You leave the hero standing in front of the king, vowing to slay the dragon, and flash back to his childhood to trace the events that explain why he's dumb enough, or desperate enough, to take on dragons.

In specific terms, get out that chronological list of actions that you made as you found and analyzed your story.

If some of those actions occurred before the complication, the first developmental focus is the time to flash back and tell about them.

While you're at it, be sure to start at the beginning and tell the whole flashback in chronological order and be done with it. The reader generally won't stand for more than one major flashback in a short story, so you've got to do it all at once.

When does a major flashback end? Usually at the end of the first developmental focus. Then the second developmental focus begins in real time. In rare cases the flashback may go on for two developmental focuses and in very, very rare cases you may proceed in flashback all the way to the resolution.

The resolution, though, since it must by definition follow the complication, must occur in real time—which is to say after the complication.

In any event, the crucial peculiarity of the first developmental focus is its ability to sustain a major flashback. You don't *have* to flash back there, but if you're going to flash back at any place, do it there.

The second developmental focus, in contrast, is structurally unremarkable. If it has any peculiar strengths, weaknesses or requirements, I haven't found them.

The third and final developmental focus, though, is definitely distinctive.

As the first developmental focus must take us deep into the story, so the end of the last developmental focus must carry us back out again. It does so by means of the character's "moment of insight," which we briefly discussed earlier.

The moment of insight, sometimes called a "plot point" in screenplays, occurs at the end of the third developmental focus, either as the climax of that focus or as a realization associated with that climax. It is there, at the end of the third developmental focus, on the threshold of the resolution, that the character visualizes clearly what he must do to solve his problem.

In the case of the dragonslayer, for instance, the third developmental focus would end with our hero finally locating the dragon. In the case of the whodunit, this is the point at which the detective suddenly has the flash of insight that reveals to him (though not to the reader) who the guilty party is. When Perry Mason gets that faraway look in his eye and suddenly changes his tactics, the point of insight has been reached.

The Resolving Focus

The resolving focus, which will end your story, may be long or short—but it will always read breathlessly fast.

All background has already been introduced, examined, and dispensed with. The character has made his agonizing choices. He has taken the actions required to bring him to this fateful point. Now he must proceed, with psychological or physical action, in a straightforward way, to solve the problem.

In a whodunit, the resolving focus consists of the detective moving in for the kill. In most action films, the resolution commonly consists of a chase. In more subtle resolutions the process involves the psychological action of the character accepting and coming to terms with the reality. In "Mrs. Kelly's Monster" the resolution describes the surgeon trying to fight after all hope is gone and finally, grimly facing the fact that he has lost and resolving to go on, as he must, with life.

A Variation on the Form

The structural form represented by "Mrs. Kelly's Monster" is the one most commonly used in marketable true stories today, but it has one major variation: the saga.

The saga, like the straight complication-resolution story, consists of a major complication and a major resolution.

But, instead of having three developmental focuses, it features a series (often five) of interlinked substories. Each substory, or episode, has its own complication and resolution.

These episodes are interlocked in the sense that each new complication is presented either before or immediately after the earlier complication is resolved, and as part of that same episode. Thus the element of tension is preserved and reinforced.

The old-fashioned Saturday-afternoon matinee serials worked in that way, each one ending with a cliff-hanger that made the audience want to come back next week and find out what happened. Modern-day television soap operas are structured in the same fashion.

The movie *Star Wars* used exactly this same trick when the villain was allowed to escape at the end of the film, thus ensuring a market for sequels. One of the best recent examples of saga form in a successful, full-length novel is James Clavell's *Shogun*.

The saga form is also extremely useful in modern newspaper journalism, where the emphasis is on brevity. Saga form allows the writer to divide his story into distinct segments, each with a cliffhanger that will ensure readership the following day. The five verses of "The Ballad of Old Man Peters" were printed on five consecutive days in *The Evening Sun*.

Now that you have a feeling for overall story structure, it's time to turn our attention to one of the most misunderstood and therefore most feared of all the techniques in the writer's bag of tricks: outlining.

VI

The Outline

PRESUMABLY YOU'RE OUT to change the world. Why else would you undergo the slow and ignoble torture of the writing apprenticeship, if not to burn the brand of your ideology or at least individuality into the hide of history?

Simply to embark on the writer's life you must look into your soul and ask yourself whether you have the courage to endure the pain of being ignored or, even more frightening, to accept the responsibilities that go with success. I must assume you have asked yourself those questions, and answered them in the affirmative, or you wouldn't be reading this book.

That being the case, it is most unseemly of you to cower and cringe at the mere mention of outlines.

But, you say miserably, you can't do it? You know you can't do it? Maybe there's something wrong with you but you've tried, and tried, and tried, and it didn't work?

And, you say—you're weasling, now—outlines are optional, aren't they? Did Hemingway outline? you ask. Did Steinbeck outline? Did Shakespeare outline?

Yeah. Sure they did, Of course. Obviously.

I don't care what you've heard, or what your literature teacher said, *or even what the writers themselves said.* Every writer of any merit at all during the last five hundred years of English history outlined virtually everything he wrote.

That's not to say that Shakespeare, before putting pen to paper to write *Hamlet,* sat down and worked through a junior-high-school Formal Outline with Roman Numerals and sub-one and sub-two and A and (a) and all that. Shakespeare was above all an intelligent man, and I'm sure he would have instantly recognized such an outline as the abomination it is.

As near as I can figure it, such outline systems were specifically designed to convince budding writers that outlining is impossible, and that the only way they can create worthwhile copy is to hack their way through the words like a hunter slashing a path through a seven-canopy jungle. It's good for the soul. It teaches humility. The Roman Numeral type of outline will henceforth in this book be recognized for what it is, the English Teacher's Revenge, or ETR for short.

If defeat in the face of the ETR outline is what convinced you that you couldn't cope with outlines, then let me confess that I, too, was a victim. I clearly remember the teacher who first forced me to my knees in front of the ETR. I would thank her one day, she sternly and knowingly assured me.

Hah! I don't normally spit on graves, but for her I make an exception. I was so thoroughly scared and demoralized that I developed a phobia about outlines, and my ability to cope with them; as a result I wasted at least five years of my writing career proceeding on the assumption that outlining could be avoided.

Well, I'm here to inform you of a grim truth: It can't be.

And even if it could, no sane writer would want to, because, believe it or not, once you understand what an outline is, it serves to make writing much, much easier.

An outline, you see, has nothing to do with Roman Numerals. It is simply a scheme, or a set of procedures, that you use to sort out your thoughts and analyze your story before you sit down to write.

In telling yourself you can't outline, what you're *really* saying is that you can't think your story through, and if that's actually the case—which I seriously doubt—then you'd better give up your writing ambitions before you become successful enough for people to discover that you don't know what you're talking about.

Obviously, if you can't think your story through you can't write it convincingly. That's why I so smugly assert that Hemingway, Steinbeck and Shakespeare used outlines. I've read their stuff, and it has integrity—that quality of all hanging together, and being an interrelated, organic whole. Integrity in a story is something you just don't get unless you did a workmanship job of thinking your story through in the first place.

What you get if you *don't* think your story through is, well . . . if you're convinced you can't outline, you've surely had the experience.

For openers, you have this great idea. Your enthusiasm is without bounds; the idea is so good you're certain it'll work. So you sit down in front of your typewriter or word processor and start banging away with a vengeance.

In the beginning the words pour out smoothly and they're nothing short of wonderful. A hundred words accumulate. Two hundred. And then . . . you start running into problems.

Something you did in the first two hundred words doesn't quite mesh perfectly with something you have to do in the next one hundred words, but you're not quite sure why. It seems to be telling you something . . . but what? You try to understand but, as you do, a certain confusion arises in your mind; that's disconcerting and dangerous, so you back off. Ah, well. You'll fix it later You push on.

You pound away some more, slower now. It's becoming apparent that you'll have to rewrite. This is not going to work totally on inspiration but, all the same, it's still a really hot story. You pound some more, slower yet. Something's getting complicated. And then you hit another glitch, another inconsistency, and then another.

You press on, but . . . it's getting harder, now; the copy is taking on the consistency of horse-hoof glue, and your mind is slowing down. You thought you knew where you were going, but your words seem to be carrying you somewhere . . . slightly different. Confusion oozes across your brainpan. But you know what you're doing . . . that is to say, you *did* know what you were doing . . . but now you're having trouble keeping it clear in your mind.

You keep forgetting to put things in; you need to go back and foreshadow, while it's fresh in your mind, but if you do that you'll loose your place . . . and you can't remember why it was that your main character had that lisp . . . oh, yeah, that was because . . . but why . . .

And then it happens. You load one more thing into your active memory and it displaces something else. The whole structure of the story, which seemed so clear in the beginning, cracks and falls into pieces. You sit there looking at your writing implements, trying to remember who you are, what you were doing, and why you didn't go into some profession that was simple and straightforward, like immunochemistry.

What happened? I have a word for it that's actually printable. I call it "spaghettiing."

I stole the term from the meteorologists who tried to teach computers to do long-range weather forecasts back in the '70s. The tale of their travails is instructive.

In the beginning, the meteorologists' idea seemed quite straightforward. The gas laws, which govern the motion and behavior of bodies of air, were well known. Beyond that, weather forecasting is mainly a matter of keeping track of large masses of trivial data—just the sort of thing that computers are good at.

So these intrepid scientists programmed the gas laws into a computer, fed in current data, and then told the computer to print out tomorrow's weather map.

It did so and the map, while not perfect, was pretty good. It wasn't bad for the day after tomorrow, either. But when it tried to push its predictions further into the future, tiny errors in the input began to accumulate, the computer seemed to get sort of . . . confused . . . and something weird began to happen.

Slowly the high and low pressure systems, which normally look like fat blobs on the weather map, began to narrow and curl around on themselves, faster and faster, multiplying insanely, until the next week's weather map didn't even look like a weather map. What it looked like was a plate of spaghetti.

The computer programmers scratched their heads and, not knowing what to do about it, gave the phenomenon a name: "spaghettiing."

The words fits nicely into a writer's universe, as well.

My point is, of course, that writing also involves the processing and integration of large masses of individually trivial bits of data. If you begin your story without knowing precisely where you're going, any mistakes you make at first, any small omissions, take on added significance as you proceed. As length grows linearly, complexity expands exponentially.

The basic reason for this is that a story, like the life it represents, is fundamentally complex. As the annotated "Mrs. Kelly's Monster" and "The Ballad of Old Man Peters" in the back of the book should serve to illustrate, each image serves a multiplicity of functions both in terms of itself and of its context. A story is not a line of dominoes, it is a web, and tugging on any filament causes the whole thing to vibrate.

To make matters worse, the web has three dimensions, and what you're saying at the polish level may have totally different connotations at the structural and outline levels. Not only do you have to remember the details and the connections between them, you have to be able to square them at every instant with three different sets of principles.

If the piece is very short, of course, you can keep all the factors in your mind at once. Jokes are highly structured and quite complex, but you don't need an outline to write one. That's because the typical joke contains only a handful of images. You can write them down and shuffle them around until it feels right; when it snaps into place you'll know it intuitively.

If you're bullheaded enough, and enough of a masochist, you can write fairly long stories that way . . . just by cramming them all into your active memory. The procedure is simple.

You start out as described above, throwing yourself full tilt into the story and writing as hard as you can until you spaghetti. Then you go in the bathroom, run cold water on your wrists, regroup, go back to the typewriter and plunge in again, from the top. Rewrite and improve as you go, and chances are you'll get a few hundred words further before you spaghetti again. Repeat the process often enough, and you'll bull your way through to the end.

Not that the story will work then, though, because the front of it will be polished to a high sheen but it won't quite match the ending, which will still be rough. So you start rewriting, again and again.

Rewriting is a plodding business, done this way, and involves typing over and over. Cut and paste. Retype. Cut and paste. Retype. If you're lucky, ten rewrites will do it. It might take twenty, or even thirty, but when you're done you'll have an acceptable story.

If you ask me how I know all this in such intimate detail, I may cry all over you.

In fact, though, the process I've just described is the one that most young writers employ, in their mid-apprenticeships. But eventually they can no longer escape the fact that it involves several drawbacks aside from simple agony.

For one thing it turns writing into an absolute grind, and in the process of getting everything right the writer loses track of what it was the story was supposed to say. As a result, the finished product has all the life and vitality of a squashed armadillo on the Dallas Freeway.

The bull-your-way-through approach also imposes severe length limitations. You can claw your way through ten pages, or even twenty, and in time you can get it under control. Given more time, much more time, you get better at the process itself and you can undertake longer and more complex projects.

But every person has some absolute limit. In my more innocent days I tried to do numerous novels that way, and no matter how hard I tried or how many times I tried them, they all spun off into utter confusion about page 90.

It was an instructive experience of course, though I might say the same thing about ten years in Sing Sing. But a writer does need the ability to hold a lot of stuff in his head—to be able to juggle a lot of balls, to use a different metaphor—and writing without an outline certainly teaches you to do that!

Thanks to my phobia about outlines, and my years-long, bullheaded attempts to write without them, I learned a lot about holding things in my head. In fact, I'm something of a phenomenon among my writer friends. On a good day I can juggle four or five thousand words in my head without dropping a single one.

But I can't do it predictably, and the stuff I write that way doesn't have the power it should have. Besides, no matter how good you are, everybody's got a limit. You add one more ball to the ones you're juggling, or cram one more piece of data into your formula, or crank in a side-image of a wet dog and . . . reality starts to bend and warp on you.

There's only one thing that will save you when that happens: Glance up at the outline you've got tacked on the wall behind the typewriter. That will remind you where you are in your story, and restore a sense of perspective. Almost instantly, the intellectual vertigo will cease.

That assumes you have an outline. If you have no outline, well, tough luck. You spaghetti.

"I say "you" because this doesn't happen to me anymore. I can't remember the last time I spaghettied.

I use outlines.

So, if you are serious in your ambition to write, will you. You have probably already begun to do so, without even knowing it.

The truth is that writing is a very complex undertaking, analogous to conducting a military campaign. Things won't simply fall into place because God is on your side. You have to plan for them, and there are far, far too many factors for you to keep them all straight without writing them down.

This being the case you naturally make notes to yourself, and you arrange those notes, and then as the campaign proceeds you refer to them. That is the basis of outlining.

That's pretty haphazard, of course. Anyone who writes well soon discovers that what the notes say, and how they're arranged, has to reflect the story form being used. If the story is to be a dramatic one, which is to say if it's going to touch the reader emotionally, the outline must be consistent with that aim.

That rules out the English Teacher's Revenge—the ETR outline follows a "logical" form (or so I'm told), and nothing is more anathema to drama than logic. The dramatic story, because it purports to be a representation of life, is not logical at all.

It is, instead, psychological, and the outlining form must match. It must, in short, be a complication-resolution outline.

The implications of that are many, and to make them stand out I've developed an outline scheme designed to direct the writer's attention at the most critical dramatic issues. I use this method myself and require my students to master it. The method has been kept as simple as possible, on the grounds that a story, to be clear, must ultimately have simplicity of structure.

The outline consists of five simple statements that describe the major actions through which the story will be told. There is one statement for each major focus.

These statements are similar, at first glance, to the topic sentences often required in English composition classes, but in the end they are not.

The most obvious technical difference is that in the method I use the statements are pared down to two or three words—a noun, a strong, concrete action verb, and (usually) a direct object.

For these purposes, the articles "a," "an," and "the" are not counted as words. They are usually left out; "Joe eats an apple" becomes, more simply, "Joe eats apple."

If this seems picky—you bet it is. I've learned the hard way that the simpler an outline is, the more it focuses your thoughts on the important relationships in your story . . . and the easier it is to get a mental grasp on the outline when you feel yourself about to spaghetti.

There is also another factor: Words count for more in outlines than they do in stories. An outline of the sort I advocate contains a maximum of fifteen words; each word then may represent several hundred or several thousand words of copy. You can use the almost-right word in copy and get away with it, but in the outline the word had . . . better . . . be . . . the . . . right . . . word.

Another key difference between a dramatic outline and the English Teacher's Revenge is that the statements in the ETR outlines represent topic sentences and therefore specify what comes at the the *beginning* of the section they are supposed to represent. The first sentence in the outline expresses the thought that opens the piece. That's because in "logical" writing the writer states his premise first, then develops it.

In storytelling, on the other hand, the dramatic action that makes your point comes at the *end* of each section, where climaxes belong. That means your statements represent endings, not beginnings.

By illustration, let's consider a dramatic story in which our hero, Joe, is unfairly fired by his company and eventually gets his job back. The complication statement in the outline might be "Company fires Joe."

That does not mean that the story opens with a scene in which the protagonist finds a pink slip in his envelope. It doesn't. "Company fires Joe" represents the complicating action, which comes at the end of the complicating focus.

Before we go any further, we need to examine the focus statement we've just proposed. Focus statements represent a lot of effort down the line, and must be subjected to a specific sort of scrutiny as soon as they're committed to paper. If there's anything wrong with "Company fires Joe," we need to discover it now, before we've written several thousands unusable words.

There are three questions that should be asked immediately about every focus statement.

The first question is: Does the verb connote action?

The answer to this question is, of course, yes. "Fires" is an action verb.

We should pause here to emphasize that while almost everything about the complication-resolution outline is critical, nothing is as critical as the use of action verbs. This is absolutely, utterly, completely, with shrieking boldface and capital letters **CENTRAL** to the dramatic outline; it is the single most important piece of wisdom I can pass along to you.

Stories consist of actions! Stories consist of actions! Stories consist of actions! If your focus statement is weak or static (if it includes the verbs *be, am, was, were, have, has, being, been, do, does, did, could, would, should*) it means you haven't properly thought through the action chronology that we discussed in Chapter 4.

The second question is: Is your main character in the statement? If he is, and in this case he is, you're safe on that one.

The third and final question concerns the statement as a whole. Can you illustrate the event described? In this case, can you imagine yourself writing a scene in which "Company fires Joe"?

The answer is yes. You can show Joe opening his paycheck and finding a pink slip inside. It's got potenial drama. You're on target.

Finally, if all three questions can be answered yes, examine the statement once more and notice where in that statement your main character is placed. Observe that Joe, in this statement, is the object of action. The company acts upon Joe; Joe himself is the victim, he is passive.

This is not a problem, in the complication at least. Quite frequently the main character is the victim, in one way or another, in the first focus. After all the complication is essentially a problem, and being acted upon, instead of controlling your own destiny, is definitely a problem.

In the resolving focus, though, a passive character would be a tip-off that the story had major structural defects. After all, the resolving focus is where he's supposed to take control of the situation and solve the problem.

My point is that the order of the three words is significant, and tells you something about your character. Listen to what they say.

Once you get your complication tentatively in place, step number two is to add a resolution. In this case it's going to be: "Joe regains job."

Is the image active?

Yes.

Is the character in the statement?

Yes.

Is the character the active force in the statement? That is, is he to the left of the verb instead of to the right?

Yes.

Can you illustrate the action in the statement?

Yes. You can show the judge banging down his gavel and ordering the company to rehire him and give him back pay. Or you can do it by strong implication, and show him strolling through the factory gates with his co-workers.

Those questions asked, and satisfactorily answered, we come to an issue second in importance only to the matter of those ever-to-be-avoided static verbs.

Does the resolution solve the complication?

In this case, it obviously does . . . but this business of making certain the complication and resolution match can get subtle. "Joe regains confidence," for instance, would not, repeat *not*, solve the complication of "Joe loses job."

If the story is going to end with him regaining his confidence, the complication should be recast into something like "Joe loses confidence." The loss of the job now becomes the background force that leads up to the loss of confidence. The story is the same, but the emphasis shifts considerably.

If your complication and resolution don't match, your story will seem to go nowhere, and no matter what you do to it, it'll never quite work.

In this case, though, they match perfectly. We have now got our beginning focus:

Complication: Company fires Joe

And our ending focus:

Resolution: Joe regains job

The next step is to structure the developmental focuses, which represent the unfolding of your story.

In this case let's say the story proceeds with Joe sinking lower and lower into depression until he becomes convinced he's useless. Then, recognizing what's happening to him, he makes an effort to pull himself out of the dumps and face reality. Having done this, he grows angry with the company and takes the positive step of hiring a lawyer and suing. Finally the judge orders the company to restore him to work.

The outline might look something like this:

Complication: Company fires Joe
Development:
    1. Depression paralyzes Joe
    2. Joe regains confidence
    3. Joe sues company
Resolution: Joe regains job

To repeat an earlier point that is often misunderstood, the focus statements represent endings, not beginnings. The first developmental focus begins with Joe's depression, follows it through as it deepens, and ends with his total paralysis.

The second developmental focus begins with his realization that his paralysis is self-defeating, and shows him working his way out of it. He may seek psychiatric help. He may talk to his buddies. Finally, he feels like himself again.

In the third focus, he decides what to do, finds a lawyer, considers his advice, and makes the decision to sue.

In the resolution the court process proceeds, and Joe wins. The story may conclude with Joe, accompanied by his buddies, lunchpail in hand, going through the factory gates on the way to work.

The outlining technique, while simple, isn't as simple as it looks—the complexity isn't in the outline method itself but in the way it forces you to think through your story. To illustrate how that works, let's examine two outlines that were handed in by my students. The first received an F, the second an A.

The first involves a story that the student summed up as being "about women at war." It was the tale of an Englishwoman who, living in London during World War II, joined the British Army. The outline was as follows:

Complication: Living During WW II
Development:
1. Life at Boot Camp
2. Communications at all cost
3. Liberty on Leave
Resolution: Tina retires to Housewife

None of the focus sentences is correct.

The complicating statement has no specific human subject and, worse, no acceptable verb (''ing'' forms, called ''gerunds,'' are technically verbs—but they won't do for dramatic outlines).

Because it has no human noun (character) or verb (action), it can't be *shown* in the story.

Consider, by contrast, the strengths of a complication rewritten as follows: ''Tina joins Army.''

With that, we've introduced the character in the first word of the outline, and even more important, we have specified a climactic action that the character will take.

''Joins'' is a good action verb—an act that implies physical movement and can therefore be written in dramatic form. The writer can *show* Tina holding up her right hand while a fly buzzes in the corner and the British sky is full of Messerschmitts or buzz bombs or whatever.

The rest of the outline is similarly faulted. The developmental focuses all lack a character and an action verb. The resolving focus also contains a preposition, which is a serious mistake.

Worse, that preposition is misused. You can ''retire to [the] farm'' or ''retire to [*be* a] housewife, but you don't ''retire to housewife.''

This grammatical distortion in the outline occurred because the student was trying at all costs to avoid the cardinal error of outlining . . . the use of a static verb. But simply leaving that verb out, as was done in this case, produces gibberish.

While the above student didn't solve her problem, at least she did acknowledge the fact that the use of a static verb in an outline was unacceptable. The use of a single static verb in the outline makes that outline impossible to write from.

In other words, you could not say in an outline that "Joe was fired," because "was" is a static verb. You are forced to think in much more straightforward active terms, and to write something like "Company fires Joe."

Beyond the focus statement in the "woman at war" outline, one gets the sense that the problem posed by "Living During WW II" would not really be addressed by "Tina retires to Housewife."

The contrast is there (bombs to babies), but if the story is about the dangers of World War II, as implied, there is a much stronger solution. If life is endangered, then the proximate resolution is survival and nothing less. The knitting you do afterward is anticlimactic in the extreme.

Any of the errors mentioned, had it occurred alone, would have rendered the story unwritable. But in the course of the semester the student turned the F into a B with the following outline:

Complication: War endangers Tina
Development:
    1. Tina avoids bombs
    2. Supplies limit Tina
    3. Environment threatens Tina
Resolution: Tina survives threats

Now we have a story of endurance (Tina endures war) that begins with Tina joining the Army, finding herself in danger, avoiding the bombs, enduring the privations and living in a generally hostile world . . . and somehow (roll the drums) surviving it.

It's neat and compact—perhaps a little superficial, but a crisp little feature for the Sunday section. Done in a craftsmanlike manner, it would be handled with respect by a discerning city editor.

The reason the outline received a B rather than an A is

demonstrated by the following outline that *did* receive an A. In it, the student managed to get much closer to the human condition and produced, as a result, a more moving story.

The story involves Thomasella, a moderately retarded mongoloid. But her story, which might run the risk of being saccharine if told directly, is here secondary to the tale of her mother's struggle to accept and love her daughter. The mother's name is Libby.

Complication: Libby produces mongoloid
Development:
    1. Guilt drives Libby
    2. Mongoloid horrifies neighbors
    3. Thomasella learns
Resolution: Libby loves Thomasella

To the inexperienced eye, this outline may seem fuzzier than the one about Tina. But that's an illusion due to the fact that the forces at play in Libby's story are more psychological than those in Tina's.

Libby's story is more powerful than the one about Tina and the war because Libby confronts a *psychological* complication. War is impersonal, at least as it was conceptualized in the story about Tina.

Libby's story, in sharp contrast, focuses on an intensely personal struggle between the character and reality. Further, the resolution implies dramatic personal growth on the part of the character.

Note that the key verb in Tina's resolution is "survives." This is a strong, action verb, but it does not imply that the character underwent a fundamental change as a result of her experience. Survival is not the same thing as growth.

Not that war didn't change Tina—it probably did. But that change is not part of the structure of the story and, as a result, can't manifest itself as the strongest theme in the resolution.

Thomasella's mother, on the other hand, emerges from the second story a profoundly changed woman. That, in fact, is the point of the story.

The plot, or sequence of events, is thus. A baby is born a mongoloid. Its mother, overcome by her love and sense of responsibility, refuses to put the infant in an institution. Instead, she ignores the advice of her doctor and takes the little girl home.

In the beginning she finds herself in an achingly human situation. As the years pass Libby lives with her daughter's limitations, attempting to protect her from danger and pain.

Libby confronts the situation, she confronts the world confronting it, and slowly she absorbs the painful truth. She watches as Thomasella grows and learns, ever so slowly, the simple skills of life. No matter how hard she tries, she can't make her daughter normal.

Finally, in teaching her daughter, Libby finds within herself the answer to her dilemma: Love is not dependent on normalcy. As a result, Libby achieves a simple acceptance of reality and, in doing so, becomes a stronger person.

(On another level the story, as it was eventually written by the student, gave the reader a thorough—and painless—education in the medical history of mongolism, otherwise known as "Down's syndrome" or "trisomy-21." The best nonfiction short stories tend to be informative as well as riveting.)

If all else is done properly, the most dramatic aspect of any story is growth and change in the main character. This growth and change should be made a central part of the outline, so that it will emerge as the backbone of the story.

Properly written, the Libby story should appeal to a wide audience. It has the makings of a solid, page 1 feature story that would stand a good chance of getting picked up by the feature wires and probably being reprinted in a major national or international magazine.

The first purpose of the outline, in other words, is to

present the drama of the story in terms of the action that will carry that story from complication to resolution.

Let's take one more example, drawn this time from "Mrs. Kelly's Monster."

When presented the facts of the story, one's first impulse is to focus on Mrs. Kelly. It is she, after all, who is taking the greatest risk, and it is she who pays the greatest price. But a complication-resolution outline based on that perception would look like this:

> Complication: Woman gambles life
> Development:
>   1. Ducker enters brain
>   2. Ducker clips aneurysm
>   3. Monster thwarts Ducker
> Resolution: Woman loses gamble

The outline immediately reveals that the story is unacceptable, and why. For one thing, the main character is totally absent throughout the bulk of the story, and she has nothing to do with the outcome. The story therefore violates the Mack Truck Rule.

As a result, while the tale would start out with a bang, it'd end with the worst sort of whimper.

That leads us to the second serious structural flaw: As outlined here it's a negative story. Remember, negative stories rarely teach us anything about the human condition, except that it's fragile—and that's something that we know all too well to begin with. So there's not much value in it.

The following version is a little better.

> Complication: Ducker challenges monster
> Development:
>   1. Ducker enters brain
>   2. Ducker clips aneurysm
>   3. Monster ambushes Ducker
> Resolution: Monster wins

This clears up the Mack Truck Problem, but the second failing remains. It's still a negative story. So we try recasting it again.

> Complication: Ducker gambles life
> Development:
>   1. Ducker enters brain
>   2. Ducker clips aneurysm
>   3. Monster ambushes Ducker
> Resolution: Ducker accepts defeat

Now, by recasting our complication and resolution, we've thrown the story into a new light and solved the negativism problem.

As the outline stands now, and as the story is written, the complication is not Mrs. Kelly's but Tom Ducker's. Mrs. Kelly's story is very much there, of course, but it's Ducker who must find the confidence and the strength to go on living. In my first perception, it was a story of death. Now it's become a story in which the proximity of death illustrates the preciousness, and the necessity, of life.

The most important point in this last illustration is that had I not outlined the piece, I might well have written the story the initial way.

Assuming I had the courage to face the fact that I'd loused up, I might have read my story, diagnosed its faults, and tried again . . . only to produce version two.

Remember, I write for a living. That means I have deadlines.

But assume I had still more time, and still more courage, and wasn't so close to the story that I couldn't see it anymore. I might once again admit the story was wrong and, once again, rewrite it. Finally, I'd have gotten it right.

Or would I have?

Would it have been as fresh, or would it have reflected my exhaustion with it?

Would it have been as clear? Or would I, in my exhaustion and human desire to cut my losses, have subconsciously pulled in metaphors and scenes from the first two versions—things that would have worked, perhaps, but not quite as well?

No, the answer is that it wouldn't have been as good a story. And that is the ultimate advantage of working in outline form.

With an outline you can think your story through, quickly and without great effort. Massive structural problems will stand out, and you can solve them with a stroke of a pen. You can think the story through, time and time again, very quickly, and still retain the energy, enthusiasm and freshness you need to do a good job when it comes time to actually write the story.

Now that you've seen the basic complication-resolution form, let's examine the most extreme variation of it: the saga form.

The saga outline uses all of the principles of the simpler outlines shown above, except that it consists of a chain of substories, held together both by an overall complication and resolution and also by interlinked minor complications.

Though the saga outline looks quite different from that, say, for "Mrs. Kelly's Monster," most of the differences are superficial. In fact, the internal focuses of "Mrs. Kelly's Monster" also had internal complications and resolutions.

In the second developmental focus, for instance, the internal complication, "Ducker attacks aneurysm," was there even though it wasn't stated in the outline. The outline stated only the resolution of that complication, and the climax of the focus, which was "Ducker clips aneurysm."

Puristically it might be possible to write subcomplications and subresolutions all the way down to the image level. When you graduate to book-length drama, either fiction or nonfiction, you will find yourself doing this automatically. But when writing the short story you normally wouldn't bother because it wouldn't be necessary; once you have the major bones in the skeleton your writer's mind will automatically insert the minor ones.

The saga form, then, differs not in kind but in degree. In saga form the reader will soon forget, in the twists and turns of the plot, what the major complication was; the minor complications, as a result, become critical for the maintenance of tension.

These same twists and turns of plot also make it easy for the *writer* to get lost. That's why, in a saga-form story, it's necessary to map out the minor structure.

This is done in the following outline for "The Ballad of Old Man Peters":

Verse 1

Major Complication: Wilk faces death
Semi-Major Complication: Wilk faces ignorance
    Development 1: World intrigues Wilk
    Development 2: Wilk finds dream
    Development 3: Dream protects Wilk
Interlinked Complication: Wilk loses father
Semi-Major Resolution: Dream sustains Wilk

Verse II

Semi-Major Complication: Wilk loses father
    Development 1: Memory sustains Wilk
    Development 2: Wilk loses family
    Development 3: Wilk gathers strength
Interlinked Complication: Age threatens Wilk
Semi-Major Resolution: Wilk pursues dream

Verse III

Semi-Major Complication: Age threatens Wilk
    Development 1: Wilk persists
    Development 2: Wilk discovers books
    Development 3: Wilk grows proud

Semi-Major Resolution: Wilk overcomes threat
Interlinked Complication: Wilk faces ignorance*

Verse IV

Semi-Major Complication: Wilk faces ignorance
Development 1: Wilk finds profession
Development 2. Wilk discovers world
Development 3. Wilk studies world
Semi-Major Resolution: Wilk enlarges mind
Interlinked Complication: Wilk faces death

Verse V

Semi-Major Complication: Wilk faces death (Major Complication Restated)
Development 1: Wilk pursues life
Development 2: Death approaches Wilk
Development 3: Wilk looks forward
Major Resolution: Wilk defeats death

Though this appears more complex than the straight complication-resolution outlines above, appearances are deceiving. Details aside, it's in fact quite similar, and the similarities serve to illustrate the universal principles of all complication-resolution structures.

For openers, notice that the entire outline is bracketed by a major complication and resolution. Regardless of particular variation on the form, any effective dramatic piece is so bracketed and therefore unified.

Notice also that the tension never flags and that, though the subject seems to change from death to innocence (and ignorance) as the major complication ends and the long flashback begins, the two subjects will merge in the end. It is the battle against ignorance that prepares Wilk to face the ultimate darkness.

---

* Note that in Verses III and IV the interlinked complication comes *after* the semi-major resolution. This weakens the structure a little, since there is a momentary drop of tension after the resolution. But the reader is moving fast enough that he won't stop and put the story down.

In the meantime, once the reader is hooked into the story, tension is periodically added by means of semimajor complications—each of which is resolved only in the close proximity of the next semimajor complication.

Perhaps the most dramatically revealing aspect of this outline is the way the minor complication, that of ignorance, dovetails with the major complication as it's restated in Verse V.

As our long flashback ends we have come full circle and Wilk once again faces death. Death is the enemy . . . or is it?

By the time we meet the complication we know a great deal about Wilk and his strengths. From our new perspective we see that, no, death is *not* the enemy. Death is inevitable but the real enemy, as FDR once admonished us, is fear.

Fear, Wilk has shown us by the example of his life, is synonomous with death.

Death has no meaning, and contains no lesson. Therefore he ignores it, as he ignored every other impediment to life. He doesn't whine about it; he lives on, looking to the future, to the life he's got left. He lives life to the hilt, his way, and in doing so he overcomes the fear of death.

Though he will die soon, that fact has no place in the context of life. By having the wisdom to understand that, the indomitable Wilk Peters defeats death itself.

It is the outline level that brings out the eternal truths of your story, and if those truths seem like clichés . . . so much the better. Eternal truths, being eternal, have all (or almost all) been spoken before by other writers in other times.

The outline of "The Ballad of Old Man Peters," like the earlier ones, allows you to see the theme, threads and flow of the story at a glance. Confined to a few statements of action, they are not buried in prose where you can overlook them or misunderstand their importance *or* misinterpret their interrelationships with one another.

Frankly, once you've fully comprehended the overall

sweep of your story, and it's crystallized in your mind, you could throw the outline away and still be well ahead of the game.

The most valuable thing about the outline isn't the outline itself but the fact that you thought the problem through thoroughly enough to create one. Unless your story is quite lengthy or complex (as is the case with ''The Ballad of Old Man Peters''), you could probably do it now without spaghettiing.

All the same, you won't throw the outline away. It is the psychological roadmap of your story, and as such very valuable. So you tack it up on the wall behind your typewriter.

Then you reach for a clean sheet of paper. It's time to write.

VII

Structuring the Rough

Now that you've outlined your story and gotten all the major focuses firmly in mind, it's time to write. But it's not, as you might be tempted to phrase it, "time to begin."

In fact you began a long time ago and the creative work of the story is almost completely finished; in terms of effort, the act of sitting down at the typewriter to expand your focus statements into rough copy marks the halfway point in the creation of a story.

It is, to be sure, the moment of truth. If you have been clear in your vision, honest in your evaluation, thorough in your analysis, painstaking in your interpretations, and precise in your statement of your story, the actual writing process will be as routine as baked potatoes. If you have not, you are in for, well . . . adventure.

In broad terms, the translation of an outline into rough

copy is a straightforward extension, into the living language, of the principles you considered and used in the construction of the outline.

But as you drop below the outline level, with its emphasis on the interactions between major focuses, and shift your concentration to the internal structure of those focuses, the process becomes less abstract and the operational rules undergo that relativistic change we talked about before.

At the structural level a cliché here and there won't harm you, necessarily—but neither will it help, the way it did in the outline phase. Words begin to become important, but they will not yet assume the importance they will have later, in the polish stage; in structural copy, word choice is critical only at the dramatic high points. Likewise the use of action verbs remains important, but they are no longer critical everywhere; again, they matter most at dramatic high points.

In the realm of structural construction your concern will narrow to the practicalities of transitions, scene-setting and -building, pacing, action sequencing and the other techniques that will allow the reader's mind to slide easily through your story.

The "rough draft" stage of storycraft is subject to a number of popular illusions, due mostly to the general ignorance of the multilevel process of writing. The most obvious misconception is that the "rough draft," because of its name, is somehow permitted to be sloppy. In reality the rough draft is only "rough" in the sense that the writer doesn't worry overmuch here about the veneer of finish. Phrase order and sentence rhythm are not yet relevant.

I think of rough copy as being analogous to the "rough-in" phase of housebuilding, in which the studs, roof beams and floor joists are cut and nailed into place. The emphasis is on laying out the material, cutting and fitting. The craftsman's attention is on function; the look of the final product, though now crystallizing in the writer's mind, is no more yet than a guiding vision.

In the case of carpentry, the rough-in process is the most time-consuming and critical period of construction. Though the studs and beams may not seem particularly pretty to the uninitiated, and though they won't even be visible to the ultimate consumer, the quality of craftsmanship that goes into them will determine the ultimate strength and durability of the house. If the rough-in is done carelessly or amateurishly it may still serve as an adequate basis for plasterboard and paint . . . but it will not long survive the stresses of seeping water, gnawing termites, strong wind or heavy snow. So it is, as well, with stories.

Another myth about the rough draft is that it is a single write-through. It is no such thing.

The rough draft is not a product, it is a process, and unless you work on a computer (in which case "rewriting" becomes "copy massaging") the procedure may involve anywhere from five to ten write-throughs. How many are necessary depends on (a) the complexity of the story, (b) the proficiency of the writer, and (c) how well the story has been thought through and outlined ahead of time.

Earlier in this book you were counseled to make your observations, do your interviews, conceive your complication, resolution and three developmental focuses, and commit the relevant actions to 3x5 cards. Now take those cards out again and lay them out before you in the order in which they will appear in your story (if you have pre-complication action you will be using a flashback and so the actions will not be in strict chronological order).

Check the actions one last time, with the same care you'd take to check your parachute if you were scheduled to make a high-altitude jump in the morning.

• Are all the relevant actions represented? By describing those actions can you *show* what happens to your character? If not, you'll have to stoop to explaining.

• Are there extraneous actions, which are *not* needed to tell your story? If there are, they will confuse the structural process and lead to terrible anguish during the "baby-killing" phase described at the end of the chapter.

• Does the action fit neatly into your outline? The major actions should dovetail with your focus statements, and the minor actions should lead inexorably up to them.

If the action sequence isn't perfectly solid, go back and repack your parachute.

If it is, it's time to turn your attention to narrative.

Narrative

What is narrative?

In its classic definition, narrative is the summarizing segments of copy in which the words carry the reader quickly over bridges of time between action scenes. They are the "as the years flew by" passages.

But here I take my usual liberties with the English Teacher taxonomy; we will use the term much more generally, so that we can apply it to the story as a whole.

By the above definition, there are three kinds of narrative: transitional, preparatory, and climactic. Transitional narrative bridges the gap between focuses of various sizes and complexity. Preparatory narrative builds toward a climactic scene or action event. Climactic narrative is the close-up description of that event.

To triangulate with a different metaphor, think back to J. R. Salamanca's explanation of "focus," and the cameraman example he used. In that context, transitional narrative is when you pan from one face to another, preparatory narrative is the act of zooming in on a specific face, and climactic narrative is when you show what that face is doing.

This brings us to a point in our discussion when we must stop and consider a potentially confusing cliché that you have probably heard about narrative—that it should "flow like a river."

Well . . . yeah . . . okay.

It certainly should carry the reader's mind along smoothly. But given that metaphor, there's a temptation to think of the narrative as a broad steady flow. The Mississippi comes to mind and, offhand, I can't think of any example that could get you into more trouble.

Remember that narrative tells your story and that your story, like the people and events upon which it is based, is a living thing—and life is constant change.

So if you're going to compare your narrative to a river, then let it be a river that rises high in the thin air of glacier-carved peaks, collecting its strengths from springs and freshets and flowing, murmuring, down mountainsides.

Let it be a river that pauses in deep, clear paternoster lakes full of bright-eyed trout, gathering strength before hurling itself over roaring cataracts and racing, boiling, through narrow gorges and then over new cataracts until it marshals its strength again in still another lake, this time turned acid by the rotting needles of conifers, visited by large mammals and bright, small birds, a river that pauses there and then moves again, slowly at first and then gathering speed and broadening into shallow rapids over small round stones and gravel bars, narrowing again in a gorge, whirlpooling around a hairpin turn, falling, crashing and roaring, down a cliff, gathering, growing, moving now in the company of piranhas through a noisy jungle full of brightly colored birds, monkeys chattering in the overhanging trees, crocodiles sunning themselves lazily on the steaming banks, rolling now toward a bay of mussel beds and wheeling seagulls and brown men in dugout canoes.

If your story is to be like a river, for heaven's sake don't let that river be the Mississippi. Let it be the Amazon.

TRANSITIONAL NARRATIVE

The dynamic, ever-changing nature of stories brings us nicely to the subject of transitional narrative.

The purpose of transitional narrative is to allow the

reader to stay with you through all the twists, turns and changes in your story without getting disoriented and lost.

The key concept in transitional narrative is that a dramatic story, whether it be the old fiction or the new nonfiction, must be a world unto itself . . . a world which the reader can enter and become absorbed in. This results from a phenomenon that short-story writers called "suspension of disbelief."

In its original meaning, "suspension of disbelief" had to do with the reader's willingness to jump from the world of reality into the world of the imagination. Conceived this way, it was strictly confined to fiction. With the rise of nonfiction drama, however, it has come to include the process by which the reader moves from his own reality to someone else's equally real world.

Whether you're writing fiction or nonfiction, good narrative will make the reader forget that he's sitting in an easy chair. He will step into your character's world to stand behind Tom Ducker as he battles Mrs. Kelly's monster, or to labor with Wilk Peters in the turpentine forests of south Texas. If you tell your story correctly the reader's identity will for a short time actually fuse with that of the character and he will live for a while through that character. He will see with his eyes, hear with his ears, and think with his brain. The ability to cajole the reader into doing that is the hallmark of good narrative.

But consider for a moment . . . how would *you* feel if you were suddenly transported from your easy chair to a different place and time?

How do you feel when you wake up in a strange hotel room, and for a moment don't remember where you are?

How do you feel when, after being totally absorbed in your writing, you look up and see that the day is gone and it's approaching midnight?

Disoriented, that's how you feel. And it's very unpleasant.

Though we don't think much about it, our minds orient themselves by means of five basic realities: time, place, character, subject and mood. We constantly keep tabs on when it is, where we are, who we are, what we're doing, and what mood we're in.

The first thing a psychiatrist asks a prospective patient, for instance, is the date. The specific day of the month isn't important, and the best of us think it's Friday (wishful thinking) when it's really only Thursday. But if the patient doesn't know the month, and most especially if he doesn't know the year . . . well, then, the psychiatrist knows he has found long-term employment.

This isn't something we normally give much conscious thought to. The cues are all around us, and the process of orientation is almost wholly automatic.

But a story is the height of artificiality. Whether or not the story is true, you cannot recreate the character's world. You wouldn't if you could. It's too complicated, too confusing, too boring. Your tale represents an extract of reality, not reality itself; to make it efficient you compress time, make time run backward, change scenes with a few words, flip from viewpoint to viewpoint and alter moods and subjects as if you were changing stations on your television set.

A story is an artifice whether it's fiction or nonfiction, and unless you religiously remember to include the cues that will allow the reader to orient himself in the alien world you're creating, he won't become absorbed at all. Instead, he'll get confused and his mind, no matter how interested he may be in the character and the situation, will flatly refuse to leave the easy chair. The reader will complain that he can't "get into" your story.

Good narrative establishes the time, place, character, subject and mood in the first few lines of the story and then maintains them to the end. I call them "threads" because they absolutely must be woven into the narrative.

In certain instances, threads are established explicitly. Some stories even begin with a newspaperish dateline:

November 11, 1889—For three weeks Joe Blow and Ann Smith had labored up the mountain, accompanied by their native guides, and now they stood on the citadel below the summit . . .

But for the most part the threads are maintained by cues embedded in the narrative. The hustle and bustle of the bazaar, punctuated with the shouted Arabic calls of the merchants, tells the reader he's in Cairo. The fact that it's important that Tom Ducker's hands don't shake tells the reader the story is going to be tense. The description of a wagon train moving west with "California or Bust" painted on the canvas canopies leaves no room for doubt that it's the mid-1800s. The silhouette of Mount Fuji on the horizon is a pretty good tip-off that the story is not taking place in Paris.

Of all the threads, time is the most delicate. This is principally because the time sequence in a story is often so radically different from the time sequence we experience in our daily lives.

In reality, in the one-foot-in-front-of-another grind of existence, we live sequentially. One moment follows another, one hour follows another, and so on through days, years and decades from the hour of our birth to the fading moment of death. But the writer, faced with the necessity of starting at the complication and flashing back to antecedent actions, of leaping forward while ignoring weeks, months and even years of inconsequential events, destroys this chronological simplicity.

If the reader gets lost in the process, nothing is more disorienting—and nothing is surer to make him put down your story and flip on the television.

The place thread is almost as critical, though as a practical matter it's easier to maintain—beginning writers, intent on creating scenery, are even likely to overdo it. Character and subject are simpler yet, and the amateur usually doesn't have much trouble with them at all.

The last of the five threads, mood, is the most tenuous and as a result is often underrated. Mood pertains to the reader's emotional state as determined by the rhythm, cadence, "sound" and the nature of the imagery in the narrative, and the writer must always be aware of it. If you've got the reader grieving for your character's dead sister, for instance, avoid making a pun. An error in mood orientation can send the reader slamming into an emotional brick wall, and he will not forgive you for it.

How specific those threads must be depends on the nature of the story and where in the story we're talking about.

A historical tale about an early pathologist, for instance, might satisfy the time and place requirements, at least initially, by making it clear in the first paragraph that it's in seventeenth-century England. Later on, in a dramatic scene, we might need to know that it's a crisp autumn day.

In "Mrs. Kelly's Monster," the first paragraph makes it clear that it's winter (and by implication a current winter), satisfying the time requirement. The place requirement is met by the mention of the University of Maryland, which is obviously not in Arizona. The character requirement is satisfied by the first paragraph's focus on Dr. Ducker and the subject requirement is addressed by my mention that he is a brain surgeon. The tense mood is implied by the last line.

That's enough to get us into the story. But "Mrs. Kelly's Monster" is a drama in which a woman's life hangs by a thread as the minutes pass. Before we go very far we must zero in tightly on the events and their sequences; while the date is irrelevant the minute isn't; we must almost hear the ticking of the clock and see the individual beads of sweat roll down the surgeon's forehead.

Conversely, it's important not to be any more specific than necessary. If you open your story at fourteen minutes and seven seconds past midnight on January 13, 1433, then you convey the sense that small increments of time are important. If your story is a pastoral love story, the confusion caused by the specificity will be as serious as if you hadn't established a time thread at all.

As the story proceeds the threads shift and change as the zoom lens of the narrative moves in, then back to pan across time and through space and events. Each motion breaks a thread, and each time that thread must be instantly reestablished.

It is the explicit purpose of transitional narrative to maintain the reader's orientation through those changes.

The complexity of any given transition is determined partly by circumstance and partly by how many threads, and which ones, are being broken.

Transitions can be major or minor. If you're going to skip ahead a few hours, you may simply begin the next paragraph with the words "A few hours later . . ." Or if you want to keep the time more or less steady, you can use the old standby, "Meanwhile."

Students sometimes feel strange using such a common trick as "Meanwhile," but they shouldn't.

In the first place, while orientation is a largely subconscious process of the human psyche, it's very efficient. The cues need to be there, but they don't need to be obtrusive. In the second place, the whole purpose of the transition is to move the reader's attention, not to attract it. By definition, the best transition is one that serves its purpose without being noticed by the reader. Creative phraseology in the transition is downright harmful.

The best transition, in fact, is the one that doesn't exist—as when a clever writer ends his focus with an image that will send the reader's mind leaping automatically toward the first image in the next focus. Lacking that, simple transitions like "Meanwhile" and "After dinner" are perfectly functional.

The simplest sort of transition involves breaking and then reestablishing a single thread. As more threads become involved, as they do in transitions like "The next day on Uncle Joe's farm," the possibility of confusing the reader becomes greater and the writer must become commensurately more careful.

As you write your story, you'll notice that the simplest

transitions are usually used to tie together subfocuses within the major focuses, and that the most complex transitions tend to come between the major focuses.

There are many types of major transitions, most of them quite obvious in purpose and method. But at this juncture I wish to call attention to three.

The first is the "break transition" in which all five threads are broken. Usually the typographer skips a line or two and inserts an ornament ❀ to indicate that a break in the narrative is taking place.

❀ ❀ ❀

These transitions have become popular in modern fiction, a fact I attribute in part to falling standards. They are intrinsically weak in that they break the narrative and therefore jar the reader more than any other type of transition. A break transition, like a commercial, is an excellent place to put the story down and go do something else. Personally, once I have my hooks into the reader I am loath to let him go.

At the same time, break transitions have their place in the best of literature, and their legitimacy may in fact be increasing. There is a case to be made that television and cinema, with their fade-outs and commercial breaks, have trained the reader's mind to make ever-greater jumps.

In any event, the salient fact about break transitions is that they totally sever the narrative. That means the five threads must be effectively reestablished within the first two or three lines of text that follows, just as though the story were beginning anew.

The second type of transition that merits an in-depth discussion here is the flashback. There is usually only one in a short story, even a long short story, and it is almost always found immediately after the complication.

I call your attention to the flashback transition because, of all the transitions in the writer's bag of tricks, it is probably the one most fraught with danger.

When you flash back you are not only tinkering with the most sensitive of all the orienting threads, time, but you are pushing the reader's mind in a direction in which it is not built to go. To make matters worse, the flashback generally breaks several of the five threads and weakens those it does not break—even if you stick with your character, for instance, he reemerges after the flashback as a younger and therefore different person. The opportunities for confusion are greater in a flashback than anywhere else in your story.

The problem is overcome by making very sure that the transition is smooth, without clunky phraseology, and by making sure that the narrative immediately following the transition is rich with carefully placed details that will serve as cues for all five modes of orientation.

But as difficult as flashbacks are to do, the greatest danger isn't that you'll somehow flub it. The greatest danger is that you'll overuse the technique.

The reader will stand for a flashback to the character's childhood, and the *real* beginning of the story, so long as he realizes that you're going someplace. This confidence is never so high as it is immediately after a strong and interesting complication has been presented.

If your story is complex, you'll be tempted to use several flashbacks in it. Resist the temptation; present your complication, go into flashback, and if at all possible tell your story chronologically from there on out.

A closely related type of transition is the flashforward. This is not the same as a time transition in which you pick up your narrative and go on, like, "Two days later, on the farm." That's a simple time transition.

The flashforward is a woebegotten technique by which the writer flashes forward to a later moment, and then attempts to bring the reader back to where he was. They usually go something like this:

> Joe chose to go to the prom with Ann instead of
> Sue. In the future this choice would come back,

again and again, to haunt him. But now he was much more attracted to Ann.

This is in fact a combination of a forward time transition ("In the future") followed quickly by a flashback ("But now"). This violates the sense that there is no such thing as a "minor" flashback.

The flashforward is most of all intrusive, because it has the effect of the writer's telling a secret, *sotto voce,* into the reader's ear. Like any other intrusion by the writer, the flashforward reminds the reader that the story is an illusion and thereby destroys the sense that the story is real.

This is not to say that flashforwards are uniformly bad. There is occasion for them; you may use two or three of them in a full lifetime as a professional writer. But the editor and critic, seeing a flashforward, automatically tend to assume the writer is an amateur. If he wasn't, he wouldn't have flashed forward; he would have foreshadowed instead. (More about foreshadowing later.)

Finally we come to an important and fascinating type of transition I call the "River City."

The River City transition is a revealing exception to the otherwise iron rule that structural narrative must always proceed in a logical fashion. The human mind, or at least the part of it that reads, is very logical, and a break in logic such as a non sequitur is usually very damaging. It shatters the illusion that the story is really happening, and that the reader is there.

But transitions are alien to start with—the average human being doesn't leap decades and flit from scene to scene in a matter of seconds. The transition is the ultimate lie of literature, be it fiction or nonfiction. It is at the same time absolutely essential to smooth narrative, and the reader accepts it because he's been trained to since the first grade.

Given that credulity—gullibility, if you prefer—a transition, if subtly artful enough, may slide the reader's mind from one idea to another with a total absence of logic.

The "River City" is a slick transition that is strictly

psychological in nature but that seems, somehow, to have a certain logic to it. My favorite example, as well as the name "River City," comes from the script of *The Music Man*, by Meredith Willson.

The male lead in the show is a huckster who travels through the Midwest during the early twentieth century, selling musical instruments for school bands. The action takes place in River City, Iowa, as the peddler desperately tries to convince local citizens that it's in their interest to start a band.

The character notes, with the keen eye of a con artist, that there's a pool hall in the town, and that the local youths are hanging out there. Suddenly, he gets an inspiration. This being a musical, he jumps up on a water fountain in the city square and starts singing:

> *Ya got trouble, folks,*
> *Right here in River City.*
> *Trouble with a capital 'T'*
> *And that rhymes with 'P'*
> *And that stands for pool!*

Now you see why I call an illogical transition a "River City."

Essentially what the music man is doing is making an emotional connection (rhyming appeals to the emotions) that makes an end run around his audience's logical processes. If the gentle folk of River City stopped to think about it, they'd realize immediately that the fact that "T" rhymes with "P" proves nothing; it does *not* mean pool equals trouble.

But they don't stop to think about it. Having made an emotional connection, the human mind is satisfied and goes on.

If you're good enough, and of a larcenous mind, the River City transition is a literary license to steal.

If you're serious about your work, on the other hand, it is the most useful tool yet devised to juxtapose images that the human mind would usually not bring together and, in doing so, to illustrate the larger truths of existence.

I do a version of this in the beginning of "The Ballad of Old Man Peters," when I use the tension between Wilk and the marauding teenagers to slide from the subject of age to the ostensibly unrelated subject of ignorance:

> Outside, beyond the double-locked doors, poor teenagers traverse the alley on the way to nowhere, casting occasional glances at the old man's rowhouse.
>
> For a lifetime Wilk Peters traveled the world in search of its people and its wisdom, and he brought his knowledge back to black universities to share with the students there—but the children who pass in the alley know nothing of that.

There is really no obvious rational connection between the teenagers' wanderings in the alley and Wilk's travelings in the world. The reader's mind slips easily from one to another merely because both represent movement.

But, his mind fixed on the tension between the young punks and the old man, the reader doesn't notice that I switched dimensions, and even realities, on him. See the pretty bauble in my right hand . . . and I'll pick your pocket with my left.

I get a certain almost childish glee out of that kind of trickery. Magicians, I suspect, get the same thrill every time they pull a silver dollar out of a child's ear. But the River City is no mere parlor trick.

The human mind, after all, is logical only on the surface. Underneath, in the churning darkness of the subconscious, logic is, at best, but a willing tool of desire. The human mind is an emotional engine, and if you would lead it along by the nose you had best remember that.

In case you haven't yet realized it, I have slipped this narrative neatly through Alice's looking glass: With the River City, we have entered the realm of stream of consciousness.

It always surprises people when I tell them that I commonly use stream-of-consciousness technique. "Oh, no," they always say. "It can't be! I can *understand* what you write."

The misconception that stream of consciousness is by definition impossible to understand goes back to the founders of the tradition, James Joyce, William Faulkner, and the rest. Their stream of consciousness worked, well . . . about as efficiently as the first Wright brothers airplane. Literary prototypes, like those of aviation, are usually pretty clunky.

Today, stream of consciousness is all around you; if you have doubts, study any well-made television commercial. How do you think the Madison Avenue folks manage to transfer the sex appeal of a semi-nude woman to the overpriced gas-guzzler she's gently caressing? Logic?

In literature, or at least the kind I write, the motive is artistic, not commercial. By sucking the reader ever deeper into the story, stream-of-consciousness technique ultimately adds to his understanding of the material.

In "The Ballad of Old Man Peters," for instance, as the story unfolds I am going to take the reader on a still different kind of journey, the journey from childhood to maturity, from ignorance to wisdom. So my River City, illogical on its face, will be legitimized as everything comes to fit together nicely in the end.

I tell you all this because you should know it. But the beginner should beware: Stream-of-consciousness technique is difficult to the point of being just plain dangerous. Before you attempt to step through Alice's mirror learn all the other writing techniques.

You'll need them.

We now move back into reality, and shift from the rubbery subject of transitional narrative to the much more prosaic one of preparatory narrative.

PREPARATORY NARRATIVE

Preparatory narrative generally follows transitional narrative in the sequence of the story and serves to prepare the reader, both intellectually and emotionally, for the coming of a dramatic high point.

A few pages back, for instance, I mentioned that a flashback should be followed by strong scene-building and character-strengthening narrative designed to make the reader become quickly absorbed into the now-changed story. This is an example of preparatory narrative.

But though the writer may use preparatory narrative to resolidify the story after a transition, the narrative itself looks forward, not backward. In its simplest form it is scene- and action-building, in which the writer prepares the reader's mind for a dramatically intense part of the story.

The preparatory narrative may itself be action; in fact, such is preferred.

It may, for instance, tell the reader that Joe got out of prison and traveled by bus to Oakton, where he lied about his past and got a job at Clinton's grocery store. It may even give us a snippet of a scene, in which we see Joe lie about his prison record to lovable old Harry Clinton.

But the hallmark of preparatory narrative is that it moves on rapidly, laying down as much information as possible and moving us to the next scene, which, in this case, may be the one which shows Joe falling in love with his boss's daughter.

The most important thing that can be said about preparatory narrative is that it has a specific reason for its existence. It's going someplace, and that someplace is a dramatic, close-up focus on action. It is not only preparatory in a general way, it is quite specific.

The fundamental rationale behind preparatory narrative can be best illustrated by digressing, for a moment, into the discussion of a technique which isn't a type of narrative per se—but which accomplishes the same purpose as preparatory narrative.

The technique is *foreshadowing*, and it's one of the most powerful pieces of magic in the storyteller's bag of tricks.

Foreshadowing is the technique by which the writer unobtrusively inserts details early in the story that will allow him to conduct his dramatic scenes without the necessity of explaining background details. This is what a good jokester is doing when he carefully sets up his situation in the narrative that precedes his punch line.

Sometimes, too, foreshadowing can be used for more subtle purposes.

One example, from "Mrs. Kelly's Monster," is the peanut-butter sandwich, banana and two fig newtons that Dr. Ducker's wife packs in his lunchbag. This is revealed in the sixth paragraph of the story, and the structural purpose it serves there is to get Dr. Ducker out of his kitchen and on to work. It also serves to emphasize Dr. Ducker's humanness, with detail. Like all good foreshadowing, it had a reason to be where it was. It serves a straightforward purpose, and the reader would never question its utility to the story.

But in the case of the peanut-butter sandwich, banana and two fig newtons, there was a hidden purpose.

Because the lunch was described early in the story, the reader needs no explanation when, at the agonizingly poignant emotional climax of the story, Dr. Ducker lays out those food items "neatly, the way the scrub nurse laid out the instruments."

In a logical sense, of course, the reader doesn't need an introduction to Dr. Ducker's lunch. He knows very well what a peanut-butter sandwich and a fig newton look like.

But by introducing them earlier, in the context of Ducker's caring wife, I give them an added "ghost image" or aura of domesticity. When they appear again in the climax of the story they subconsciously remind the reader that

Ducker is a husband and a father—no god, but just a human being like all the rest of us.

In addition, the fact that the lunch has been specifically introduced earlier gives the food items the added weight they deserve as symbols for my structural message that life goes on. We notice things more the second time around. Foreshadowing, in this sense, can contribute emphasis.

But one thing I could *not* have done was to interrupt that final scene to explain where the food came from. The mundane does not belong in climaxes.

Foreshadowing is such a fundamental and powerful technique that, over the years, readers have gotten used to it and come to trust the writer to use it according to the unwritten rules. As a result there's an expectation, an implied guarantee, that the writer won't put something into a story if it isn't germane.

This principle was codified by Anton Chekhov, the late-nineteenth-century Russian playwright and master short-story writer. Chekhov's Law specifies that if the opening of a story mentions a shotgun hanging over the mantel, then that shotgun must be fired before the story ends.

Foreshadowing may also serve an out-and-out educational purpose, to be used when the writer needs to introduce a concept that he knows the reader is going to have a tough time dealing with, either because it's emotionally unpalatable or because it's unfamiliar and complex.

You could, of course, set aside a dozen paragraphs or so at the top of your story and give a mini-lecture on the subject at hand. You could . . . but you won't, not if you want to sell your story.

What you'll do, instead, is teach as you go, tucking concepts into the action, positioning your reader's mind to understand. A phrase here, a sentence there, and by means of foreshadowing your educational message will unfold with your story.

As it does, the reader's subconscious mind will have a chance to digest the lesson before it becomes a serious issue in the story. Sometimes, when dealing with a very technical subject, I will seed my story with increasingly detailed references to what's coming.

I am, by the way, practicing what I preach. Chekhov's Law, introduced a few paragraphs ago, is going to emerge later in a most unpleasant form. By the time it does, the law will have worked itself into the deep recesses of your mind. It won't make its reincarnation any less pleasant, but it will at least make it less unfamiliar.

Foreshadowing, of course, by definition is not a separate part of the narrative; as in the case of the peanut-butter sandwich in "Mrs. Kelly's Monster," it has a perfectly good reason for being where it is. Foreshadowing by definition serves double duty, and may be found anywhere in the story.

But the purpose it serves, in preparing the reader's mind, is the same as that served by preparatory narrative—which, like transitional narrative, is a discrete and identifiable chunk of copy. Preparatory narrative in a sense is a simpler and much more explicit form of foreshadowing which leads directly to a dramatic event.

Implicit in the idea both of foreshadowing and of preparatory narrative is the principle that some parts of a story are more fragile than other parts. Early in a focus, the writer is using preparatory narrative to position the reader's mind for what will happen later. Later, when that something starts to happen, there's no time for explaining.

A final characteristic of preparatory narrative is that, all else being equal, it is generally quite short and very efficient. It is, in a sense, a transition itself . . . between the transition and the full-blown scene. Like the transition, its purpose is to get somewhere; also like the transition, it can sometimes be dispensed with altogether.

The overriding similarity between transitional and preparatory narrative is that they are ultimately subsidiary. They serve support functions, and exist only to get the reader to the dramatic high points of the story and to ensure that, once those high points are reached, they aren't slowed down by explanation of background.

CLIMACTIC NARRATIVE

As the name implies, climactic narrative is used to express the dramatic action in the story—the action you earlier listed on your 3x5 cards. In a tight, active story like "Mrs. Kelly's Monster," climactic narrative in fact makes up the bulk of the story . . . and accounts for virtually all of its emotional impact.

The distinguishing characteristic of climactic narrative is that it focuses tightly on events and their supporting details. It's the close-up in J. R. Salamanca's cameraman analogy, and it never tells the reader anything. It *shows* him.

This concept, of showing your story occur rather than telling how it occurred, is a theme that reemerges over and over in this book—and in the apprenticeship of the writer.

Wherever possible, the master storyteller scrupulously avoids telling the reader how a character feels, or why he does a thing. Instead he shows the reader what happens, and what the character does in response, and what happened then. If he does this correctly, the reader will automatically understand where the character is coming from.

The reason this technique is so effective is that it echoes the mental processes by which the reader conducts his own daily life. Though we listen to each other's words, actions speak far louder and more accurately. Does a politician promise justice in every pot? Well, we say, all right . . . but what's his voting record? What's he *done?*

This is the habit of human thought—a valid habit—that the master storyteller seeks to capitalize on. He does this by relating specific actions.

Consider, for instance, the example used a few pages back in which an ex-con gets a job at a grocery store and falls in love with the grocer's daughter.

The writer could go on for several paragraphs explaining that the ex-con is still not completely rehabilitated, but we speak much more eloquently (and efficiently) when we show the man lie about his past record to his prospective boss. We may sympathize with his reasons for doing so, but we are warned when the lie jumps so readily to his lips.

All the same, few stories can be told without using *some* sweeping statements. There are times when the writer needs to make generalizations about the nature of the situation. But when you examine a powerful story you discover that such generalizations almost always appear in transitional and preparatory narrative. They almost never appear in climactic narrative.

Preparatory narrative may tell us that Joe's father was an awful guy who beat his son, but you would never see such a statement in effective climactic narrative.

Climactic narrative instead would let us watch in horror as Joe's father beat him. We would hear the father's grunts, the son's screams. We would see blood running down the left corner of Joe's mouth, and watch his father suck angrily on his bruised knuckles as he glares at his son. Climactic narrative focuses down, tight, emphasizing with detail.

Finally, and most important, climactic narrative never, never, never, never tells us how the characters feel. It doesn't describe emotion, it *evokes* it.

It doesn't tell us that Sam feels sad because his girl left the dance with another guy—it *shows* Sam standing forlorn in the corner of the dance floor, watching Bruce leave with sweet Suzy on his arm.

Together, stories are woven of the three types of narrative. As he writes the rough copy, the master storyteller is at every moment acutely aware of which kind of narrative he's using. He does not, as a result, use a sparkling phrase in a transition . . . or a dreary one at a climactic high point. He compresses his preparatory narrative and stretches out his climactic narrative with active detail.

As a result, his story soon takes on a certain structural rhythm, or pace.

Pace, Intensity, and Excitement

There is a definite flow to narrative, from transitional narrative to preparatory narrative to climactic narrative.

Transitional narrative switches scenes and keeps the reader oriented. Preparatory narrative takes over and tells the reader what he needs to know to understand the dramatic scene that's coming. Finally, climactic narrative lets the action explode, with its full significance, in the reader's mind.

Then, in the calm after the storm, transitional narrative kicks in and moves us to the next time and place so that preparatory narrative can accelerate us toward the next scene.

Perhaps nothing illustrates this principle as well as a study of sentence and phrase lengths in a good piece of writing.

Sentences, by and large, tend to be longest in transitional and preparatory narrative. That, after all, is where the writer is trying to relate events and tie things together. But as the narrative switches into action the sentences become short and clipped, moved quickly along by strong verbs, devoid of modifiers, rich in action, action, action.

This sequence, transitions emptying into calm, smooth preparatory narrative pools before cascading over the falls and into the boiling rapids of dramatic scenes, gives rise to an element called "pace." Each story, and each part of each story, has its own.

A major focus, for instance, may consist of a single narrative sequence. After the transition, there may be as much as two or three hundred words of preparatory copy that culminates finally in a single long and complicated scene.

Another major focus may have a much more rapid pace. It may consist of two, or three, or even more simple climactic scenes (each preceded by transitional and then preparatory narrative). In this case, each scene builds on the one before. The final scene draws on the drama of those that came before and is the most exciting scene of all.

How rapidly the narrative moves from climactic point to climactic point determines how many climactic points there are in the major focus, and that in turn determines the "pace" of that focus. The pace of different major focuses may vary within the story; the overall pace of the story is determined by the combined effect of the major focuses and how they build, dramatically, toward the resolution.

Pace alone, however, is not the sole determinant of how exciting the story is. That depends, as well, on another factor we shall call "intensity."

Intensity is a measure of how closely the storyteller focuses his narrative camera on the story's participants and scenery. The interplay between pace and intensity is quite complex, and can produce a variety of effects. This is illustrated by a comparison of "Mrs. Kelly's Monster" and "The Ballad of Old Man Peters."

"Mrs. Kelly's Monster" is an especially fast-paced story. The complicating focus, though the second-slowest focus in the story, is fast compared to that of the average story. The first developmental focus, which carries us into the technical background of the story and is in its own way a preparatory focus, is the slowest of the five.

The pace then picks up as the subfocuses become smaller and more numerous, and the sentence length shrinks. As the narrative plunges ahead the effect of pace is heightened by the drumbeat of the popping respirator and the moment-to-moment references to the clock. By the last focus the pace is racing ahead with breakneck speed, carrying the reader's heartrate along with it.

In addition, "Monster" is very intense. The climactic narrative zooms in through a literary microscope to focus on the throbbing brain, the beads of sweat on Dr. Ducker's forehead, the probing of the tweezers, and the millimeter-by-millimeter advance toward the ultimate confrontation with the monster. The intensity of scene dramatically increases the effect of an already rapid pace and leaves the reader with a wrung-out feeling.

In sharp contrast, "The Ballad of Old Man Peters" covers a much longer period of time. The complication was not nearly so clear, in the beginning at least, and there was no single capping realization. By the very nature of the story the narrative does not build rapidly; the story doesn't plunge ahead, as it did in "Monster." Instead, it seems to march inexorably from decade to decade.

In fact, though, the pace of "Ballad" is almost as fast as that of "Monster." That's one reason "Ballad" holds the attention.

But in "Ballad" that pace is not amplified by intensity of scene. We don't see the turpentine forests in nearly the detail that we saw the operating room. The effect of pace is also kept moderately low by the lack of pacing devices, such as "Monster's" "pop-pop-pop."

This muting was no accident. The excitement you felt when reading "Monster" typically can't be maintained for a very long time without turning into melodrama. Though there are dramatic high points in each verse, "Ballad's" ultimate power grows from the steady accumulation of events and experiences as they shape Wilk's life.

As a result the story is absorbing. Wilk becomes a much more real character than either Dr. Ducker or Mrs. Kelly ever does, and whatever his tale lacks in excitement it makes up for in depth.

Those are two stories; the number of variations is infinite. Booklength fiction and nonfiction novels, in fact, give the writer the freedom to combine the two characteristics. Early focuses tend to be fast-paced but of low intensity. Once characterization and story flow are established, the pace may even drop off a little but the scenes become much more intense. Overall, the excitement level builds steadily to the end.

Though the pace of good modern drama is always very high, compared to literature of the past, the variations of intensity and ultimately of excitement depend on the nature

of the story being told. Some stories, like "The Ballad of
Old Man Peters," are marathons. Others, like "Mrs. Kelly's Monster," are hundred-yard dashes.

Your story, if you have planned well, will choose its
own pace and intensity, and will reach its own individual
level of excitement.

The Moment of Truth

Now, the moment approaches.

Roll a fresh sheet in the typewriter . . . but before you
touch the keys, I have another caution.

One of the chief errors that a beginning writer is likely
to make in the rough-draft stage, and one that consumed
horrible gobs of my own artistic youth, is to start at the
beginning and write your way through, making every sentence as perfect as you are able.

This is a human temptation; creating the rough is in
many ways the most fluid and therefore frightening step in
the writing process, and it's natural to want to escape that
confusion by imposing some order on it. But I shake my
bony finger at you and recite a doleful warning: That way
lies madness.

For one thing, copy that you spend a lot of time on
becomes precious. After all, you've invested yourself in it.
The words are pretty and, damn it all, they're *your* words.

This makes it very difficult for you to see when they
don't belong, no matter how pretty they are. A critical part
of the rough-draft process involves throwing things away,
and that's hard enough even if you haven't, as they say,
"gotten married to it."

For another thing, no matter how logical the polish-as-
you-go temptation may seem, it does not make sense to
begin at the beginning. The story doesn't pivot on the
beginning, it pivots on the ending—so write that first. That
way you know exactly what it is that you need to
foreshadow.

Sort through your cards and find, toward the bottom of the pile, the point of insight—that pivotal moment at the end of the last developmental focus when the situation first crystallized in your character's mind.

Write that climactic scene; follow it with transitional narrative and then the preparatory narrative that sets up the first scene of the resolution. Then (assuming you have several scenes in the resolution) write on through until you reach the end of the story.

Read what you have written. Can you make it structurally better, tighter, more exciting? Should one scene be larger, and another smaller? Probably.

So rewrite, emphasizing structure over polish, until the flow and pace is more or less to your liking. That done, you will have sketched out the single most difficult segment of the story.

If it gets worse, and not better . . . well, then you've made some grievous error in thinking through or outlining your tale. If so, starting where you did will make the horrible truth become immediately apparent. If you have to trash the story and start over, at least you didn't waste the effort of writing the whole thing.

If it works, now go to the beginning of the last developmental focus and write that. Since you have already written the end of that focus, you'll know exactly where you're going and exactly what you have to say to get there. You should find it comparatively easy.

When you're finished with that, go to the beginning of the story and write the complication.

Don't worry about the first few lines of the story; that comes later. Dive directly into the story, introduce your character, set up the situation, and bring him face-to-face with the complication. The shorter the sweeter; you want to hook the reader quickly, before he puts your story down and turns on the television.

You now have your story's beginning; keep going. Write the first two developmental focuses, and you have nailed your story down. Congratulations.

Calibrating

If it's that easy the first time, though, be very careful the rest of the week. You may have totally used up your luck.

Chances are good to overwhelming that you're going to hit a serious snag somewhere. A scene that you thought was going to be powerful turns out to be cut-and-dried boring. Or something you thought was a minor detail gets out of hand and threatens to take over the show.

Such occurrences shouldn't be considered failures; often they are quite the opposite. The story is taking over and making course corrections for you. This is why nobody, but nobody, ever writes only one "rough draft."

For one thing, the simple (or not so simple) process of writing the story through, if you've invested yourself in it, has changed *you*.

You're no longer the same person who found that story and analyzed it. In a sense you have lived it, and you can see it from the inside now as well as from the outside. As you reconsider the story now you should be able to see it with much more insight and a keener understanding of the forces at play in the character and his story.

It's not really the story that's trying to tell you something—it's your own subconscious, wiser now, working through the medium of your story.

So, whenever your story seems to be going awry . . . stop right then. Don't attempt to push farther. You're trying to tell yourself something, and you should listen. The trouble is that by this time you're so close to the story you can't hear.

That's one of the basic reasons you didn't throw away the outline.

Read it, carefully. Where, precisely, did you deviate from it? Why did you do that? Where did you go instead?

If you deviated for no good reason, but just because you got lost, then throw away the last few paragraphs and start again, following the outline.

But the chances are at least even that you deviated from

the outline because the story was stronger that way. If that's the case, don't change the copy—change the outline. The outline is not, after all, an inviolate blueprint. It's an evolving roadmap of your copy, and it's not finished until the story is.

Don't forget that when you change one thing in the outline, the entire outline must be reevaluated. A change in one focus may affect the content, or the emphasis, of related focuses.

For example, if the outline's resolving statement is changed, it's necessary to reexamine the complicating statement. It will often have to be changed as well, to ensure that the complication and resolution match.

As you grow comfortable with this process, you'll find yourself using your outline to calibrate and recalibrate as you press through the first rough draft.

When you are finally finished, sit back and look at the outline again. Does the story still reflect the outline? The odds are that it does, more or less. But not exactly.

Where does the story deviate from the outline? Which do you like the best? Change the other to match.

Assume, for illustration, that you like the story best. Okay, then reoutline it. With your new understanding, the outline should be much improved.

Once you've finished, compare it to the story again. It probably still won't match, at least not perfectly.

Change the story to reflect the outline.

Again, you won't quite be able to do it. The story, as you try to make it match your improved outline, will change on you again. But by this round, or perhaps the next one, you'll begin to perceive a pattern to the changes . . . they're not "changes" at all. They're *refinements*. Your story is beginning to crystallize.

Continue with the process, revising the story to fit the outline and then the outline to fit the story, until the two match. When they do, stop.

Woodwork

Earlier, during our discussion of foreshadowing, I warned you I was softening you up for something. The time has now come, as one of my writing buddies so neatly phrases it, to kill babies.

Yours.

Chekhov's Law, as you should remember, was that if the opening scene of the story mentioned a shotgun hanging over the mantel, then that shotgun had to be fired before the story ended.

The rationale behind this is that the reader has become accustomed to trust you not to include anything in your story that doesn't have meaning within the story. The reader will assume that whatever you tell him will have some importance to the story, and if that meaning isn't immediately apparent he'll be waiting, with part of his mind, for the other shoe to drop. If it drops, you were foreshadowing.

But if it never does drop, you will have only one reader: the editor who slips it into the stamped, self-addressed envelope and sends it back to you.

Is this a problem with the particular story you're writing? In a word, yes.

Throughout the writing process you've incorporated many ideas and perceptions in your story, woven them into the plot and character, lived with them, grown used to them . . . and some of them are bound to be totally unnecessary.

I call this woodwork . . . as in "wandering off into the woodwork."

Woodwork usually creeps into a story in the guise of things, events and people that seem to be too interesting or important to leave out. One example that comes to mind has to do with my first book, *Shocktrauma,* and an electrifying scene I witnessed in an emergency room.

An ambulance crew had brought in a young man who had put a .45 caliber pistol to his right temple and pulled the trigger. On the right side of his head was a small hole, the size of a dime. On the left side was an opening you could put your fist in.

Yet, incredibly, he still lived—legally, at least. That is to say, there was a flicker of electrical activity in his brain-stem.

The team, headed by a young surgical fellow, worked almost automatically. They followed the protocol, quickly hooking the young man up to a respirator and the other life-support systems.

Then, suddenly realizing what he had done, the surgeon stopped. He stood, immobilized, at the foot of the bed, staring in horror at the living corpse in front of him.

The doctor could have refused to hook the patient up to the lifesupport system in the first place. The wound was, as they say, "incompatible with life." He should have refused, but a doctor's first reaction is rarely to turn his back.

And now . . . having provided the support in the first place, the doctor was legally obligated to keep that support going. And yet, and yet . . .

On the one hand, medical technology was capable of supporting that flickering life for days or even weeks—at great expense not only to the taxpayers but to the young man's family, who were waiting outside. But no amount of medical expertise or equipment could restore to the young man anything even approximating human life.

Minutes passed. The nurses silently moved back from the patient, saying nothing, their eyes on the doctor.

So intense was the situation that the doctor committed an unusual oversight. He forgot that there was a reporter in the room.

I could see the indecision in the doctor's face. If he satisfied his legal obligation the state would pay tens of thousands of dollars for nothing and the grieving family outside would undergo days of torture. Or he could discon-nect the life-support system . . . and be guilty of murder.

The doctor stood there for a long time. Once, he reached

out toward the respirator, then withdrew his hand. The nurses' eyes followed his every movement.

Another minute passed, then another.

Finally the young doctor reached out, again, his hand trembling, and turned off the respirator.

In my whole career of reporting medicine, a career that has allowed me to witness hundreds of operations and many deaths, that was one of the most dramatic moments to which I have ever been privy.

Naturally, it went in my book.

In the first draft, anyway.

But there was a problem. The scene raised dozens of questions—medical, ethical, legal and emotional. Why, for instance, was the doctor so certain? Why did the nurses all step back and remain silent? What *is* death, anyway?

These questions, once raised, begged to be answered. But to answer them would have been to digress far from the main points in my book. My book was not about the realities and potential abuses of modern medical technology. It would treat those issues, of course, but not as a main theme. My book was about the development of emergency medicine.

It was a wonderful scene, a gut-wrenching scene, emotional and at the same time revealing . . . a reporter's dream.

And that was why it had to go.

It was woodwork, and as such its dramatic impact made it all the more distracting, and therefore dangerous to the story I was committed to tell. (As I deleted the anecdote, I promised myself that I would someday, somehow, use it somewhere. Now, many years later, I have fulfilled that promise.)

The woodwork problem arises inevitably in my students' stories:

A story about an unforgettable character who runs a suburban farm in Maryland, for instance, digresses into the character's views on the fascinating and important issue of soil erosion in Iowa.

A story about how a widow copes emotionally with the loss of her husband includes the unrelated but interesting substory about how the woman, as a child, once saw President Roosevelt.

A story about a man's battle with the utility bureaucracy over a foul-up in billing includes the irrelevant but chilling information that the man, a right-wing gun nut and survivalist, has built a bomb shelter in his back yard.

If there is something that seems more fascinating than the story you're telling, as may be the case in the last example . . . why, maybe you're telling the wrong story.

But unless you are willing to totally redefine your story, and in the process cut out information that pertains only to the original story, the distracting woodwork has to come out. The more interesting it is, the more dangerous.

The point is that you have to choose a story *and stick to it*. Remember, it is not the storyteller's mission to portray the confusion of life—the reader is already well supplied with confusion, thank you. The storyteller's function is clarity.

However, in the process of writing, and in the enthusiasm of the moment, no human being can write a story totally without woodwork. That means you have to go back, identify it, and take it out.

Apply that to your own story.

Go back through it, perhaps with the help of your worst enemy, and pinpoint the places where you went off into the woodwork.

Once you identify the woodwork, you will discover to your absolute horror that it represents your best prose. In fact, one way you can identify woodwork, if you have the stomach, is to automatically turn to the sections where the writing is, well . . . beautiful.

Chances are good that it's beautiful because you had a free hand there . . . a 707 transport can do fancy aerobatics too, when it's not carrying a load and has no specific destination to reach.

But it *is* beautiful, isn't it? Indulge yourself for a moment and admire it.

Now, take it out.

No, I don't want to hear your eighty-three justifications for leaving it in. None of them is worth listening to.

Take it out.

No, it's not screaming. That's your imagination.

And don't cry on my shoulder. I've got my own problems.

You have now finished with your rough draft.

Unless you're on deadline, put the story aside. Go plant petunias, tie tin cans onto the tails of cats, whine to your shrink, or do whatever it is you do to clear your mind.

VIII

Contemplating the Structure

THERE COMES A MOMENT in any project to sit back, put your feet up on the desk, and contemplate what you've accomplished. In the storytelling business the most fertile time for this is after you've got the tale roughed in and before you begin the polish. Unless a pressing deadline forces you to push on, it's an excellent idea at this juncture to let a few days or more pass before you embark on the polish phase.

A rest, now, is not a luxury. Producing rough copy is typically the single most exhausting step in storytelling (probably because the writer learns so much in the process) and if you're not mentally tired you've probably been holding back. Letting yourself rest up while the story cools off will give your subconscious time to digest what you've done.

When your mind is rested and clear, go back and read your

story without a pencil or a pen within reach. Try to read it as though you had never seen it before, as a reader would read it.

Who is your character? What happens to him? What does he learn from the experience?

As you read the story, does it make you *feel* anything? It should, now. If your structure is sound, your interest should rise steadily as you read the preparatory passages, soar during the climactic sections, then bank down as you go into the transitional turns.

This is the time when errors of proportion should be most apparent to you. Do you have a transition that's too long? In your anxiety to finish, did you short-change a scene in the second focus? Did you allow too little breathing room for the reader to make the transition from complicating scene to flashback?

If there are parts of the structure that seem wrong, and the problem isn't immediately apparent, consult your outline. What were you trying to do at that place? Did you do it? Did you overdo it? Were you telling instead of showing?

Go back, now, and make the minor structural corrections.

When you are finished, put away the outline. The only reason you put it away instead of throw it away is that you may need it again if an editor spots something you missed, and wants revisions. Otherwise, it's history.

It's time to polish.

IX

Polishing

POLISHING IS THE PROCESS by which the writer converts his rough copy into clear, active, well-integrated narrative that moves the story along smoothly without intruding into it. It is the final, simplest and most widely understood step in the creation of a story.

If literary quality and depth of message are important, polish is critical. At the same time, polish is probably the most overemphasized aspect of the writing craft.

As I explained in the Preface, my motivation for writing this book was a general lack of literature on the subject of craft. Polish, however, is a spectacular exception. Perhaps because polish is so visible, and because so many people erroneously believe it to be the most important part of writing, there have if anything been too many books on it.

This being the case, and because some of those books (however limited) are quite good, I'll not try to duplicate them here. Instead I'll concentrate on dispensing warnings, squelching myths, and putting the various principles into a usable perspective.

Concerning myths, the most damaging one of all to the beginner is the idea that the writer produces polished copy out of whole cloth. If you've stuck with me so far, you already know better than that.

Polish is but the plaster on the walls of structure. Done in a craftsmanlike fashion it reflects and highlights the dramatic architecture of the story, but it is never more than a facade. Structural flaws will inevitably show through.

If the character's personality does not square with the story's approach to the complication, for instance, no amount of careful polish-level explanation of why he acts as he does will make him seem less wooden.

If the resolution doesn't satisfy the complication, the polish in that section will seem flaccid and off point no matter what you do. If the structure lacks action, the climactic narrative will inevitably sag under the leaden weight of static verbs—you can't find action verbs to adequately fit the narrative because what the narrative describes is itself passive.

The brutal fact is that structure is far more fundamental to storytelling than polish. If you doubt this, examine the polish techniques used (or, accurately, not used) by most of the popular writers on the current best-seller list at any given time. Readers will buy story without polish, but I defy you to find a best-seller that has polish without story.

Unfortunately, the polish phase of writing has about it its own intensity, and we all tend to get lost in the fascinating landscape of our own words. As a result, when we are polishing along and come to a section that doesn't work for some reason, our natural response is to polish harder. We all make this mistake, and in doing so waste immense gobs of time and energy. The best polish can't correct structural defects, no matter how much elbow grease we apply.

To guard against such wasted effort we must constantly

remind ourselves that *polish should not be agonizing*. When we find ourselves sweating bullets over some paragraph that should be simple, we must be willing to step back and reexamine structure. Maybe the paragraph doesn't go there. Or maybe it's saying something structural that we didn't crank into our design.

Another myth about polish is that its laws are very flexible. This grows out of the observation that professional writers are inclined to amuse and indulge themselves by appearing to break those laws at will. This can be horribly misleading to a neophyte writer who seeks to develop his skills, as we all do, by imitation.

In the first place, the professional is not exactly breaking the rules. Like a good tax lawyer, he understands the system so thoroughly that he knows where all the loopholes are; and those loopholes, once you know where to find them, are large enough to drive a tank through.

The linguistic flights of fancy indulged in by an Ernest Hemingway or a Tom Wolfe are the polish-level equivalent of the woodwork we discussed in an earlier chapter. The master craftsmen can get away with it because they know precisely where the narrative can stand the strain of an exuberant loop-the-loop and where it can't.

But unfotunately those idiosyncrasies stand out, and, standing out, they catch the attention of the neophyte. In his innocence, he assumes that the story works *because* of them. So he calls them "style" and mimics them.

The result is disaster.

If the beginner is to become a professional, he will eventually learn that there are indeed right and wrong ways of doing things. Particular rules of polish apply in some circumstances and not in others, which is how there come to be loopholes. But where the individual rules apply, they have all the inherent flexibility of a bowling ball.

Eventually, after you have written enough and mastered the laws of structure and rules of polish you too will understand where the rules apply and where they do not. Then you can break them. In the meantime, the only safe course is to pay your dues like we all did and follow the rules of polish as though they were handed down by God.

So, you ask, what are these rules?

The bad news is that there are a whole lot of them. The laws of structure are solidly based in human psychology, and have a consistent logic about them, which is why I could provide a general outline of them in a single chapter. The rules of polish, however, are one part logic, one part prejudice, one part authority and one part tradition. There are hundreds and hundreds of rules, each with its own exceptions, each changing in time, each contested hotly by some half-dozen card-carrying Authorities.

But there is good news as well. The laws of structure are comparatively few, but they are exceedingly abstract and have complex ramifications. The rules of polish, on the other hand, are rarely abstract and have very straight-forward applications.

The back-and-forth squabbling of the experts, for instance, has only marginal relevance for the practicing writer. It doesn't much matter who is right or who is wrong, or whether you conservatively use ''as'' in its traditional function or steer the liberal course and substitute ''like'' whenever it sounds right.

Personally, like most professional writers in this part of the century, I am a moderate conservative who tries to avoid fanaticism. But all that really matters is that you study and understand the various arguments until you can make a reasonable choice that fits your professional personality.

This is reflected in the First Iron Rule of Polish: *Do it consciously.*

The Second Iron Rule is to go out and buy a copy of a thin little book called *Elements of Style,* by William Strunk, Jr., and E. B. White, now in its umpteenth edition. It's clear, it's concise, it's in paperback, it touches virtually all the important bases, and in recent years it's become a sort of writer's bible.

The original copy was composed by the late William

Strunk, Jr., who was professor of English at Cornell. It was written for the use of his students but years later one of those students, E. B. White, revised the original and put together an edition for the general public. Among other things, White added a chapter of his own at the end in which he sought to lead the reader, as the book jacket says, ''beyond mere correctness toward distinction in English style.''

Not that *Elements of Style* is perfect, though. It has two major flaws, but as long as you're aware of them they will do no great harm.

The first flaw can be laid, I suspect, at White's feet. In the last chapter in particular the book tends to mix conceptual, structural and polish-level rules without making any distinction between them. But since you now understand the difference between the levels, you shouldn't have any trouble making those distinctions for yourself.

The other drawback of the book parallels its single greatest strength: its terseness.

In less than eighty pages the authors succinctly summarize all of the basic principles of polish. The result is so condensed as to make the book practically indigestible without the context of other books on grammar and usage.

I won't recommend any particular books; there are a number on the market. Which ones you should use depends on the weakness in your skills, which will be duly pointed out to you by teachers and editors.

The important thing is that you do not limit your studies to Strunk and White. Good polish requires a deep and personal insight into the language, and such insight is gained only by diligently studying different sources—and by experience.

Finally, and perhaps most important: Read. And read good stuff.

Early in our careers, most of us pick up most of our polish technique through osmosis as we go about reading for study and pleasure. Keep your eyes and mind open, and watch how various writers use words. Notice how their styles match their subjects and presentations; the use of language is not independent of what that language is being used for.

And as you choose what you will read, keep quality in mind. Unlike structure, polish rubs off easily—especially on impressionable beginners. The young would-be writer who yearns to write high-power prose but who reads mostly romances and whodunits will have to learn polish the hard way, out of Strunk and White, or not at all.

Above all, try not to forget that polish has an ultimate purpose, and that purpose is to tell a story.

Good polish grabs the reader with its active imagery and propels him into the story, where he is captured and moved along by the underlying structure. The active images follow one another like the frames of a moving picture, catapulting the reader from focus to focus as the story unfolds.

Like the character, the reader becomes so deeply involved with the events as they occur that he perceives only occasional glimmers of the realities behind those events.

A good writer, like a good magician, never gives his audience a moment to think. Effective polish is so unobtrusive, so subservient to the structure, that it's impossible to study it on a first reading—you get too caught up in the story. If you can study a writer's polish on the first reading, it's not worth studying.

Now, on to the process of polish itself.

Transition from Structure to Polish

The procedure for polishing, as opposed to the rules of polish, is similar to the procedures for outlining and rough composition. For one thing, you never begin at the beginning.

In one sense, the transition from structural craftsmanship to polish is a smooth one. As the writer satisfies himself that the major focuses of his story are sound, he naturally narrows his attention to the sequencing of the minor focuses; as those come under control, he looks to the subfocuses.

As this process continues, and he nears the level of the image, concepts and procedures that were germane before no longer apply. The attention now is on image sequencing and clarity, and the outline fades into uselessness as a whole new set of principles kick into action.

In practice, the shift to polish is differential. As you sketched out your dramatic high points first, and gave them your best energy throughout the structural process, they will naturally be the best developed and the smoothest.

The dramatic scene that climaxes the complication, for instance, along with the whole of the resolving focus, may already be on the verge of being finished. Many less-critical parts of the story will still be in very rough form.

This is as it should be, and you should polish your story the way you wrote it, without regard to sequence, concentrating first on the most critical scenes and then working down the list in order of importance.

The writing process is, after all, also a thinking process; this remains true until the last word is written. By polishing the dramatic high points first, you achieve a clearer grasp of exactly how you must lead the reader up to those high points.

The important-scene-first approach is also the most efficient. The dramatic high points of a story are the first ones nailed down and the ones which, once nailed down, are most likely to remain as they are.

If you invest technical and psychological energy in polishing other parts of the story first, when you finally get to the dramatic high points you may find they don't work exactly as you had envisioned—you must approach them in some slightly different fashion. Once you do, you must then go back and change the lead-in narrative to match.

If you've already invested effort in polishing that lead-in and background narrative, that effort is lost. Worse, polishing is a particularly emotional process for many beginners, and they consequently have a tendency to become married to polished copy.

This can make the writer psychologically incapable of comprehending that the copy needs to be recast or deleted; when that happens the whole story is destroyed for all but the neophyte's mother and best friend.

This brings us to the subject of beginnings.

The lead, or in fiction terms the "narrative hook," is reputed to be the toughest problem in all of storycraft. This is pure baloney, a durable myth that has evolved from the penchant of amateurs to begin at the beginning.

Beginning at the beginning of a story is like trying to aim a spacecraft at a particular crater on the moon and having it hit the target without even knowing what or where it is. That's why beginners labor so hard over leads, writing them again and again and again because they somehow . . . don't . . . seem . . . right.

They are absolutely correct. They can write them a million times and still not hit the target, for the simple reason that it's not yet clear where they're going.

The lead, you see, is a transition. It bridges the psychological gap between the story and the reader's world.

The only inherent difficulty is posed by the fact that the details of the reader's world are almost totally unpredictable for the writer. The reader may be anybody, anywhere, doing anything.

In itself this uncertainty can be solved. But it is dramatically compounded, and rendered all but insoluble, if the lead is written before the story is complete. Until then, the writer is ignorant not only of where he's transitioning from but of where he's transitioning *to* as well.

Once the story is completed, he at least knows where the lead is going, and the problem is reduced to human proportions.

In terms of the story, the lead-in transition must establish (or begin to establish) all five threads.

In the case of mood, for instance, the lead should foreshadow emotional elements that will appear in the story. "Mrs. Kelly's Monster" does this by telling the reader that coffee makes Dr. Ducker's hands shake. The clear implication is that it matters whether or not Dr. Ducker's hands shake, which further implies that Dr. Ducker is going to face some challenge.

The important thing is that the lead should match the story. No such challenge-to-come is implied in the lead to "The Ballad of Old Man Peters." Instead, I talk about the inexorable movement of time and the countervailing struggle against ignorance.

In addition, the lead must somehow make contact with the reader's unknown world. A good lead does this by creating images with which any reader can identify. In the case of "Mrs. Kelley's Monster," the image is all but universal . . . a family sitting around a breakfast table. In "The Ballad of Old Man Peters" an equally familiar image, of a man at a desk, is used.

Another possible approach, if the story involves exotic scenery, is to entice the reader with that exotica. A story about a Navy pilot, for instance, might begin in the cockpit of a Fury as the plane approaches the USS *Saratoga*, wallowing in a rough sea.

Whichever method you choose—and, so long as you keep the above requirements in mind, you should be inventive—the lead should not be difficult to write once you've completed the rest of the story.

It is, after all, the final ironic touch in the convoluted procedure that readers call art and writers call craft. We began at the ending; where better might we end than at the beginning?

Now that we've put the process of polish in perspective, and discussed the general order in which things must be accomplished, let's focus down to the process itself.

Image Clarity

As you undertake to polish your story you will confront two separate and overriding sets of principles. One set applies to the image itself, and the second to the sequencing of images. First, the image:

The "perfect image" is the precise image that all the images before have prepared the reader for, the image he already half-expects, the image that crystallizes in his mind the instant his eyes touch the words. There should be no need for him to hesitate, or to reread, or to stop and figure out what the writer *really* meant.

The easiest way to create the perfect image is to begin with the perfectly appropriate action verb.

The verb is the core of the image, and if your verb is a strong one, the other words in the image will tend to align themselves properly around it—it will sound best one way, and one way only.

This is because verbs are the center of gravity of the active image, a fact that echoes the iron rule of structure that stories must be told in terms of action. Likewise paragraphs, sentences and phrases must capture the kinetic energy of life . . . they must *do* something, or they have no dramatic point.

If the verb is weak, on the other hand, the surrounding words will fit almost any way you put them. No one way will sound appreciably better than any other, and chances are that none of them will sound exactly right. In that case you must return to the rules laid out in *Elements of Style*.

You can often get away with static verbs at the trough of the dramatic waves, and particularly in preparatory narrative. You can even get away with them, sometimes, in supporting images in climactic narrative. But when the image must bear the full weight of the drama, weak verbs are to literature what rain is to a garden wedding.

WORD CHOICE

Beyond the consistent use of good strong verbs, the key to image clarity is the proper choice of words. Clemens was right; the difference between the right word and the almost right word *is* the difference between lightning and the lightning bug.

The point is that words have specific meanings, and those meanings, dwelling as they do in the reader's mind, are not flexible at all. They are the "given" of polish.

Beginning writers commonly have a great deal of difficulty getting this inflexibility of word usage through their artistic young noggins. They use words to mean what *they* think they mean, and they are baffled when the teacher or editor circles them in red.

The only ready therapy for this is a dictionary, but even that is not curative. The dictionary is much more likely to represent the reader's definition of a word than is the young writer's own prejudice, and so The Great God Webster reigns throughout the writing apprenticeship.

But there is truth beyond Webster, and a seasoned writer's experience often carries him beyond the dictionary—at least with words that he knows and uses frequently.

How does a seasoned writer get seasoned? First of all, by going through the apprenticeship, making mistakes, and getting his ears pinned back. This makes him very conservative, on the one hand, and very observant of language on the other. The former makes him actually more likely than the apprentice to reach for a dictionary; the latter cues him in on the few instances where the lexicographers are fuzzy or slightly behind the times.

Fortunately for the diligent apprentice, there are easy ways to get the jump on experience. There is an active cadre of writers who specialize in explaining word usage and the theories that lie behind it.

My own library contains Fowler's *Modern English Usage*. Also, like thousands of other writers and language buffs, I enjoy reading the likes of William Safire.

I also have a *Roget's International Thesaurus,* but I can't say that I get much use out of it. Neither have I ever found another professional writer who says it's been helpful to him.

My suspicion is that the book, despite its popularity among laymen (and especially among bureaucrats), is founded on an erroneous principle—the principle that there is such a thing as a "synonym."

The more years I devote to writing the stronger my suspicion becomes that words are just as Samuel Clemens implied. They are as unique as people. Roget's perception that they have any useful degree of interchangeability represents a total misunderstanding of what the language is about.

If this is the case, word usage is something that must be learned piecemeal by the writer, one word at a time. The average writer, whatever that is, understands and can use about 100,000 words—or so I've heard.

I can't give you a list, though, and neither can anyone else. The specific words that you must know and be able to use with precision will be determined by the perceptions you have and the images you will use, as a professional, to express them.

While there will be many similarities between the words in your bag of tricks and those in mine, there will also be significant differences. What's more, the vocabularies we hold in common will be used in different ways by each of us, depending on the nature of the stories we tend to choose.

The bottom line, then, is that with the help of people like William Safire you must develop your own vocabulary, and learn by experience how to use it correctly. This process generally accounts for a significant amount of an apprentice's mental energy.

SPECIFICITY AND UNIVERSALITY

The key to word choice, as well as to the inherent power of active images, is specificity.

Specificity is a concept that applies exquisitely to the level of polish. On the conceptual level, stories benefit from sweeping summarizations and even from clichés: "Man Seeks Love" is a powerful complication.

But at the polish level, the story must be told in terms of unique individuals and their specific actions and thoughts. As in poetry, the universal is finally achieved by focusing down, tightly, even microscopically, on specific events and the details that surround them.

Clichés, precisely because they are so widely applicable (and not, in my opinion, because they are "tired"—whatever *that* means), destroy the writer's effort to be specific and therefore universal.

SIMPLICITY UNTO ELEGANCE

Simplicity, or the quality of straightforwardness, is a key concept in polish. Clarity of image is as sensitive to complexity as structure is to woodwork. If you have any doubts, read *Huckleberry Finn* and then follow it, without pause, with Faulkner's *The Hamlet*. Or try to. The sensation is something like running full-tilt into that familiar brick wall.

This is not a total criticism of Faulkner. Faulkner, like Joyce before him, was an experimenter and inventor. To criticize him for lack of clarity is much like criticizing the Wright brothers because their airplanes couldn't carry troops. Still, the example makes my point.

The quest for simplicity is complicated by two great dangers. The first is that the image will not be simple enough; the second is that it will be too simple.

Simplicity ultimately boils down to the use of as few words as possible. If you need very many words to create your active image, and particularly if very many of those words are modifiers or if the image is bracketed by prepositions, you probably aren't using the right words.

This is the reason that virtually all polish experts issue frequent dire warnings against the use of modifiers (adjectives and adverbs), prepositions, and words that end with "ing."

Modifiers, prepositions and so forth are not in and of themselves evil. The problem is that the writer tends to need them only if he is trying to make do with an almost-right word. If you need a modifier to alter the meaning of a word, then the chances are very good that you don't have the right word. If you did, it wouldn't need modification.

If this is the case, simply cutting out the modifiers and prepositional constructions may simplify the thought, but it will also make it inaccurate. The situation calls to mind Albert Einstein's observation that he liked things as simple as they could be . . . but not any simpler than they really were.

At the same time, lest the apprentice hide behind Albert's baggy trousers, it should be pointed out that Einstein was the same fellow who summed up the entire physical universe in a single mathematical image.

The writer's pursuit, like the physicist's, is a combination of simplicity and accuracy. A master craftsman by choosing exactly the right words, can sum up great segments of the psychological universe. What he achieves in the process is not mere simplicity but elegance.

Sequencing

The final and most portentous element of polish has to do with the flow of paragraphs, images and finally words. I have saved it for last because it leads us to The Secret.

Sequencing pertains to the need for your story to unfold, image by image, in a fashion that best achieves your structural (which is to say dramatic) goals.

Sequencing represents the downward extension of structure into the polish level. Because it has a direct connection to structure, sequencing is the most important of the two principles of polish. At the same time, if you have a good structural foundation, image sequencing is by far the most logical of the two.

One useful analogy to sequencing in prose is the frame-by-frame progression of a movie film. Each frame is different enough from the one before that the viewer gets an impression of motion, but not so different that the motion seems jerky.

In the chapter on structure, as you may remember, I cautioned you against using the Mississippi as a metaphor for narrative. Now I reverse that advice; on the polish level, ''smoothness'' is usually a positive quality.

To achieve this illusion of smoothness you arrange your paragraphs, images and words in an order that allows the reader's mind to jump easily and automatically from one image to another.

This means, first, that the order of images within a sentence and the order of sentences within the paragraph must either be logical or phychological, but never random. Each image must make sense within the context of the images that came immediately before.

Complex sentences, combined with the heavy use of prepositions and other devices that contort the straightforward flow of thoughts, should alert you to the possibility that you have extraneous or insufficiently thought-out images.

If your copy seems confused, or if others say it is, bracket off the individual images and look at them, instead of the sentences they compose. Are they in the right order? If not, switch them . . . and *then* figure out how to incorporate them into new sentences.

If it doesn't seem important which of two images comes first, you should stop and scratch your head. Something is wrong. Ask yourself whether both are necessary—if one doesn't build on the other, what's its purpose?

It needs to be noted that sophisticated polish-level sequencing also incorporates the almost musical principles of rhythms and word sounds.

A series of long sentences may establish a slow rhythm, for instance, that is then shattered by a short, pithy summation. The breaking of the rhythm adds impact to the conclusion.

An example of the use of rhythms can be found in "Mrs. Kelly's Monster." Much of the narrative is blank verse. Though few readers recognize this fact, it has a definite psychological effect that contributes significantly to the overall dramatic nature of the story. (For a more complete discussion of these techniques, I recommend Richard A. Lanham's *Revising Prose* [Scribner's, 1979]).

Finally, since images build on one another, they must build *into* something, right?

Right! They do, which finally brings us around to the thesis of this book.

From the beginning I have talked about subunits of story, which we have called focuses, and at one point we discussed the fact that the smallest focus was the image and the largest was the story itself.

But we have looked at this concept from the top down. That's the way a writer *has* to look at it, but it's a perspective that's difficult to get used to.

Now that we have reached the bottom level, that of the image, we can look up and see the mountain of story in its full majesty, lowlands building to foothills, foothills to shoulders, shoulders to citadels, citadels to stairstepping peaks, peaks to the final lofty summit.

As a mountain rises, so rises a story.

Images build on one another, collecting force as they do so, until finally reaching a dramatic crest in a capping and preferably emotionally laden statement that comes at the end of a paragraph. Then the dramatic level falls off into a minor transition (if necessary) and another dramatic foothill of preparatory prose begins to rise.

Several such foothills, each one building on the one before and therefore rising ever higher, finally reach the climax of a small focus. That climax is the expression of the most dramatic cluster of images within that focus. That final statement summarizes the dramatic content of all the dramatic statements that built toward it.

Such small focuses, in turn, drop away through transitional valleys and then build toward higher ones, and those to still loftier ones, each cresting in a summary dramatic statement, until the level of the major focus is reached and the focus statement (the one that appears in the outline) is demonstrated.

This is a dramatic peak. The narration then descends through the high valley of a major transition before beginning the long up-and-down ascent toward the next such peak. At the end of the story, in the final few images of the resolution, the narrative finally tops the summit of the highest dramatic peak of all. That accomplished, the story ends.

Like mountain chains, the dramatic heights of stories, and the steepness of the ascent, vary widely. "Mrs. Kelly's Monster" is a volcano that rises sharply upward, like Fuji-no-yama or Kilimanjaro. The views from its peaks are breathless, but the mountain itself is not all that high. "The Ballad of Old Man Peters" is more of a McKinley, rising slowly, ridge by ridge, into the stratosphere.

The number of focuses, like the number of rises and falls in the trail upward, varies accordingly. The number of images within a major focus is determined by the length and the complexity of the story.

As you examine the dramatic rises and falls of a story, the most striking thing is that the valleys, where the images begin to build, are where you find the greatest proportion of passive statements . . . and also the longest sentences. Those often pastoral images are like pleasant trails through hanging valleys; they make up the preparatory narrative.

A few dozen images later in the sequence, as the drama

builds toward a dramatic crest, the sentence length falls off and the proportion of static verbs drops.

This is a relative phenomenon and repeats itself again and again, changing in nature as the air thins. Early in a major focus, where the preparatory narrative is progressing, the verbs may be mostly static throughout each gentle rise and fall of the narrative, with a few action verbs kicking in at the crest.

Later on, toward the end of the major focus and when the climactic narrative is at play, the verbs may be entirely action verbs—but they grow ever stronger, and more dramatic, on the crests.

The master craftsman is acutely conscious of this rise and fall in his drama. He knows that the narrative of the valleys is the least sensitive of all; here, if circumstances are otherwise appropriate, he can wax poetic over the forests and the clear lakes. He can employ static verbs, if they seem to suit his purposes more than strong ones—or if he is in a hurry and can't think of a good action verb.

But as the wave builds and the sentences shorten, his latitude diminishes. Now, as the ascent becomes steep, the possibility of a misstep increases and the danger grows. Each step, now, carries great risk, and the writer, as the climber, grows conservative. Each image must be ever more clear and ever more active.

As each dramatic rise builds toward its climax, the demands on the language become greater and greater until finally, at the end of the major focus, the writer has no choices left at all. The words he uses, now, are totally dictated by what has gone before and by the heavy dramatic weight each image must bear.

The Secret of the professional writer, then, is an elegant fusion of craftsmanship with artistic vision—of not only having the tools but also understanding the purpose for which each is intended. The successful writer is one who grasps the separate components of his story and, at the same time, sees how those components work together to produce a compelling and dramatic tale.

The Secret, in other words, is that there *is* no secret beyond knowledge and experience; writing is no different than conducting an orchestra, performing surgery, flying an airplane, or climbing a mountain. It is a human endeavor and the skilled professional in any field, including writing, is one who has first mastered the techniques and then accumulated the experience necessary to know when, and to what purpose, each technique is used.

To continue the mountain metaphor, the writer's art is his ability to see the mountain of story rising through the fog and haze of reality—and to dream the great, insane dream of climbing it.

Structuring is the act of planning and analysis, of hiring sherpas, accumulating equipment and buying tickets. It is the antithesis of dream, as unartful as anything the writer does. Yet it is absolutely necessary to his survival.

The laws and rules of craft are the tools you carry in your pack.

You don't need many of those tools in the valleys, of course. If you are a coward there, and rock-engineer your way over every little rise and rockfall, you'll never get where you're going. But in the dramatic high country you'll need every tool in your pack and every skill you can muster.

Any idiot can amble through the valleys, and any fool can fall off a cliff. The master craftsman is the one who knows mountains, and where the dangers are, who can stride whistling through the vales but turn serious on the high rocks, who can expertly and safely work his way up the sheer walls of the citadels that guard his objective, placing his pitons solidly and at perfect intervals, pinning the psyche of his reader firmly to the living rock of the story, each hammer-blow image ringing bell-clear and perfect in the thin air of high drama.

X

The Nature of Art and Artists

BUT, YOU MAY OBJECT, is that all there is? Is it really so
. . . mechanistic? In all this technical discussion about
complications, resolutions, actions, plot points and characters, structure and polish, haven't we left something out?

At one level, the level of craftsmanship, your uneasiness
probably comes from the accumulation of buncombe you've
heard about the mysteriousness of it all.

In truth, storycraft *is* mechanistic. These are the tricks
of the magician-writer, the blue smoke and mirrors with
which the master craftsman makes his living even on bad
days when there is no inspiration, no insight . . . only a
blank piece of paper in his typewriter and overdue bills in
his top drawer. Without technique you cannot be a writer.

But on a more personal level, your feelings of vague
uneasiness are justified. While writing cannot be performed
without mechanism, it is more than mechanism. We *have*

left something out. There *is* something magic that occurs behind the smoke and mirrors.

What we have left out of our discussion of craft is the artist. You.

A general misunderstanding of this issue, of art and of the artist's feelings, composes what is perhaps the single greatest bar to the growth of the writer as craftsman. Unresolved, it fosters an attitude that distorts the simple truth about craftsmanship and turns it into something unpleasant and fundamentally threatening. Until the issue is put to rest the writer must keep some part of himself reserved; he can't open his mind and *learn*.

So, in this last chapter, we confront the nature of art. To do so we must go back to that yearning and excruciating era of life called adolescence when, for most of us (myself included), it all began.

From the very beginning the very young writer knows certain eternal truths. He knows art is a delicate flower, an innocent thing of great beauty. And he knows that its bud swells promisingly in his own mind.

Why him? That, he doesn't know. But he knows, though he knows not to talk about it, that there is something special about him. Something unique. Something acutely individual. And he knows that whatever that something is, it must be protected at all costs from those who would pound him into the common mold—family, friends, teachers, ministers, policemen, grocery clerks and all the other lockstep zombies who have already sold their souls to the devil of conformity.

"*Conform!*" the world seems to hiss, threateningly, at the young writer. "*Think as you are told to think! Do as we all do! Adopt, as your own, the rules and perceptions of your elders!*"

He doesn't know how he escaped these pressures as long as he has. Maybe a certain resiliency goes with the specialness. But whatever the explanation, he did escape; if he hadn't, he wouldn't think the thoughts he thinks, or have that desperate craving to put them down on paper.

However his specialness survived this far, now that he's old enough and savvy enough to see what life's about he consciously resists the pressures that would tend to damp out the differences between him and Everybody Else. He is generally suspicious of rules of all sorts, and especially of those that purport to teach him how he should write.

Art, he well knows, comes from Inside. It can be protected and nourished. It can be destroyed. But it can't be taught.

The principles of grammar, on the other hand, and the rest of the catechism of "correct writing" are essentially superficial. This catechism is a drab accumulation of detail, of tradition and its nonsensical exceptions, of pedantic nuances and literary abstractions. What's more, as anyone who compares the pronouncements of experts can see, it's largely a matter of opinion.

Being arbitrary, the laws of composition have their principal value in the minds of English teachers, power-drunk editors and other purists who, lacking creativity themselves, have vested interests in squelching it anywhere they find it. Of course "craftsmanship" can be taught—always assuming you can find a student so devoid of originality that he takes it seriously. The same can be said of fashion design, shoemaking, accounting or Sanskrit.

It also doesn't escape the writer that the overwhelming majority of the rules of composition are negative. Do *not* use static verbs. Do *not* use incomplete sentences. Do *not* use words contrary to the meanings determined by The Great God Webster.

And just how, after all, are these different from the barrage of edicts he encounters every time he finds himself in close proximity to an adult? Don't forget to wash behind your ears. Stay out of the mud. Don't play with that thing in here. Stay out of that it's for supper, don't pick your nose, don't point, don't put your hands in your pockets, don't slouch, don't stay out after eleven, don't, don't, don't and don't.

The adolescent may be young but he's not dumb; the

edicts of everyday existence are clearly contrived for the convenience of adults and, as such, they are fundamentally repressive. What reason is there for him to believe that the rules of writing are any different?

Art, on the other hand . . .

Rules are imposed from the outside but art comes from within, and it should not be bound by petty shackles imposed by small minds. It, and the artist within whose breast the creative heart beats, should be free.

Alone in his room, the beginner vows to the assembled muses that he will not, repeat not, *not,* allow the Authorities of Formal English to pound him into creative submission. He writes, by God, what he sees.

Then he shows what he's written to his friends, parents, and favorite relatives. They love it. Encouraged, he commits it to the U.S. mails. He waits nervously.

In the fullness of time his manuscript comes back to him in the company of a printed rejection slip.

Well, for art one must suffer. The girl next door, looking at him with big hazel eyes, understands and sympathizes.

He puts the manuscript in another envelope and hesitates before sealing it. Perhaps . . . perhaps he shouldn't include return postage. Maybe that's too much of a temptation. His better judgment prevails.

Sure enough, the editor yields to the temptation.

The news is not all bad, of course. Occasionally he gets a handwritten note from a kindly editor who assures him that he is obviously very talented.

It is a bright day when such a note appears in the mailbox; somebody out there understands his suffering. That fires him with optimism that he is indeed on destiny's trail.

He sends out a poem. It comes back.

Sometimes, a note from an editor contains a small piece of advice—an observation that he might get further if he'd bite off smaller chunks, for instance, or if he'd minimize the background about the whichness of the what and write more about individual people. Nonfiction might be worth trying, too, as there isn't much demand these days for lyric poetry and short fiction.

This advice, of course, the young writer summarily rejects. Nonfiction is out; it stunts the imagination. One day editors will understand what he's doing, and meanwhile he will forgive them for their shortsightedness.

He sends off another manuscript. It comes back. He sends off another. It comes back. He sends off another. It comes back. Defiantly, he puts the rejection slips in a shoebox. When he's a literary idol he'll use them to paper his bathroom.

But with the passage of time, and as he continues to write and to mature in other ways, rejection inexorably takes its toll. One day his courage wavers for a moment, and a frightening thought occurs.

He quickly pushes it to the back of his mind, far back . . . far, far back, where it can keep company with other things best not examined too closely, like sex and death.

But this particular thought is terribly compelling, relentlessly urgent, and the young writer's mind dredges it up again and again, masochistically, like a tongue repeatedly seeking out and exploring a newly discovered cavity.

The unthinkable thought has to do with the fact that, well . . . the notes from editors, no matter how encouraging and sympathetic they may be . . . it occurs to him, once he thinks about it, that . . . they are nevertheless eternally accompanied by a rejected manuscript.

Something . . . isn't . . . working.

The idea settles in the pit of his stomach like so much indigestible grease. It enters the mind unbidden, like Marley's ghost, at the brink of sleep. It intrudes while he's writing, tainting the artistic process with the poison of self-doubt, ruining the rhythm, deadening the inspiration, and generally creating pandemonium among the muses.

A manuscript goes out, a manuscript comes back. A manuscript goes out, a manuscript comes back.

Something . . . isn't . . . working.

Perhaps he can't be a writer. Perhaps he hasn't got it.

Perhaps . . . no.

A manuscript goes out, a manuscript comes back.

Perhaps . . . just perhaps . . .

No. Never!

Like an alcoholic warily circling the possibility that he may share the blame for his condition, the young writer struggles with himself, art versus reality.

Well, he finally and reluctantly concedes, maybe the Authorities of Formal English aren't entirely wrong.

That is not to say, of course, that they are right. But maybe, in that snowstorm of trivial admonitions they get such pleasure out of throwing at him, they know some important secret that he, the innocent young artist, does not.

If so, he must have it.

He must open his mind, if only a crack, to the possibility that his writing might be improved by outside forces.

He must be vigilant, of course, lest the Authorities catch him napping. Given the opportunity, he knows they will dart into his psyche and rip out his creativity; he must be prepared to slam his mind shut again in an instant.

But he's got to take the chance. He's growing up, you see, and his manuscripts keep coming back. He doesn't know what to do and he must do *something* or he's going to end up washing cars for the rest of his life. So he takes one tiny, pragmatic step away from artistic purity.

Artistic purity, though, is like virginity. One step is all it takes.

He is now an apprentice.

Keep your nouns close to your verbs!

Avoid prepositions!

The apprentice listens, and thinks about such things, and gingerly even tries to apply one or two of them to his prose. To his surprise, he finds they work.

One by one, he discovers that at least some rules of

composition seem to have some vague basis in . . . in art?
It's painful to admit, but . . . and there is a place for, say,
incomplete sentences, but . . . but perhaps, the apprentice
concedes . . . perhaps in his enthusiasm he overused them
a bit.

Use action verbs!

Well, yes. His copy *is* brighter if he uses action verbs,
though it's not at all clear to him why this should be so.
And didn't Shakespeare use static verbs?

To be or not to be, that is the question? Where does *that*
fit into the rules?

Learn to follow them first, and then you can break them.

And as for nonfiction, well, it *would* be nice to get
published. Fact isn't as creative as fiction, of course—you
don't create fact, you dredge it up from the muck of reality
around you—but all the same, it might do for practice.

Later he'll write short stories that'll knock their socks
off, but for the moment he starts interviewing people.
Unfortunately, the people he interviews aren't very interesting.

Show, don't tell!

*One example is a contention, two is an argument and
three is proof.*

*The difference between the right word and the almost-
right word is the difference between lightning and the
lightning bug.*

Language, the professors say, is an extension of the
human mind and it shares with that organ its characteristic
complexity. In this instance, at least, the professors are
correct.

The rules are so many, and they are so confounded by exceptions, and are transformed by such a confusion of factors and levels, that the mere struggle to keep them all in mind comes to dominate the young writer's existence.

They would be easy enough to memorize, but that doesn't help. There's a relationship between them, some pattern that he can't quite grasp, and in the meantime his mind is awash in what seems like trivia but isn't.

Once the words had flowed easily from his pen, uncluttered by technique, filling the blank paper before him. But now, as he looks at each word, self-consciousness sets in. As he struggles to keep track of the principles he's trying to follow he loses his grip on the concepts he is trying to convey and his narrative collapses.

In despair he remembers his vow not to let his art, his soul, be overwhelmed by trivia. Little by little, he's losing the battle.

An inspiration sends him back to his old stories and poems, the ones he liked so much. Certainly *they* weren't awkward, and that should inspire him.

They don't though. Instead, he's horrified to discver that if anything they're even worse than what he's producing now. They sound like the enthusiastic blather of a child! Why couldn't he see that before?

It suddenly occurs to him that while *he* couldn't see it, others probably could. The realization makes him burn with humiliation.

Shaken, he wonders if he's lost the art he once had in his soul. Or, worse, if he never had it in the first place.

He forces himself to write. He pounds out a story, doesn't have the nerve to look at it, tells himself it's wonderful, and sends it off. It comes back like a boomerang.

Perhaps, he thinks . . . perhaps if he only had an interested editor. He looks for one but finds that the editors, the good ones anyway, are occupied with published writers. He's not quite so young, anymore, and he gets the distinct impression that they don't think he's cute. In fact, they hardly acknowledge that he exists.

The weeks pass, and turn into years. Other young writers quit in favor of engineering, business, and agronomy. Our hero, however, hangs on desperately.

Language is a great intellectual onion, layer upon layer upon layer. The more he learns, the more the apprentice is hemmed in on all sides by laws and processes that limit his options.

High school gives way to college.

Somehow the apprentice thought the study of literature had to do with reading great poetry and discussing the themes in the *Iliad*. But he feels more like a student in physics, trying to keep the various colors and flavors of quarks straight in his head.

The muses sing only rarely, now; most of his material comes from books, interviews and direct observations. Only occasionally does an odd inspiration assure him that his art is not dead.

His stories still lack something, and when he sends them out they invariably come back, but he's having better luck now finding subjects who are good stories. His sentences are also beginning to flow a little more smoothly.

But at the same time he's becoming more conscious of an indefinable awkwardness in his organization.

The strongest thought should always appear at the end of a sentence, a paragraph, or a passage.

Nothing is more damaging to narrative than a good example of something that isn't germane.

Organization is maddening! He cuts and pastes, cuts and pastes, cuts and pastes, and what was poorly organized before becomes incomprehensible.

The purpose of narrative is to guide the reader's thoughts from one action to the next.

But if he puts this up here, then that's out of place. If he moves that, then the other doesn't go anywhere!

Chekhov's Law: If the opening scene of your story shows a shotgun hanging over the mantelpiece, then that gun must be fired before the end.

Foreshadow! Foreshadow! Foreshadow!

His stories, while improving, lack something critical, something structural.

Or something artistic? Something the Authorities snatched away while he wasn't looking?

He rejects the thought. It has to be structural.

He digs through the library, looking for old textbooks on short stories, and discovers the complication-resolution form.

That helps. That helps a lot. There is a quantum jump in the quality of his efforts. His days are filled with excitement; he's finally there. After all these years of effort, he's finally cracked it! He writes a story, examines it, rejects it, and writes another. Wonderful! He sends it off.

It comes back.

His elation changes to outrage. What the hell? The story has a complication, a resolution . . . why, it's the best thing he ever wrote! And the editor didn't even send along an encouraging note! Who do they think they are, anyway? "Not suitable for our audience!"

But deep within his mind, the apprentice is afraid he knows what was wrong. This fear has been growing for some time, getting more insistent with every improvement.

What's the use of writing if you've nothing to say?

His story was technically perfect. He is certain of that. He did everything right, and that's what's wrong. There was too much technique, not enough . . . not enough . . . *soul*.

He lies awake at night, staring into the darkness and listening to his roommate snore.

What's happening, anyway, to the art that he once felt within him? He answers himself: It's withering from disuse.

He's got to find some outlet for his art. If he doesn't,

he'll never become a Steinbeck, or a Hemingway, or even a Capote. He will become, instead, a hack.

This dilemma, he believes, is compounded by the modern insistence on nonfiction. At least young Hemingway, while tied to the formula of his time, could create the story itself. But now editors don't want that, they want only fact, fact, fact . . . what they don't want is the writer.

If he can't even create the story, the apprentice asks himself, what *can* he create? Where, in all this technique, can he find an outlet for *himself?*

By and by, the magic answer dawns on him: It's not what you say, anymore, it's all in how you say it!

His creativity must go into the use of words, into the warp and flux of the syntax itself. Isn't that what Tom Wolfe did, with his trademark boom-bang-pow-man-oh-wowie? Wasn't that how e. e. cummings did it?

Given a new purpose, a new hope, the apprentice snaps out of his doldrums. In one week he reads every scrap Tom Wolfe ever wrote. In two weeks he's playing around with unique constructions, using more phrases that tie back to the sentence before, a little stream of consciousness in the lead, maybe, and not just one flashback. Naw, five. Ten. Give the thing a fluid feeling. Break a few rules.

For the first time in years, inspiration pounds in his temples, art flows in his veins, and the muse croons sweetly in his ear. He knows the rules; now he breaks them in an orgy of creativity. This is fun!

He takes his story to his adviser.

"You gotta read this right now!" he says. "It's the best thing I ever did." The professor takes the manuscript and starts reading.

The apprentice sits on the edge of a chair and waits, trying not to fidget. His stomach writhes, and he fights back nausea. Must be the lunch he ate. College chow is awful.

The professor finishes the manuscript and then goes back and reads it again, slowly this time. That gives him a chance to figure out what in the world he's going to say to the intense young man in front of him. Finally the professor sighs and decides that the lesser of all the many possible evils is to tell the truth. So he does.

The apprentice looks at him in disbelief. He'd thought his adviser *liked* him!

What does he mean, he can't figure out what I'm trying to say? What does he mean . . . unclear? What does he mean, why don't I just tell the story?

That's style, man! Can't you tell that's style?

The apprentice leaps to his feet, snatches the manuscript out of the professor's hands, and stomps out. He throws the story into the dumpster outside, walks to the park, finds a secluded tree to sit under, and cries like a baby for forty-five minutes.

The tears are for the flower of his art, and his pristine dreams. It was his last chance, and he blew it. There's no other way out. It's over.

The next day he changes his major to biochemistry, brushing off his adviser's questions with noncommittal grunts.

The adviser peers at the apprentice, speculatively, then reaches into his top desk drawer, pulls out a copy of Somerset Maugham's *The Summing Up*, and gives it to the apprentice along with the signed change-of-major form. The apprentice, the ex-apprentice, sticks both in his knapsack and walks out.

That night the ex-apprentice doesn't read Maugham, he reads a biochemistry textbook instead. It doesn't make sense, but at least he knows it's not magic. A lot of dunderheads have mastered biochem.

But the next morning, or soon, his curiosity gets the best of him and he opens the book the professor gave him.

The Summing Up is a thin book, totally without artistic reverence, and Maugham gets right to the point. The arts, he notes, is the only human endeavor in which the label "competent" is pejorative. Well, horsefeathers! Maugham, for one, was proud of his competence.

The apprentice reads on, fascinated. He can't believe

what this fellow's saying. *He's saying you can do it without art!*

What a strange idea. And yet, and yet . . .

All right then, the ex-apprentice says, he won't run if he doesn't have to. If he can't be an artist he'll by damned be a hack. But he'll not be just any hack—he'll be a good hack. He'll be so good a hack that nobody will dare call him a hack.

He'll be a craftsman.

Craftsman. He rolls the word around in his mind. It doesn't fit as well as "artist," but it seems a lot more natural, somehow, than "biochemist." The next day the ex-apprentice switches his major back to English.

But he doesn't become an apprentice again. There are some processes that run in only one direction: You can't rediscover virginity, unbreak an egg, or unsee the fact that there is no art in you.

He is now a journeyman writer.

Now, the protecting shield of art stripped away, he has nothing left to fall back on but craft. As a result, he is fiercely pragmatic.

He no longer shows his stories to his friends and lovers; he doesn't want their painful lies about his "art." He tries showing them, instead, to disinterested critics.

He even shows something to someone he knows doesn't like him, and the experiment works surprisingly well. His enemies are far more inclined than his friends to tell him the truth.

Humbler now, he no longer aspires to write masterpieces. He dreams a smaller and more attainable dream, of writing a clear sentence.

In the pursuit of that limited goal, he makes a profound discovery. The reason he couldn't put much art into the exercise of language is that language isn't nearly as flexible as it appears to an apprentice.

Language is more like mathematics than magic. It is a program code, for the computer called the mind, and its sequencing is not arbitrary at all. The choice and flow of words is guided by a complex, interlocking system of straightforward principles. While experts may snarl at one another over fine points, most of composition is ruled by the iron hand of grammar, usage, fine-scale structure, rhythm and the other laws of polish.

For a while he's sidetracked into the matter of colloquialisms. He'd thought he'd weeded them out of his style long ago, but now that he's less egotistical about his words he discovers that he's using the verb "get" in a strictly colloquial fashion. That gets him started, and he finds more, and still more.

Suddenly he's overtaken by a fascination with rhythms. Used properly, rhythm can raise or lower the reader's excitement level. And . . . there's an interesting phenomenon about rhythm. The principles involved seem to change slightly, depending on what part of the story they're in.

That means something, he suspects. He wishes he knew what.

The journeyman learns so rapidly that he begins to see patterns in the process of learning itself. Every time he solves a problem, or discovers a principle that improves his work, he unmasks a new weakness. It's like eating peanuts.

Life, since he abandoned art, is guiltlessly, almost joyfully, technical. His ability improves, story by story. His mind is feverish with questions and current interests.

Right now it's Clarity. Clarity. Clarity is the new God.

The journeyman's style begins to change, becoming more direct and straightforward. He no longer uses fancy words where simple ones will do.

Simplicity, coupled with clarity, equals elegance.

As he concentrates on clarity, his sentences tighten and become crisper. They almost crackle, now, they are so information-dense, and yet on good days they flow with the ease of fiction. He starts thinking about paragraphs.

As an outgrowth of his concentration on clarity, it occurs to him that there's an easy way to improve the effectiveness of his writing.

Though his ability improves with glacial speed, what if he simplified the story? What if he scaled his ambitions downward, and limited his stories to those he thought he had a realistic chance of writing well? A simple story, well told.

He tries it, and it works beyond his wildest expectations. He shows the story to his adviser, and three days later he gets a call from the editor of the school literary magazine. That spring, the journeyman's first nonfiction drama is set in type.

He reads it, expecting to enjoy the warm flush of accomplishment, but instead . . . Damn! There's something about cold type that dramatically emphasizes flaws! Good Lord but his transitions are clunky! In type, for everyone to see!

Why? he asks himself, in embarrassment. Where did he go wrong?

He asks his professor. The professor hazards some theories, and hems and haws until it becomes obvious that he doesn't know. And besides, they don't look so terrible to him.

The writer goes away and rereads the story. Is he being too critical, too hard on himself? Unfortunately, he decides, he's not. The transitions are even worse than they looked at first.

The professor's ignorance unnerves him. He feels very alone.

He spends a weekend in the library, trying to find something on transitions, and what makes them tick. He doesn't find anything, which amazes him.

Every book in the library is chock full of transitions, some of them good and some of them bad. Transitions are the glue that holds together the collective perceptions of modern man . . . and yet nobody has ever written a book on them.

That is sobering. Now the journeyman *really* feels alone.

The problem wedges itself into his mind and nags at him. For three months he thinks about almost nothing but transitions, transitions, transitions, and he still can't figure out what he's doing wrong.

Then one morning at 3:25 he awakens with a start and sits straight up in bed.

There's nothing wrong with his transitions, nothing at all!

What's wrong is that the stuff he's trying to glue together isn't supposed to be glued together! It doesn't mesh! He might as well have tried to stick a marble to a pigeon's foot!

He reorders the structure of the story, writes new transitions, and is pleased with the result. So is his adviser. He sends it off.

It comes back.

But it is accompanied by a full-page letter from the editor. The editor says he is mightily impressed with the story, but that it seems fuzzy. As near as he can figure, there's something wrong with the character.

The character? The writer reads the story, and shows it to the professor. The professor, on second reading, has to agree. The character's motivation isn't quite clear.

They talk about it, and decide what changes need to be made. The writer makes them.

But, as he does, something strange and dismaying happens. In strengthening the character the action of the story, though unchanged, seems . . . different. It's shifted its focus, somehow, and is slightly off point.

The writer feels his grasp of the story slipping, so he lays it aside and does another, to clear his head.

Exactly the same thing happens.

He can't believe it! He was doing so well, and now . . . he's not doing anything different except . . . except he's a little better at it.

The obvious answer is that his writing has improved enough that he's discovered something else, some other weakness. But this time he can't put his finger on exactly what it is.

Or, maybe not. Two stories does not a trend make. So he writes another. This one is worse than the first two, and in exactly the same mysterious way.

He takes it to his critics and they point out many small flaws, no single one of which is fatal. Taken together, however, they ruin the story.

He corrects those flaws, but when he does new ones appear. His advisers still don't like the story, but their reasons are different now.

Something systematic is happening.

Suddenly language itself begins to fail him. As he tries to make his story work as a whole he must twist his sentences, and they grow murky and convoluted.

What's happening? He fights panic. He goes to his professor, and his professor says he shouldn't worry about it.

Thanks a lot.

He looks at his recent stories, one by one. There's no mistaking it. He's definitely getting worse.

Worse.

Desperately, he chooses a story and tries again to rewrite it. But when he sharpens the character, the resolution goes out of focus. When he brings the resolution up to the clarity level of the character, the complication doesn't fit anymore.

He starts buttonholing English and journalism professors he barely knows and begging them to read his stuff. They are unanimous that something is wrong, but they disagree on what.

The literary magazine wants another story. He gives them one. The editor looks at it and reconsiders. It turned out, he apologizes as he returns the manuscript, that space was more limited than he'd thought.

The writer is disconsolate. Suddenly everybody's picking at him. This is wrong. That's wrong. Everybody points a red pencil at something different. Brooding, the writer tries to describe to himself how he feels and comes up with a perfect metaphor. It's like being nibbled to death by ducks.

His confidence drops precipitously. He goes off by himself, and thinks about it, and sulks, and thinks about it, and sulks.

His mind goes back to his young days, when he had the confidence of art. He mourns the loss.

His mother and his friends see him brooding, and worry. Someone gently suggests he see the campus psychiatrist. He tells him to drop dead.

Okay, he says to himself, reason it through.

He tries, but his mind slithers away. A psychiatrist, indeed!

He forces his mind back. It's something systemic, something fundamental to the whole story.

He has a sudden, acute urge for an ice cream cone.

That's a clue!

His mind won't focus on the problem. He's run into that before. It means the answer is something he doesn't want to see.

He puts his mind back where it belongs. What things are systemic? What touches every part of the story, and might distort it?

But his mind slides away again, and he sulks. It's not fair. After all this time, all this work . . . he catches himself, and brings his mind back again.

Again it skitters away, and this time he can't bring it back. He is exhausted. He goes out and buys the ice cream cone.

Days pass. Weeks. He persists.

Think it through again.

It takes a long, long time, longer than makes sense.

Eliminate possibilities.

It's not the words. It can't be the words, or the phrases, or the paragraphs. If it were any of those things he could fix them, and they'd by golly *stay* fixed. So the problem is something larger, in the structure. It has to be a structural problem.

What is structure?

It's how he tells the story.

But that doesn't mean anything, not right away, and his mind slips back into the sulks.

He remembers the rejection slips, too many to count now, and the humiliation he endured. He remembers the effort, the years of effort, the sweet certainty of art that he sacrificed on the cold altar of technique, the promise he once showed . . . the work, the work, the work.

He remembers the times before, when he solved one problem only to find that, in doing so, he had revealed an underlying weakness in his technique. This is like that, only on a far larger scale.

Try it again.

What is structure?

It's how he tells the story.

He remembers the pain he felt when the art died, the pain when he learned that criticism always hurt, the pain, the pain, the pain.

Try it again.

What is structure?

Don't you ever finish? Don't you ever get there?

Plod.

One thought in front of the other.

Structure is how you tell the story.

What lies behind the story?

What lies behind the story is, is . . .

It's raining, and the splash of the raindrops against the window is distracting.

He sulks. It's not fair!

He calculates how much money he would have if he'd put the same hours and effort into frying hamburgers at the local fast-foods emporium. The dollar figure is astonishing. He could buy a Mercedes . . .

Try it again.

What lies behind the story?

He pushes.

His mind resists.

He pushes harder.

What force is behind the story?

Suddenly, deep in his psyche, in the tunnels of his self-perception, some supporting structure gives way and an overarching assumption caves in. Abruptly, pressures change. Another structure disintegrates, and another. Equilibriums shift. A shockwave propagates. Along some major fault line of the soul, the weld fails. Slowly, ponderously, something very large rumbles into motion.

The writer is the force behind the story.

A swirling tidal wave of emotion explodes upwards, into the writer's conscious mind, carrying with it the aches and yearnings of childhood, the broken dreams of adolescence, the sorrow of all things that never were and never can be. Out of turbulence, the worst of all possible answers crystallizes.

There is something fundamentally wrong with his stories because there is something fundamentally wrong with him.

Instantly, as though he has always somehow known, he grasps the implication.

He has already given up his art, but that's not enough.

Now he must give up himself.

And there is no turning back.

The pain is blinding.

I can generalize with confidence about the pain the adolescent writer feels as life disabuses him of his sweet certainties. I can speak with broad authority about the chronology of his development as he studies his craft and grows ever more professional in his approach to the written word.

After all, I followed that same path myself, as did my colleagues; I watch my students as they follow it today. And while it varies somewhat with time, circumstance and personality, the variation is not very great. Our hero, as he

wends his way through the twists and turns of his professional development, fairly represents us all.

But when the final layer of the onion is peeled back, and
the writer comes face-to-face with himself . . . that is an
event that cannot be generalized. The only universality
about that moment is that it always comes, and that the
agony is exquisite.

It's not a kind of agony that translates very well beyond
the confines of the human skull, so writers don't talk about
it much except in metaphorical terms. So, in hopes that
you will be a little better prepared than I was, I'm going to
do my best to describe how it was for me.

I remember the moment exactly. I was sitting in the
driver's seat of my blue Dodge van at a stoplight at the
corner of Ritchie Highway and Furnace Branch Road in
Glen Burnie, Maryland. My girlfriend was sitting beside
me. She was wearing a red skirt and a white blouse.

The van was in the left-turn lane, waiting for the arrow.
There was a beige Ford waiting across the highway to turn
left in the opposite direction. It was 2:35 in the afternoon,
on a crisp autumn day in 1978.

For several years I had been grappling with a nonfiction
novel about accident medicine. I had written it again and
again, and each time it had been rejected. I didn't know
why, but I was at the threshold of despair.

As I look back on the moment, my memory mingles
with a strange fact I had noticed, in the shocktrauma unit,
about pain.

The traffic victims most likely to shriek out their agony
and terror were those who were injured the least. The most
horribly mangled ones, the ones whose intestines were
ripped away, or who had been partly dismembered . . .
they seemed protected, somehow, from their pain. As they
died they were almost calm; in the rare event that they
lived, they would have no memory of even being conscious.

This fact hangs in the back of my mind as I re-create the
scene at the stoplight.

I sat there, clutch in, eyes focused on the red light, mind

empty, defenses down, and the truth sort of arched up out of my subconscious mind and exploded in my forebrain.

My book wasn't working because I had avoided looking directly at what my characters were feeling.

Why had I avoided it? Because I had built my whole psychic apparatus, my whole world view, on the premise that I was somehow different (which is to say better) than the people I wrote about. To look at them was to realize that I was no different, and that what was happening to them could as well happen to me. I was, in short, nothing special.

It happened much faster than I can explain it. I knew instantly that most of what I believed was wrong, most of what I thought about myself was fraudulent, and most of what I depended on for my emotional security was pure fantasy. I cannot begin to describe the pain. In that instant a young man named Jon Franklin died.

I use his name, and his memories. I love his children, know his friends, and use his bank account. But I am to a very large degree someone else.

I suppose the light changed, the green arrow glowed, and I made my left turn. My girlfriend has no particular recollection of the moment, so I guess I didn't scream. Obviously, to judge by my insurance rates, I didn't run over anyone. But I don't remember a thing; the next three months are a total blank.

It is only years later, having heard of similar experiences from other writers, that I can go back and reconstruct, intellectually at least, what must have happened.

The crisis has to do with belief, and with the pattern of self-deception that we use to protect us from unpleasant truths as we bumble through the minefield of life.

The writer, like everyone else, is equipped in infancy with a thick padding of things he believes to be true, but which aren't. Some of his beliefs, like Santa Claus and the infallibility of his parents, are obvious frauds; he loses them fairly quickly. But others are more subtle falsehoods or, worse, they are the most deceptive lies of all—half-truths. These he keeps. They allow him to see life as he thinks it is (or if it isn't, should be), rather than as it is.

It was one such cluster of prejudices, for instance, that led the adolescent writer to diagnose the rules of craft as threats to his artistic freedom, and to resist them. That particular aspect of his innocence, since it interfered with his profession, died rather quickly.

That's not unique to writing. The physicist, likewise, must give up his preconceptions about the physical universe long before he reaches graduate school.

But the physicist's loss of innocence can be limited; he can cling for a lifetime to naïve preconceptions about biology without losing his job or his reputation. That's why so many first-rate physicists reject the theory of evolution. On the subject of biology they are free to believe any sort of buncombe that fits their fancy.

Likewise biologists, though they must accept evolution to be professionally successful, can entertain a mind full of ludicrous notions about physics.

The realm of the writer, though, is far less limited. He must see clearly, wherever he looks, and if he is to be a first-rate professional he must look at all of life—and especially at its most basic, and therefore most frightening, aspects.

Take, for example, the touchy subject of religion.

Say the young writer, as many do, believes strongly in God. What happens if he attempts to write about a character whose growth process, and whose action in the story, leads him *away* from his former faith in God? What happens when the character ignores God as a possible solution and instead chooses some other, equally valid, method of coping with his problem?

Is the writer, blinded by his own beliefs, capable of seeing the true dynamics of such a story? Of course not.

This dilemma is very democratic; it arises with equal force if the writer believes strongly that God does *not* exist. How does he then handle the character who relies heavily on God for strength, and whose religion is part and parcel of his ultimate triumph over his complication?

If we were talking only about religion the solution would be straightforward: The writer could steer clear of the subject.

But, as any psychiatrist will testify, the normal human being has so many preconceived notions about reality that it is virtually impossible for him to find a story of any breadth or depth that does not encompass a half-dozen of them.

Religion, politics, abortion, economics, patriotism, insanity, addiction, justice, consumer rights, the nature of health and disease . . . the list goes on and on and for almost every entry the typical precocious adolescent has a conviction as unyielding as it is superficial.

There is nothing philosophical about the problem. There is nothing abstract, or even subtle, about what happens when the writer attempts to apply a prejudice where only an insight will do.

Proceeding blindly toward his preconceived conclusions, he asks his character (whether real or imaginary) the wrong questions; compounding the error, he twists the answer to make it match what he would prefer to hear. His goal immutably fixed in his mind, he ignores clues that would lead him to the unacceptable truth.

The stories the young writer produces in such ecstasies of self-assurance are as unpalatable as green persimmons. As everyone but he can see, the characters are shallow, reflecting the biases of the writer rather than the contradictions and complexities of the protagonist. The action is forced, leaving the reader to sense that important turning points have been left out. The sentences are filled with clichés and platitudes, and the overall effect of the story is that it somehow grievously misses the point.

This dilemma does not appear, in its full-blown form, until the writer's craftsmanship has progressed to the point where he can say precisely what he means; only then does it become clear that what he means makes no sense.

And so it is that the last and greatest crisis of a writer's development emerges not from art but from craft, and is delayed until that craft is almost completely developed.

Then, when the editor can see the characterization clearly, he can point out that it's somehow faulted.

The writer goes back and fixes the character, but as he does, the stronger character throws the failure of the action into sharp relief. The writer fixes the action, but now the resolution no longer matches the complication. He fixes the resolution, and the character . . . the character seemed right before, but now, now . . . somehow the character is inadequate again.

Then comes the thinking, the sulking, the brooding and, finally, in a flash of insight and pain, the answer.

Now, once the answer is fully accepted and the writer has recovered his equilibrium, craftsmanship shifts to a higher level. The object is no longer to write clearly but to see clearly.

Now each story presents the writer with agonizing choices. Each time he sits down to write he discovers he must once again choose between a precious belief and the integrity of his story.

The choice is stark and terrible.

The story is important. Success is important. If it weren't, the writer wouldn't be in this pickle in the first place.

But the belief . . . the belief . . . is *him*!

It tears free slowly. The psychic pain is almost unbearable as, with each story, another part of him dies.

Why is it, he asks himself, that the truths he holds most precious are always the ones that are most in error?

It is a relentlessly Darwinian process; the writer writhes in internal agony as he sacrifices piece after piece of himself; he feels, sometimes, as though his very soul is being ripped out.

At the same time his stories get better and better. He sends them off in the mail. They come back. He sends off another.

A check comes back.

The writer looks at it.

Part of his mind rejoices but another part, the part that once contained the gossamer flower of his art, throbs with a hollow ache. He has sold out. The check is from the devil.

With time his writer's vision grows ever more clear, and he finds himself increasingly interested in the lives of the people around him. Where once he had to search long and hard for an interesting true story, he now sees them everywhere.

His stories improve rapidly, and the checks get more frequent and ever larger. A reporter knocks on his door to interview him. The hollowness within him aches.

At night he stares into the dark and thinks it through again and again.

From pain, comprehension.

From reality, stories.

True stories?

That's what they call them. But as the writer lies awake at night and thinks about his stories, he wonders.

Granted they are taken from real life, and that every detail is painstakingly researched fact. But all that, to-gether, does not add up to Truth. Truth, with a capital T, requires something more.

Doesn't it?

The writer stares into the darkness.

Does the reader want reality?

No. Not really.

Reality is confusing, Reality is boring. It lacks empha-sis. It turns out bad and we never understand why. It teaches us little—or it teaches us much, at great cost. Besides . . . why should a reader pay good money for reality? He's got reality up the gazatch!

No, reality is not what he wants. What he wants is *extract* of reality, shaped by . . . by what?

The reader and editor want a story with a minimum of loose ends, a tale that's been simplified and crystallized in such a way that it clarifies and enlarges the mind. They don't want reality, they want Truth, and that's not the same thing at all.

Truth is . . . art?

Long, long ago, in the throes of adolescence, the writer had sensed a thing in himself that he called art. Throughout his apprenticeship he had sought desperately to preserve some little piece of it.

That was his greatest mistake; what he sought to protect wasn't art at all. It was nothing more than the combined platitudes and wishful thinking of childhood, the soft beliefs of an undisciplined mind, the flaccid, self-indulgent fantasies of immaturity. His allegiance to it was slavery.

Now, incredibly, having fought and struggled to preserve his innocence, he has lost it and, losing it, he is finally free; being free, he is entitled to look for the art within himself.

To his shock and amazement, he finds it.

It is the embodiment of what's left of his belief system, composed of the truths that *didn't* melt away under the fire of reality, the ones that stood the test, that emerged stronger for it, tempered now with effort and discipline.

And that's not all. Other beliefs, beliefs he had never had, perspectives he had never dreamed of entertaining, emerge from the ashes of those that were destroyed.

His belief in God and Jesus Christ, if it served him and his readers, will have grown stronger during the trial by reality. Or it may have withered and dropped away, to be replaced by a clear-eyed pantheism.

They are strong, and so is he. And so, he discovers, is the individuality he thought was dead.

He doesn't stop growing, of course—quite the opposite. He grows, now, with each story, and his growth takes on a new individuality and that new individuality, in turn, illuminates each new story.

His individuality, now so firmly in contact with reality, becomes the centerpiece of his craft. It is the scale upon which he weighs each story for its intrinsic worth, the measure against which he analyzes each character, each complication, each action, each resolution. The story, when it emerges from his mind and his typewriter, bears the unique imprint of his mind.

Now the tedious details of craftsmanship that once ruled his life are second nature to him. He understands them intimately, and fully appreciates the nature of the great web of language of which they are a part. He knows where each principle of grammar and usage applies, and where it does not.

But he doesn't think about his craft, not while he writes. His craftsmanship now functions in the service of art, subsidiary to the thematic relationship of character to complication, and complication to resolution, and story to reality, and reality to Truth.

His fingers move across the keyboard without much effort, following the rules where they serve him, effortlessly bending and breaking them where they do not.

Sometimes, when there's time and he's feeling especially mellow, and when there's no one around to catch him, the master craftsman-artist drags out the stories he wrote as a young man and chuckles over them.

The artist reads the purple prose and the vague, static descriptions that wander off into nowhere, and smiles wryly at the memory of the innocent adolescent who was utterly convinced that prejudice was art, fantasy was courage and ignorance was freedom.

He was born with a specialness, all right—but there's nothing special about specialness. Anyone who watches a kindergartner work with crayons realizes that talent is a hallmark of the species.

And as for the fragile flower of art . . . ha!

Art is what remains after the apocalypse, after everything else is burned away. Art is the bedrock of existence, the steel structure of intelligence, the single most durable component in the entire human psyche.

He was blind, poor kid, to all that was.

He had thought art was innocent, but it wasn't art that was innocent.

It was he.

APPENDIX A

The Annotated Monster

Complication. Ducker gambles
Development:
    1. Ducker enters brain
    2. Ducker clips aneurysm
    3. Monster ambushes Ducker
Resolution: Ducker accepts defeat

Mrs. Kelly's Monster[1]

BY JON FRANKLIN

Complication: Ducker Gambles

In the cold hours of a winter[2] morning Dr. Thomas Barbee Ducker, chief brain surgeon at the University of Maryland Hospital, rises[3-4] before dawn.[5] His wife serves him waffles[6] but no coffee. Coffee makes his hands shake.[7]

In downtown Baltimore,[8] on the 12th[9] floor of University Hospital, Edna Kelly's husband tells her goodbye.[10] For 57 years Mrs. Kelly shared her skull[11] with the monster[12]: No more. Today she is frightened but determined.

It is 6:30 a.m.[13]

"I'm not afraid to die," she said[14] as this day approached.[15] "I've lost part of my eyesight. I've gone through all the hemorrhages. A couple of years ago I lost my sense of smell, my taste. I started having seizures. I

216

smell a strange odor and then I start strangling. It started affecting my legs, and I'm partially paralyzed.

"Three years ago a doctor told me all I had to look forward to was blindness, paralysis and a remote chance of death. Now I have aneurysms; this monster is causing that. I'm scared[16] to death . . . but there isn't a day that goes by that I'm not in pain, and I'm tired of it. I can't bear the pain. I wouldn't want to live like this much longer."[17]

As Dr. Ducker leaves for work, Mrs. Ducker hands him a paper bag containing a peanut butter sandwich, a banana and two fig newtons.[18]

Downtown, in Mrs. Kelly's brain, a sedative takes effect.

Mrs. Kelly was[19] born with a tangled knot of abnormal blood vessels in the back of her brain. The malformation began small, but in time the vessels ballooned inside the confines of the skull, crowding the healthy brain tissue.

Finally, in 1942, the malformation announced its presence[20] when one of the abnormal arteries, stretched beyond capacity, burst. Mrs. Kelly grabbed her head and collapsed.[21] After that the agony never stopped.

Mrs. Kelly, at the time of her first intracranial bleed, was carrying her second child. Despite the pain, she raised her children and cared for her husband.[22] The malformation continued to grow.

She began[23] calling it "the monster."

Developmental Focus 1: Ducker Enters Brain

Now, at 7:15[24] a.m. in operating room eleven, a technician checks the brain surgery microscope and the circulating nurse lays out bandages and instruments.[25] Mrs. Kelly lies still on a stainless steel table.

A small sensor has been threaded through her veins and now hangs in the antechamber of her heart. The anesthesiologist connects the sensor to a 7-foot-high bank of electronic instruments. Oscilloscope waveforms begin[26] to build and break. Dials swing. Lights flash. With each heartbeat a loudspeaker produces an audible popping sound. The steady pop, pop, popping[27] isn't loud, but it dominates the operating room.

Dr. Ducker enters the O.R. and pauses before the x-ray films that hang on a lighted panel. He carried those brain images to Europe, Canada and Florida in search of advice, and he knows them by heart.[28] Still, he studies them again, eyes[29] focused on the two fragile aneurysms that swell above the major arteries. Either may burst on contact.

The one directly behind Mrs. Kelly's eyes is the most likely to burst, but also the easiest to reach.[30] That's first.

The surgeon-in-training who will assist Dr. Ducker places Mrs. Kelly's head in a clamp and shaves her hair. Dr. Ducker checks to make certain the three steel pins of the vice have pierced the skin and press directly against Mrs. Kelly's skull. "We can't have a millimeter[31] slip," he says.

Mrs. Kelly, except for a six-inch crescent of scalp, is draped[32] with green sheets. A rubber-gloved palm goes out and Doris Schwabland, the scrub nurse, lays a scalpel in it. Hemostats snap over the arteries of the scalp. Blood spatters onto Dr. Ducker's sterile paper booties.[33]

It is 8:25 a.m. The heartbeat goes pop, pop, pop, 70 beats a minute, steady.

Today Dr. Ducker intends to remove the two aneurysms, which comprise the most immediate threat to Mrs. Kelly's life. Later, he will move directly on the monster.[34]

It's a risky operation, designed to take him to the hazardous frontiers of neurosurgery. Several experts told him he shouldn't do it at all, that he should let Mrs. Kelly die. But the consensus was that he had no choice. The choice was Mrs. Kelly's.

"There's one chance out of three that we'll end up with a hell of a mess or a dead patient," Dr. Ducker says.[35] "I reviewed it in my own heart and with other people, and I thought about the patient. You weigh what happens if you do it against what happens if you don't do it. I convinced myself it should be done."

Mrs. Kelly said yes. Now Dr. Ducker pulls back Mrs. Kelly's[36] scalp to reveal the dull ivory of living bone. The chatter of the half-inch drill fills the room, drowning the rhythmic pop, pop, pop[37] of the heart monitor. It is 9 o'clock when Dr. Ducker hands the two-by-four-inch triangle of skull to the scrub nurse.

The tough, rubbery covering of the brain is cut free, revealing the soft gray convolutions of the forebrain.

"There it its," says the circulating nurse in a hushed voice. "That's what keeps you working."[38]

It is 9:20.[39]

Eventually Dr. Ducker steps back, holding his gloved hands high to avoid contamination. While others move the microscope into place over the glistening brain the neurosurgeon communes[40] once more with the x-ray films. The heart beats strong, 70 beats a minute, 70 beats a minute.[41] "We're going to have a hard time today," the surgeon says to the x-rays.[42]

Dr. Ducker presses his face against the microscope. His hands go out for an electrified, tweezer-like instrument. The assistant moves in close, taking his position above the secondary eyepieces.[43]

Dr. Ducker's view is shared by a video camera. Across the room a color television crackles,[44] displaying a highly-magnified landscape[45] of the brain. The polished tips of the tweezers move into view.

Developmental Focus 2: Ducker Clips Aneurysm

It is Dr. Ducker's intent[46] to place tiny, spring-loaded alligator clips across the base of each aneurysm. But first he must navigate[47] a tortured path from his incision, above Mrs. Kelly's right eye, to the deeply-buried Circle of Willis.

The journey will be immense. Under magnification, the landscape of the mind[48] expands to the size of a room.

Dr. Ducker's tiny, blunt-tipped instrument[49] travels in millimeter leaps.

His strategy is to push between the forebrain, where conscious thought occurs, and the thumb-like projection of the brain, called the temporal lobe, that extends beneath the temples.[50]

Carefully, Dr. Ducker pulls these two structures apart to form a deep channel. The journey begins at the bottom of this crevasse.[51] The time is 9:36 a.m.

The gray convolutions of the brain, wet with secretions, sparkle beneath the powerful operating theater spotlights. The microscopic landscape heaves and subsides in time to the pop, pop, pop of the heart monitor.

Gently, gently, the blunt probe teases apart the minute structures of gray matter, spreading a tiny tunnel, millimeter[52] by gentle millimeter, into the glistening gray.[53]

"We're having trouble just getting in," Dr. Ducker tells the operating room team.[54]

As the neurosurgeon works, he refers to Mrs. Kelly's monster as "the AVM," or arterio-venous malformation.[55] Normally, he says,[56] arteries force high-pressure blood into muscle or organ tissue. After the living cells suck out the oxygen and nourishment the blood drains into low-pressure veins, which carry it back to the heart and lungs.

But in the back of Mrs. Kelly's brain one set of arteries pumps directly into veins, bypassing the tissue. The unnatural junction was not designed for such a rapid flow of blood and in 57 years it slowly swelled to the size of a fist. Periodically it leaked drops of blood and torrents of agony.[57] Now the structures of the brain are welded together by scar tissue and, to make his tunnel, Dr. Ducker must tease them apart again.[58] But the brain is delicate.

The screen of the television monitor fills with red.

Dr. Ducker responds quickly, snatching the broken end of the tiny artery with the tweezers. There is an electrical bzzzzzt[59] as he burns the bleeder closed. Progress stops while the blood is suctioned out.

"It's nothing to worry about," he says. "It's not much,

but when you're looking at one square centimeter, two ounces is a damned lake.''[60]

Carefully, gently, Dr. Ducker continues to make his way into the brain. Far down the tiny tunnel the white trunk of the optic nerve can be seen. It is 9:54.

Slowly, using the optic nerve as a guidepost, Dr. Ducker probes deeper and deeper into the gray. The heart monitor continues to pop, pop, pop, 70 beats a minute, 70 beats a minute.

The neurosurgeon guides the tweezers directly to the pulsing carotid artery, one of the three main blood channels into the brain. The carotid twists and dances[61] to the electronic pop, pop popping. Gently, ever gently, nudging aside the scarred brain tissue, Dr. Ducker moves along the carotid toward the Circle of Willis, near the floor of the skull.

This loop of vessels is the staging area from which blood is distributed throughout the brain. Three major arteries feed it from below, one in the rear and the two carotids in the front.

The first aneurysm lies ahead, still buried in gray matter, where the carotid meets the Circle. The second aneurysm is deeper yet in the brain, where the hindmost artery rises along the spine and joins the circle.

Eyes pressed against the microscope, Dr. Ducker makes his tedious way along the carotid.

''She's so scarred I can't identify anything,'' he complains through the mask.

It is 10:01 a.m. The heart monitor pop, pop, pops with reassuring regularity.[62]

The probing tweezers are gentle, firm, deliberate, probing, probing, probing, slower than the hands of the clock. Repeatedly, vessels bleed and Dr. Ducker cauterizes them. The blood loss is mounting, and now the anesthesiologist hangs a transfusion bag above Mrs. Kelly's shrouded[63] form.

Ten minutes pass. Twenty. Blood flows, the tweezers

buzz, the suction hose hisses. The tunnel is small, almost filled by the shank of the instrument.

The aneurysm finally appears at the end of the tunnel, throbbing, visibly thin, a lumpy, overstretched bag, the color of rich cream,[64] swelling out from the once-strong arterial wall, a tire about to blow out, a balloon ready to burst, a time-bomb the size of a pea.[65]

The aneurysm isn't the monster itself, only the work of the monster, which, growing malevolently, has disrupted the pressures and weakened arterial walls throughout the brain. But the monster itself, the x-rays say, lies far away.[66]

The probe nudges the aneurysm, hesitantly, gently.

"Sometimes you touch one," a nurse says, "and blooey, the wolf's at the door."

Patiently, Dr. Ducker separates the aneurysm from the surrounding brain tissue. The tension is electric.

No surgeon would dare go after the monster itself until this swelling killer is defused.

Now.[67]

A nurse hands Dr. Ducker a long, delicate pair of pliers. A little stainless steel clip, its jaws open wide, is positioned on the pliers' end. Presently the magnified clip moves into the field of view, light glinting from its polished surface.

It is 10:40.

For eleven minutes[68] Dr. Ducker repeatedly attempts to work the clip over the neck of the balloon, but the device is too small. He calls for one with longer jaws. Soon that clip moves into the microscopic tunnel. With infinite slowness, Dr. Ducker maneuvers it over the neck of the aneurysm.

Then, in an instant, the jaws close and the balloon collapses.

"That's clipped," Dr. Ducker calls out. Smile wrinkles appear above his mask.[69] The heart monitor goes pop, pop, pop, steady. It is 10:58.

Developmental Focus 3: Monster Ambushes Ducker

Dr. Ducker now begins following the Circle of Willis back into the brain, toward the second, and more difficult, aneurysm that swells[70] at the very rear of the Circle, tight against the most sensitive and primitive structure in the head, the brainstem. The brainstem controls vital processes, including breathing and heartbeat.

The going becomes steadily more difficult and bloody. Millimeter, millimeter after treacherous millimeter the tweezers burrow a tunnel through Mrs. Kelly's mind. Blood flows, the tweezers buzz, the suction slurps. Push and probe. Cauterize. Suction. Push and probe. More blood. Then the tweezers lie quiet.

"I don't recognize anything," the surgeon says. He pushes further and quickly finds a landmark.

Then, exhausted, Dr. Ducker[71] disengages himself, backs away, sits down on a stool and stares straight ahead for a long moment. The brainstem is close, close.[72]

"This is a frightening place to be," whispers [73] the doctor.

In the background the heart monitor goes pop, pop, pop, 70 beats a minute, steady. The smell of ozone and burnt flesh hangs thick in the air.[74] It is 11:05 a.m., the day of the monster.

The operating room door opens and Dr. Michael Salcman,[75] the assistant chief neurosurgeon, enters. He confers with Dr. Ducker, who then returns to the microscope. Dr. Salcman moves to the front of the television monitor.

As he watches Dr. Ducker work, Dr. Salcman compares an aneurysm to a bump on a tire. The weakened wall of the artery balloons outward under the relentless pressure of the heartbeat and, eventually, it bursts. That's death.

So the fragile aneurysms must be removed before Dr. Ducker can tackle the AVM itself. Dr. Salcman crosses his arms and fixes his eyes on the television screen, preparing himself to relieve Dr. Ducker if he tires. One aneurysm down, one to go.

The second, however, is the toughest. It pulses dangerously deep, hard against the bulb of nerves that sits atop the spinal cord.

"Technically, the brainstem," says Dr. Salcman. "I call it the 'pilot light.' That's because if it goes out . . . that's it."

On the television screen the tweezer instrument presses on, following the artery toward the brainstem. Gently, gently, gently, gently it pushes aside the gray coils. For a moment the optic nerve appears in the background, then vanishes.[76]

The going is even slower now. Dr. Ducker is reaching all the way into the center of the brain and his instruments are the length of chopsticks. The danger mounts because, here, many of the vessels feed the pilot light.[77]

The heartbeat goes pop, pop, pop, 70 beats a minute.[78]

The instrument moves across a topography of torture, scars everywhere, remnants of pain past, of agonies Mrs. Kelly would rather die than further endure.[79] Dr. Ducker is lost again.

Dr. Salcman joins him at the microscope, peering through the assistant's eyepieces. They debate the options in low tones and technical terms.[80] A decision is made and again the polished tweezers probe along the vessel.

Back on course, Dr. Ducker works his tunnel ever deeper, gentle, gentle, gentle as the touch of sterile cotton. Finally the gray matter parts.

The neurosurgeon freezes.[81]

Dead ahead[82] the field is crossed by many huge, distended, ropelike veins.

The neurosurgeon stares intently at the veins, surprised, chagrined, betrayed by the x-rays.

The monster.

The monster, by microscopic standards, lies far away, above and back, in the rear of the head. Dr. Ducker was to face the monster itself on another day, not now. Not here.

But clearly these tangled veins, absent on the x-ray films but very real in Mrs. Kelly's brain, are tentacles of the monster.

Gingerly, the tweezers attempt to push around them.

Pop, pop, pop . . pop . . . pop . . . . pop . . . . pop.[83]

"It's slowing!" warns the anesthesiologist, alarmed.

The tweezers pull away like fingers touching fire.

. . . . pop . . . pop . . pop. pop, pop, pop.

"It's coming back" says the anesthesiologist.

The vessels control bloodflow to the brainstem, the pilot light.

Dr. Ducker tries to go around them a different way.

Pop, pop, pop . pop . . pop . . . pop . . . .

And withdraws.

Dr. Salcman stands before the television monitor, arms crossed, frowning.

"She can't take much of that," the anesthesiologist says.[84] "The heart will go into arrhythmia and that'll lead to a . . . call it a heart attack."

Dr. Ducker tries a still different route, pulling clear of the area and returning at a new angle. Eventually, at the end of a long, throbbing tunnel of brain tissue, the sought-after aneurysm appears.

Pop, pop, pop . pop . . pop . . . pop . . . .

The instruments retract.

"Damn," says the neurosurgeon. "I can only work here for a few minutes without the bottom falling out."

The clock says 12:29.

Already the gray tissue swells visibly from the repeated attempts to burrow past the tentacles.

Again the tweezers move forward in a different approach and the aneurysm reappears. Dr. Ducker tries to reach it by inserting the aneurysm clip through a long, narrow tunnel. But the pliers that hold the clip obscure the view.

Pop, pop . pop . . pop . . . pop . . . .

The pliers retract.

"We're on it and we know where we are," complains

the neurosurgeon, frustration adding a metallic edge to his voice. "But we're going to have an awful time getting a clip in there. We're so close, but . . ."

A resident who has been assisting Dr. Ducker collapses on a stool. He stares straight ahead, eyes unfocused, glazed.[85]

"Michael, scrub," Dr. Ducker says to Dr. Salcman. "See what you can do. I'm too cramped."

While the circulating nurse massages Dr. Ducker's shoulders, Dr. Salcman attempts to reach the aneurysm with the clip.

Pop, pop, pop . pop . . pop . . . pop . . . .

The clip withdraws.

"That should be the aneurysm right there, says Dr. Ducker, taking his place at the microscope again. "Why the hell can't we get to it? We've tried, ten times."

At 12:53, another approach.

Pop, pop, pop . pop . . pop . . . pop . . . .

Again.

It is 1:06.

And again, and again, and again.

Pop . . . pop . . . pop, pop, pop . . . pop . . . pop-pop-pop . . .

The anesthesiologist's hands move rapidly across a panel of switches. A nurse catches her breath and holds it.

"Damn, damn, damn."

Dr. Ducker backs away from the microscope, his gloved hands held before him. For a full minute, he's silent.

"There's an old dictum in medicine," he finally says. "If you can't help, don't do any harm. Let nature take its course. We may have already hurt her. We've slowed down her heart. Too many times." The words carry defeat, exhaustion, anger.[86]

Dr. Ducker stands again before the x-rays. His eyes focus on the rear aneurysm, the second one, the one that thwarted him. He examines the film for signs, unseen before, of the monster's descending tentacles. He finds no such indications.

Pop, pop, pop, goes the monitor, steady now, 70 beats a minute.

"Mother nature," a resident growls, "is a mother."

Resolution: Ducker Accepts Defeat

The retreat begins. Under Dr. Salcman's command, the team prepares to wire the chunk of skull back into place and close the incision.

It ends quickly, without ceremony. Dr. Ducker's gloves snap sharply as a nurse pulls them off.[87] It is 1:30.

Dr. Ducker walks, alone, down the hall, brown paper bag in his hand. In the lounge he sits on the edge of a hard orange couch and unwraps the peanut butter sandwich. His eyes focus on the opposite wall.

Back in the operating room the anesthesiologist shines a light into each of Mrs. Kelly's eyes. The right pupil, the one under the incision, is dilated and does not respond to the probing beam. It is a grim omen.

[88]If Mrs. Kelly recovers, says Dr. Ducker, he'll go ahead and try to deal with the monster itself, despite the remaining aneurysm. He'll try to block the arteries to it, maybe even take it out. That would be a tough operation, he says without enthusiasm.

"And it's providing that she's in good shape after this." If she survives. If. If.

"I'm not afraid to die," Mrs. Kelly had said. "I'm scared to death . . . but . . . I can't bear the pain. I wouldn't want to live like this much longer."[89]

Her brain was too scarred. The operation, tolerable in a younger person, was too much. Already, where the monster's tentacles hang before the brainstem, the tissue swells, pinching off the source of oxygen.

Mrs. Kelly is dying.

The clock on the wall, near where Dr. Ducker sits, says 1:40.

"It's hard to tell what to do. We've been thinking about

it for six weeks. But, you know, there are certain things . . . that's just as far as you can go. I just don't know . . ."

He lays the sandwich, the banana and the fig newtons on the table before him, neatly, the way the scrub nurse laid out the instruments.[90]

"It was triple jeopardy," he says finally, staring at his peanut butter sandwich the same way he stared at the x-rays. "It was triple jeopardy."

It is 1:43, and it's over.

Dr. Ducker bites, grimly, into the sandwich.[91]

The monster won.

Annotations: Mrs. Kelly's Monster

1. Published in *The Evening Sun,* December 1979. Received Pulitzer prize in feature writing in May of 1979.
2. You must set the mood early in the story. Dr. Ducker also rose to a warm house and a bright future, but those facts are not relevant to the story being told.
3. It is no accident that the first verb in this story is an action verb.
4. The use of present tense tends to make the story more immediate, but it increases the pressure on the writer, who must supply an endless stream of detail to make the immediate nature of the story seem real. Because of the increased technical problems with present tense, the technique must never be used lightly. Also, present tense is usually unsuitable for longer pieces.
5. This provides sense of time. Sense of place is implied, here: It's in Dr. Ducker's house, in Baltimore.
6. Be specific with symbolism. Also note how the food imagery here dovetails with the food imagery in the ending. Food is a life process. In the morning the food is warm, and served lovingly. In the end, the food is dry, cold, and packed in an anonymous paper bag.
7. Straight news technique requires the writer to sum up the story in the first paragraph. Feature style often requires that it be implied. The implication here is that it is very important that Dr. Ducker's hands *don't* shake.
8. Place transition.

9. Be specific . . . but only when it doesn't interfere with the story you're telling. You need a good *literary* reason for the inclusion of each fact. In this case, it was rhythm.

10. This implies danger, building on the implications of the "shaking hands" line above.

11. Note the perception that Mrs. Kelly *is* her brain. Such a unity, once established, must be carried out throughout the piece.

12. This perception was Mrs. Kelly's, not the author's nor the surgeon's. Your subject will do much of your head work for you, if you'll be observant.

13. Pacing. Pacing must begin before the need for it becomes apparent. This story picks up a definite beat later. It begins here, with the stipulation of an exact time. To make it an odd number, such as 6:32, would have been enameling the lily, and would have lost the effect when the story shifts to specific time later, as the pace increases.

14. Flashback to material gleaned in an early interview.

15. This sentence marks the transition from the opening, or lead, into the complication.

16. And we're back to present tense.

17. The reader must clearly understand the motivations of your characters. In this case, Mrs. Kelly has decided to go for broke because the disease had made her life not worth living.

18. Foreshadowing is the magic of the dramatic feature writer. In this part of the story, the lunch helps get Dr. Ducker out of the house and shifts the reader's attention toward his work. (The information does double duty, another hallmark of good dramatic writing.)

19. Flashbacks provide supportive, background and character information.

20. This personifies the malformation. Personification of objects is a tricky, tricky business and should be done only with the greatest care—and only with the principal forces in the story. It would not do, for instance, to personify the peanut-butter sandwich.

21. The story does not say how Mrs. Kelly felt. Rather it implies and shows it. Action (grabbing one's head and falling) tells much more than attempts to describe her feelings. The first rule of feature writing is "Show, don't tell."

22. She is never said, specifically, to be courageous. Rather, by her actions, she is shown to be.

23. Today I would hesitate to use "began." I would say, instead, "She called it 'the monster.' " Words like "begin, began, commenced" and "started" are usually unnecessary and tend to give the sentence in which they reside a distant and passive cast.

24. Fifteen minutes past the hour is more specific than thirty minutes past. A minor point, but the tempo is building.

25. Always use action. If you want to tell the reader that the operating room is ready, then show the crew getting it ready.

26. This word is unnecessary.

27. The value of sound as a pacing and descriptive device is widely overlooked. Clocks tick. Babies cry in the background. Pencils tap restively on tables. Rain clatters on a tin roof. Notice those things, and use them.

28. This serves to emphasize the danger.

29. By using the eyes, what's going on in the brain can be illustrated.

30. If you're taking your reader into unfamiliar territory, it's necessary to step back periodically and tell the reader, in brief and nontechnical terms, what's going on. Otherwise, certain readers will become disoriented and quit reading.

31. The word "millimeter" is rather unfamiliar to the reader. It is necessary to run it through the reader's mind once, in a relatively slow-paced situation, so that it will seem more familiar later when it's used under more dramatic tension. The rule is never to use an unfamiliar word for the first time in a fast-paced part of your story, because it'll slow the narrative down. (It is, incidentally, not relevant here exactly how large a millimeter is. It is sufficient that the reader know it's small.)

32. Here, you'll note, she's draped. Later, the image is "shrouded."

33. Gore, like sex, is sometimes more effective when it occurs off camera.

34. This is another orientation paragraph. Note that it is used also as a pacing device, to keep the action from getting too fast here. We want the action to build.

35. Says to whom? The reporter, of course. But imagine how awful it'd sound to say, "said to this reporter." Keep yourself out of the copy and let your subject talk directly through you to your reader. Remember, as a feature writer who puts himself into the action, you are a surrogate for your reader, and your existence on the scene is totally unimportant.

36. Were I to write this today, I'd use "her," instead of "Mrs. Kelly's."

37. Pacing devices must be heavily foreshadowed. The pops are going to be critical later, so they have to be firmly embedded in the front of the story.

38. Greek choruses are very useful. Watch for the opportunity to use them.

39. The times are getting more specific.

40. The difference between the right word and the almost-right word, Mark Twain said, is the difference between lightning and the lightning bug.

41. Repetition can add dramatic tension and emphasize building tensions in the story. Most professional writers understand that events and ideas must be foreshadowed, but few apply the principle to gimmicks, like repetition, as well.

42. Actually, of course, he doesn't expect the x-rays to hear him. The words are directed to the occupants of the operating room—or to the readers, in the persona of a reporter, who is standing beside him. Here is another example of physical action (his voice is aimed at the x-rays) being used to keep the story concrete while implying moods and tensions.

43. This is the pause before battle. A romantic novel uses the same technique when the writer describes the knights settling into their stirrups just before the heroic charge. Some things never change.

44. Sounds, like smells, are extremely effective in putting the reader into your story. The senses of hearing and smell are ancient, and are more closely connected to the emotional brain than is the sense of sight. That's a good anatomical fact for a professional writer to know.

45. This is the hardest-won word in the piece. I wanted something that implied a bigness. The word "landscape" is commonly applied to continents and planets, and so carries an aura of great spaces. Few people realize how big a drop of water becomes under a microscope, and how the viewer can actually get lost and disoriented in it. Getting disoriented and lost is one of the most important dangers of neurosurgery.

46. Any time you start talking about something that happens in the subject's head, you almost automatically slow the narrative and move into background discussion. So, when you do that, make sure you're doing it at a place you can afford to slow down.

    Also, this does double duty as another orientation paragraph.

47. "Navigate" is something you do over a landscape, or sea-scape. See the footnote on "landscape," above.

48. Now, the perception of "landscape" fully established, we can make the story's most important metaphysical leap, from the brain to the mind. When I wrote this piece I was beginning an unusually technical series on the brain, focusing on the brain-mind connection. I decided to do this story as the lead piece because I thought it would embed that point firmly in the reader's brain/mind.

49. As the instrument and its movement become the focus of the reader's attention, it becomes a surrogate for Dr. Ducker. Thus the instruments get a very specific personification.

50. More orientation. Note the regularity of orientation paragraphs, and how they fall off as the pace picks up.

51. This paragraph should have read, ". . . Dr. Ducker pulls these two structures apart to form a deep *crevasse*. The journey begins at the bottom. The time is 9.36 a.m." Some heat-of-the-moment awkwardness is, sigh, unavoidable in the newspaper feature writing business.

52. Never use an awkward word for the first time in a poetic passage. It takes the reader's brain longer to process it the first time, and that will throw off the rhythm you're trying so hard to establish. Foreshadow!

53. Count the number of "m" sounds in this paragraph. Then count the number of "g" sounds. That is a very, very tricky gimmick and can be used only with care. Very much of it, and an otherwise elegant piece turns saccharine.

54. Here, action is used to foreshadow.

55. Shift here to background.

56. This attribution is unnecessary and slows down the flow.

57. Parallel construction tugs compellingly at the mind. It makes things seem related that aren't, and makes for slick stream-of-consciousness transitions. The concepts "drops of blood" and "torrents of agony" come from separate universes . . . or do they?

   This piece was written specifically to make the reader ask that question.

58. This statement brings us back to story action.

59. A good feature writer learns to observe noises and, when possible, bring them to his reader. Sometimes this can be tricky. I've got an hour invested in "ka-Glup, ka-Glup, ka-Glup," used to describe a heart-sounds amplifier in a recent book.

60. Driving home the idea, again, that the microscope magnifies everything, including the problems.

61. Verbs are everything.

62. This implies that irregularity is not reassuring, and foreshadows trouble ahead. When the heart slows, the reader will know instantly something is wrong. He won't have to have an explanation, which would slow him down.

63. Note the switch from "covered" to "shrouded." This kind of foreshadowing operates on the reader's mind at a subconscious level. With such subliminal devices, the reader never knows what hits him. But hit him it does.

64. When you've taken the reader to an alien and frightening place, it's necessary to use as many familiar images as possible. But they have to be very apt. If it's the almost-right word, you end up looking like an idiot.

65. Relate sizes to something the reader knows.

66. This should have been foreshadowed, first, very early in the piece. Another example of deadline-related awkwardness.

67. A paragraph is, most of all, a unit of thought. If the thought is elegant, the paragraph is short.

68. When you've got rapid action, keep writing down times in your notebook. Later, you can select what you need for pacing.

69. Action can sometimes be heightened by hinting at it. The alternative would have been, "He smiled behind his mask." That's a more direct statement of fact, but has less dramatic impact. Both statements are accurate.

70. Word choice can be used to bolster imagery. In this case, the word tends to remind the reader of the nature of the aneurysm.

71. It should have been "he."

72. Again, repetition emphasizes. If you're interested in rhythmic techniques, by the way, read Edgar Allan Poe's poetry. Bells bells bells bells bells bells bells. And not one single bell more.

73. "Whispers" is a word that amplifies the nature of the frightening place in which Dr. Ducker finds himself. Reserve this category of attribution trick for dramatic passages only. Usually, the word "said" will suffice. Repetition of the word "said" is rarely a serious problem.

74. Pacing images are used to put the reader into the scene while also serving to slow the story action down. This implies that you've got to have enough action that you can afford some slow passages. If you don't have enough action to withstand the imagery slowdowns, you've probably got a boring story.

75. Minor characters do not have to be introduced at the top of a story but, if not, they must be foreshadowed. In this case

that was easy, since Dr. Salcman came in and hung around for a while before he started taking important (structural) action.

76. A glance at something he's met before, in this case the optic nerve, gives the reader the sense that he understands where he is. That is strictly smoke and mirrors, of course, but it puts his mind at rest and he can read on. After all, the reader isn't here to learn brain anatomy. He's here to find out what happens, and how the story comes out. The moral of the story is don't explain any more than the reader needs to understand the story. Explanations beyond that are flab.

77. In a less rushed world, this would have been better foreshadowed.

78. And the beat, now in a separate paragraph, begins to take on a life of its own.

79. And a tip of the hat to Abe Lincoln. Immature poets, some guru said, create. Mature poets steal. When possible, steal from the masters. Steal from romance novels and other trash at your peril.

80. Going too deeply into the technical would only confuse the reader, and is not necessary to the action. Deciding what to leave out is one of the writer's most important functions. The iron rule is that if you don't need it to make the climax work, then you don't need it at all. Some of the best stories are written backwards. This one was, sort of, and at times.

81. When your action is being carried along by active, fine-scale description, then *action* is defined not as motion but as change. Thus freezing in the face of danger is, in this story, a very active thing for Dr. Ducker to do.

82. Symbolism can be layered on top of symbolism. The word "dead" is symbolic in its own right, and the phrase "dead ahead" is a term used for *navigating* across *topography*.

83. Consider the foreshadowing that led up to this.

84. Note the absence of the phrase "told this reporter." Unless you're writing about yourself, *stay out of your story*.

85. This makes Dr. Ducker's fatigue more real.

86. It is better to let action carry emotion, even if the action is no more than inflection on words.

87. This punctuates the end of the action. It is a specific, active, concrete, sensual (sound is used) symbol.

88. This paragraph and the two short paragraphs that follow are worse than unnecessary. They bring up images that are irrelevant (Mrs. Kelly is going to die and Dr. Ducker knows it), and distract the reader. Some readers were left uncertain

as to whether or not Mrs. Kelly died. These paragraphs are the culprit. Together, they constitute the worst structural failing of the story, and if the rest of it hadn't worked well enough to offset the problem . . . the piece as a whole would have failed.

89. Flashbacks late in the story provide dramatic perspective. It is time that the reader remember that Mrs. Kelly went into this with her eyes open. Otherwise, our hero becomes tarnished by failure. One of the points of the piece is that he is *not* tarnished, because he tried.

90. Foreshadowed, this becomes a very dramatic, human action.

91. He must go on. Food symbolizes life.

APPENDIX B:

The Annotated Ballad

Verse I
    Major Complication: Wilk Faces Death
    Semi-Major Complication: Wilk Faces Ignorance
        Development 1: World Intrigues Wilk
        Development 2: Wilk Finds Dream
        Development 3: Dream Protects Wilk
    Interlinked Complication: Wilk Loses Father
    Semi-Major Resolution: Dream Sustains Wilk

Verse II
    Semi-Major Complication: Wilk Loses Father
        Development 1: Memory Sustains Wilk
        Development 2: Wilk Loses Family
        Development 3: Wilk Gathers Strength
    Interlinked Complication: Age Threatens Wilk
    Semi-Major Resolution: Wilk Pursues Dream

Verse III
    Semi-Major Complication: Age Threatens Wilk
        Development 1: Wilk Persists
        Development 2: Wilk Discovers Books
        Development 3: Wilk Grows Proud
    Semi-Major Resolution: Wilk Overcomes Threat
    Interlinked Complication: Wilk Faces Ignorance

Verse IV
    Semi-Major Complication: Wilk Faces Ignorance
        Development 1: Wilk Finds Profession
        Development 2: Wilk Discovers World
        Development 3: Wilk Studies World
    Semi-Major Resolution: Wilk Enlarges Mind
    Interlinked Complication: Wilk Faces Death

Verse V
    Semi-Major Complication: Wilk Faces Death (Major
       Complication Restated)
          Development 1: Wilk Pursues Life
          Development 2: Death Approaches Wilk
          Development 3: Wilk Looks Forward
    Major Resolution: Wilk Defeats Death

The Ballad of Old Man Peters[1]

BY JON FRANKLIN

VERSE ONE

Major Complication: Wilk Faces Death

TIME IS PRECIOUS as it runs out, and Old Man Peters spends long hours at his desk, writing and studying, fighting for a little more knowledge.[2] Death is near,[3] but he brushes away the comprehension. There has never been time for fear,[4] and there is none now.

Prudence, though . . . prudence is another matter.[5]

Outside, beyond the double-locked doors,[6] poor teenagers traverse the alley on the way to nowhere, casting occasional glances at the old man's rowhouse.[7]

For a lifetime[8] Wilk Peters traveled the world in search of its people and its wisdom,[9] and he brought his knowledge back to black universities to share with the students there—but the children who pass in the alley know nothing of that.

Their minds are filled with the hormones of youth, and

to them the old man is . . . an old man, that's all, an incomprehensibly ancient old man, 82 years old. Spent. Finished.[10]

To some of them, he is prey. For those Mr. Peters has locks on the doors, locks on the garage, steel screens on the windows . . . but he doesn't consider moving. Moving would take precious time.[11]

He sits at his desk, a book of Italian grammar[12] open in front of him. He stares at it. The mind behind the eyes is old,[13] years beyond the average life expectancy of, as the actuaries so succinctly put it,[14] a black male.

Outside, a truck thunders down The Alameda.[15]

He reads a line, loses it, reads it again.[16]

The scientists say that there are two kinds of memory, short-term and long-term. It is as though life writes its current experiences upon some blackboard in the mind and, as the days pass, the brain copies the information into a permanent library.[17]

But at 82 the blackboard often goes blank prematurely. Then what Mr. Peters learned today, a moment ago, is lost. When that happens, he stubbornly begins again. In recent years he has learned to make notes to himself, lest he forget an appointment, or an important fact.[18]

Semi-Major Complication: Wilk Faces Ignorance

But he needs no notes[19] to remember his childhood,[20] and the romantic, impossible dream[21] that saw him safely through decades of racism, poverty, and ignorance . . . the dream that guides him still.[22]

The dream began[23] in Trinity County, Texas,[24] in the southern forest east of the great prairie,[25] the part of Texas that had enough rainfall for cotton[26] to grow; Klan country,[27] where the nights were ruled by racial paranoia[28]

Wilk's father John had once owned his own farm, but that was a violation of the racial code. After a series of night attacks by anonymous riflemen he abandoned the land and fled for his life.[29]

Wilk was born a few years later, in 1900, in a share-cropper's cabin. His mother, Martha, carried him with her when she went to work in the fields,[30] and soon he was joined by another baby, and then another.[31]

With each season the family changed farms, hoping for a better life[32] but finding hard labor[33] instead. Wilk learned to supervise his younger brothers and sisters, then to hoe.[34]

At the age of eight he was an American serf walking behind a plow mule.[35]

Developmental Focus 1: World Intrigues Wilk

But even then there was some special, indefinable thing about Wilk Peters. Somehow he sensed that the world stretched far beyond the Texas horizon.

Though he had never seen them, he knew from school[36] that the earth included seas and mountains, and was home to people who were hues of brown, red and yellow. To the north was Oklahoma, somewhere to the southwest a place called Mexico.[37]

Mexico . . . he liked[38] the way the word slid along the tongue.[39]

It was a foreign country—exotic in the poor boy's mind, yet near enough that he occasionally heard Spanish[40] spoken by travelers. It had a romantic sound, rich with rhythm and vowels, and to hear the incomprehensible words filled him with a restless, inarticulate lust[41] to . . . to . . . *to go*.[42]

Developmental Focus 2: Wilk Finds Dream

His parents had attended grammar school, and though they had never learned to read without effort they understood enough to know that education was the path to

emancipation.[43-44] And they recognized that Wilk's . . .
specialness . . . if it was to flourish, required tangible
aspirations.

Considering his son's future, father John groped far
beyond his own experience.

He had never seen a library or a college campus. He
knew nothing of engineers and scientists, of economists or
accountants. There was only one educated man in his
humble experience, an awesome figure in a tall black
hat—the doctor.[45]

Wilk would be . . . a doctor.

A doctor.

Developmental Focus 3: Dream Protects Wilk

The word was a gift from father to son, and it settled in
the boy's mind and lodged there, a kernel of reality around
which his inchoate yearnings could coalesce.[46] The word
gave definition to his life and focus to his mind, and it led
him to an instinctive understanding of the enemy.[47]

The doctor represented knowledge. The antithesis, the
enemy, was ignorance.

The dream gave school a special urgency, and while his
classmates daydreamed Wilk diligently pursued the art of
penmanship and the abstract rhythms of mathematics.[48]

He learned that there was a country called France, beyond
the Atlantic Ocean, and another called Russia. Switzerland
was a place of mountains. In Spain, matadors challenged
enraged bulls. Armies marched in Germany. Boatmen poled
gondolas through the canals of Venice.[49]

The boll weevil[50] was by virtue of its six legs an insect,
and separate from the eight-legged family of spiders.

Wilk was wary of spiders, snakes and white men, but he
wasn't afraid of them.[51] In his nightmares he recoiled from
a far more horrible evil, ignorance, and with his entire
being he concentrated on the desperate need to beat it
back. Step by encouraging step, he saw himself succeeding.

Another sister was born, then a brother, then another sister, finally seven in all. Mother and father slept in the main room of the cabin, the children in the side room.[52]

John Peters was a good and provident farmer, and though there was little cash there was no hunger. The family raised its own poultry, grew its own garden, smoked its own hams and kept range cattle.[53]

The seasons changed and Wilk grew. With the approach of Christmas and Thanksgiving the cabin began to smell of baking cookies and cakes. The holiday table was laden with turkey, stuffing, bowls of home-grown vegetables and woman's most wonderful contribution to man, sweet potato pie. If there was no Christmas tree with gifts beneath it, no one felt the lack.[54]

They were years of innocent hope, of family laughter and poverty lightly borne, when life stretched on toward infinity and dreams were indistinguishable from reality. Of course Wilk would be a doctor. Why not?[55]

Interlinked Complication: Wilk Loses Father

Then, in the spring of 1913, his father returned from an errand and collapsed heavily on the bed, disoriented. The next day he couldn't move his left side.[56]

Somehow the family got through the summer. From his bed John gave orders, advice and encouragement to his wife and eldest son. Leaning on one another, Wilk and his mother hoed the corn, tended the livestock, and struggled to keep the farm and equipment in good repair. In late summer the whole family helped pick the cotton and Wilk drove it to market.[57]

Then, in the autumn, as the days began to grow short, Wilk's father died. They buried him in a small cemetery not far from the farm he'd been forced to abandon. There was no money for a tombstone.[58]

Semi-Major Resolution: Dream Sustains Wilk

Wilk stood, numb, by the grave.[59] Without his father's strength and knowledge, the poverty was suddenly crushing.

When school began a few days later, Wilk's brothers and sisters went but Wilk stayed home. He was needed to take his father's place on the farm [60]

As the boundaries of Trinity County closed in around him,[61] the 13-year-old clung desperately, hopelessly, to the only thing he had left: his dream.[62]

VERSE TWO[63]

Semi-Major Complication: Wilk Loses Father

In the early years of the 20th century, the dream that a black sharecropper's son could become a doctor was an audacious one. But while Wilk had his father to encourage and instruct him, it had somehow seemed possible.

With the approach of the winter of 1913, however, his father lay in an unmarked grave and Wilk, as the eldest of seven children, inherited adult responsibilities. For him, there could be no more school.

Developmental Focus 1: Memory Sustains Wilk

His father had taught him the fundamentals of farming, and Wilk could plow, hoe, chop, pick, milk and do most of the other chores. But the boy's best efforts had gone into books, and he lacked the practical savvy that had allowed his father to support the large family.[64]

The winter passed, followed by a summer of hard work, followed by a poor harvest, followed by a desperate winter. The next year was no better. Nor the next. Wilk yearned passionately for the sound of his father's voice, a voice that knew all things, a voice . . .[65]

A voice that spoke clearly in his the boy's memory, a voice that still said, with proud love: "I want you to be a doctor."

A doctor.

The dream had no place behind a plow, no application to the process of butchering a hog, no meaning at all for a boy who had dropped out of school so early. And yet . . . somehow . . . without it he would perish.

The dream sustained him as he fought for the family's survival, and it comforted him when he failed.

Developmental Focus 2: Wilk Loses Family

He worked hard, but hard work didn't suffice when the rains didn't come, or when they came too early and beat down the tiny cotton seedlings. Hard work didn't stop the boll weevil[66] or the worms that burrowed into the ears of corn, and hard work couldn't help his little sister.[67]

Wilk's youngest sister had always been sickly, but now she grew increasingly thin and weak. A doctor was called.

Wilk watched with awe[68] as the man examined his sister, but the outcome wasn't any comfort. The girl was very sick, the doctor said. But he didn't know why, and he had no medicine that would help.[69]

Harvest brought still another failure. The family needed money for food and Wilk and his mother looked around for something to sell.

There was nothing left but the mules. They brought very little.[70]

It was then that the Reverend Eva Johnson entered their lives.

The Reverend Johnson was part black and part American Indian, a man with a bible, a bible and a job, a real job, in the turpentine forests . . . and a man with an eye for Wilk's mother.[71]

Wilk instinctively[72] disliked the preacher. He watched suspiciously as the courtship developed, but was helpless to prevent the marriage. Then, when the family moved to the turpentine camp, the boy's worst fears were confirmed.

Soon he and his brothers and sisters were at labor in the long-leaf pine forests, scarring the trees to bring the resin out, collecting the sap and pouring it into barrels, hauling it to the distillery for conversion into turpentine.[73]

As for the preacher . . . sometimes he read a few words from the bible, but he wasn't a *real* preacher after all. Sometimes he worked in the turpentine forests, but he usually had something more important to do,[74] like hunting and fishing.

The turpentine work was difficult, menial labor, from dawn to dusk, and the days blended into one another.[75] With the passage of time Wilk's image of himself as a doctor deteriorated into fantasy, a fantasy that grew increasingly difficult to capture.

Wilk was in the forests, scarring trees, when word came that his youngest sister was dead.

Then he stood, at age 16, in another anonymous free cemetery, miles from where his father was buried, watching them lower his sister's wooden coffin into the ground.[76]

For two more years he worked,[77] taking orders from his stepfather.[78] But he balked when the man decreed that the family would move again, to work for a new turpentine company.

Wilk, for his part, suspected that one turpentine forest was much like another,[79] and, anyway, he wasn't going anywhere[80] . . . nowhere, at least, with the preacher.

He stayed and the family moved on. For the first[81] time in his life, Wilk was alone. He was 18.[82]

Developmental Focus 3: Wilk Gathers Strength

Confused and unsure of himself, he hung around the turpentine forest and grappled with the future. The dream was all but gone now, and it offered no inspiration.[83]

Finally, hearing of work in the lumbermill town of Diboll, and having no reason to stay where he was, he took his few belongings and headed down the dirt road, one foot in front of another.[84]

Diboll was a sawmill town of perhaps 2,500, a collection of greenwood shacks, dirt roads, and a company store . . . and it was always in need of another strong back.[85] Within a few days of his arrival Wilk was pushing slabs of lumber toward a howling planer.

It was a tiny, humble place, lost in the hot south Texas forest, a transient town that would vanish as soon as the timber was gone.[86]

But to the young farmboy it was a wonder.[87] Model A Fords, used by the lumber company, frightened horses on the street. There was electricity, a boardwalk in front of the store,[88] and a bewildering number of faces.

And some of those faces, he found as he settled into the first of a long line of cheap rooming houses, had intelligence behind them.[89]

Almost all the residents of Diboll could read and write, and most had at one time or another journeyed down to Tyler, 125 miles away . . . Tyler, the place of dreams, home of the black place of learning, the Methodist-owned Texas College.[90]

Wilk found that some of the other young men at the lumbermill had also dreamed of getting an education, and that some of them had actually gone to Tyler and enrolled. They had failed, however, and had returned to the mill in Diboll.[91]

This intelligence had a dramatic impact on young Wilk.[92] If they could go, so could he! The gossamer fantasy instantly solidified in his mind,[93] from possibility to dream to goal to necessity.

Yet . . . the men he talked to had failed.[94]

In Tyler they had somehow lost the dream, forgotten their priorities, mismanaged their money, failed to apply themselves to their studies, flunked out . . .[95]

It was said in Diboll that an illiterate, once he became an adult, was done for. The mind was set, firm, impossible to teach.[96]

The thought filled Wilk with cold terror. He couldn't believe it was too late; he refused to believe it. If he ever got the chance, he promised himself, *he* would not drop out.[97]

If he got the chance?

Wilk looked around him, at the automobiles, at the sawmill, at the goods in the company store, at the simple machinery he operated at the sawmill. To make those things, somebody, somewhere, had to know something. To make the trains run, somebody had to know something.[98]

Desperately, he wanted to be one of those people.

So it wasn't *if* he went to college. Not if.

When.[99]

He would have to save money, and in the meantime he would have to study, to make up for lost time.

The resolution made, his ignorance became suddenly intolerable, and he couldn't wait. He borrowed some primers and, when he wasn't working, he reviewed arithmetic and grammar. Then he found a book on mathematics. It was incomprehensible, but he refused to put it down.

By day he worked at the sawmill, by night he studied, on Sundays he went to the local church, on payday . . .

On payday, every two weeks, he carefully divided his money into three small stacks. One stack was for home—for shoes for his sisters, a dress for his mother,[100] for whatever was needed. The second stack was for his own modest requirements.[101]

The third stack was the smallest, by far, but by far the most precious. It was for the dream.[102]

A dollar became, with the addition of another, two

dollars. Five dollars grew into ten, ten became twelve, twelve became thirteen.[103]

Wilk began to worry about security.[104] There weren't any banks in Diboll, and he didn't dare leave the money in his room.

The solution was to fold it and knot it into a handkerchief. Before he went to work he put the handkerchief into his right pants pocket, then tied a string around the bottom of the pocket so that the handkerchief couldn't possibly fall out. At night, he slept with the handkerchief pinned into his pajama pocket [105]

A year passed in work and study, then two.[106] The more he learned, the more voracious his appetite for knowledge became. Slowly the puzzle of mathematics yielded to his stubborn attack, and he was captivated by the sweet logic of it.[107]

As he learned, the idea of learning itself broadened. When some of the townspeople talked of forming a band, for instance, he was mesmerized by the idea [108]

Back in the turpentine forests some people had played a guitar, but . . . a band! All those different instruments!

Music was still another thing for a young, hungry mind to learn, and Wilk spent precious money on a used clarinet. After that he worked, he studied, and he played.

The handkerchief got too full to carry with him. He walked to a nearby town, located a trusted aunt, and gave her $50 to hide for him [109]

And another year passed, and another. He sent off to Tyler for a college catalog. He pored over it, neglecting the clarinet.[110]

Soon, now.

One Sunday a note appeared on the church bulletin board, announcing an educational meeting. Dr. W. R. Banks, the president of Texas College, would give a lecture and be available afterward to answer questions.

Semi-Major Resolution: Wilk Pursues Dream

Wilk returned to his room and re-counted his savings. The total, including the money that had been left in the care of his aunt, amounted to almost $300.[111]

That evening Wilk was at the church early, and when the program began he listened spellbound to the tall, unbelievably erudite gentleman[112] who seemed to know every word in the dictionary and could make ideas dance in the air like notes on a page of music.[113]

Afterwards, Wilk overcame his intimidation, went up to the man, and demanded his attention.

Wilk confessed that he was 23, and had only a sixth-grade education. But he'd saved some money. And he could work hard.

Was it possible?

Interlinked Complication: Age Threatens Wilk

The college president studied the intent young man. Experience told him Wilk was too old, but he hadn't the heart to say so.

Nothing, he equivocated, was impossible.

It was all Wilk needed to hear.

That autumn, almost precisely ten years after his father had died, Wilk packed his belongings, bought a ticket on the lumber train, and headed for Tyler.[114]

VERSE THREE

Semi-Major Complication: Age Threatens Wilk

Intimidated, but firm in his resolve, Wilk Peters demonstrated his knowledge to the admissions officials at Texas College. He could do sums, and he could do take-aways.[115] He knew nouns and verbs . . .

The officials shook their heads, sadly. The fellow knew a little, but too little, and he spoke in the condemning, ignorant slur of the field hand. A pity.

The illiterate adult who showed up on campus, hat in his hands and life savings in his pocket, was a familiar story to black educators. The eagerness to learn had somehow survived in such men as Wilk, but the youthful plasticity was gone from their minds. They tried, but they failed.[116]

Wilk was too old . . . but who would tell him so?

No one. He would have to learn that himself.

Developmental Focus 1: Wilk Persists

They gave him a job shoveling coal in the furnace room of the girls' dormitory, showed him a tiny cubbyhole where he could sleep, and explained to him where the path to knowledge began.

And so Wilk found himself, at age 23, a full-grown man with callused hands and hardened muscles, sitting with his knees jammed under a tiny desk,[117] wrestling with long division, surrounded by prepubescent sixth-graders.

The effect was not what the admission officials had predicted.

Wilk viewed his place in class as opportunity, not insult.[118] If the children laughed at him he didn't notice, preoccupied as he was with the serious business of fractions, with the parsing of sentences and the memorization of poetry.[119]

The college maintained a secondary school on campus, so that the student teachers could get experience teaching neighborhood children. If Wilk could survive sixth grade, he was sure that next fall he would be allowed to enroll there. If he survived secondary school, then . . .[120]

Wilk had never known security, but neither had he ever had anything to lose. Now, he had opportunity. At night, scooping coal into the big dormitory furnace, he was sometimes overwhelmed with fear.[121]

What if something happened?

What if he got sick? What if one of his family got sick, and he had to drop out and support them? What if . . . what if, now that he stood on the threshold of a world which he wanted desperately . . . but which he didn't understand . . . *what if he lost his courage?*[122]

If there might be no tomorrow, he would have to study harder today.[123] In that way, the sixth grader progressed. The following summer he went to Dallas to work and save money.

Developmental Focus 2: Wilk Discovers Books

When he'd left in the spring the Texas College faculty had assumed they'd seen the last of him. Their surprise showed on their faces when he returned in the fall and asked to enroll in secondary school.

That year he met Shakespeare. Shakespeare seemed to speak directly to him, over a span of four centuries, from beyond an ocean, across the immense chasm of race.[124]

He read the famous words, "To be or not to be: that is the question," and then he read them again, and again. At night, as he shoveled coal, he thought about the English bard, he considered the symbols of elementary algebra, and he memorized Latin.

He also discovered the library.[125]

It was a sacred place, as hushed as a church, and it occupied the entire top floor of one of the college buildings. The library had books on every subject Wilk had ever heard of . . . and many he hadn't . . . and there were more titles than he'd ever imagined could exist. They were all neatly arranged by some scheme that he didn't immediately grasp.

The young man walked the aisles in wonder, looking at the words on the spines and touching the bindings.

The librarian was Govina Banks,[126] the president's wife, and she, as much as her husband, was responsible for the careful nurturing of the black community's meager intellectual resources. Thoughtfully, she watched the young man.[127]

A year passed, another. Sometimes on Saturday and Sunday Wilk found odd jobs in Tyler, a thriving metropolis of perhaps 11,000 souls. One Christmas a package arrived from Wilk's mother. It contained a blanket.[128]

He found his support and courage[129] in books. When he discovered something he considered particularly valuable, he transferred the words to memory:

"The stones are sharp, and cut my hands. But I must build . . . and build . . . and build . . . until this temple stands."

In a volume of obscure quotations he discovered the motto, "Keep on keeping on." He soon forgot who said it, but he would never forget the words.[130]

Slowly, so slowly that he would not perceive it for many years yet, Wilk began to change.[131]

Developmental Focus 3: Wilk Grows Proud

In part it was knowledge that changed him, the simple accumulation of historical dates and geometric theorems, of Shakespeare and the exotic sound of Latin. But he also responded, on a more fundamental level, to his own success.[132]

He had been a dreamer. Now, in beating back the ignorance, he was turning his dream into reality.[133]

He had always respected knowledge.

Now, he began to respect himself.[134]

If he could survive the junior year of high school, what else might he do? Might he . . .

What, he wondered, was Shakespeare's England like? What was it like in Hamlet's Denmark? What was a place called "France?" And what would it be like to walk the streets of Italy?[135]

His thoughts moved in another direction, as well. One of his student teachers was a young woman named Geneva

Crouch . . . and . . . and she was one of the prettiest women he had ever seen.[136]

Sometimes, as he listened to her, his mind wandered far off the subject of English . . .[137]

He said nothing to her, of course. It was against the rules for students to date teachers, and he didn't dare risk the anger of the administration.[138]

When he graduated from high school in the spring of 1928 there was a small ceremony, but Wilk missed it because he had to work. He didn't feel sorry for himself, though. It wouldn't be the last time he graduated from something; of that he was certain.[139]

His fear of failure had vanished. If he had made it this far then he could keep on keeping on all the way to . . . where?

It didn't matter. Somewhere. Medical school.

That fall, the year he turned 28, he enrolled as a freshman in Texas College.

Though his education was still far from completed, life was different now. As a laborer in grammar school he'd been nothing, a nobody, an inevitable failure who would probably be back in the fields by next year.

But a college student . . . now, *that* was different. In the black community in South Texas at the close of the Roaring Twenties, a college student merited respect.

The next two years were consumed by work and study. Wilk traded Latin for French. He wrestled with higher algebra, and won. Analytical geometry followed, and history, and sociology, and biology. Such were the threads of fantasy, that went into the fabric of dreams.[140]

As he grew, the little Methodist campus seemed to shrink.[141] There were, after all, only 300 students—and the college lost substantially in appeal when Dr. Banks, the president, quit to take over as president of the state's Prairie View A & M College some 150 miles distant.

Worse, the pretty teacher, Geneva, left for Prairie View too.[142]

Then in the autumn of 1929 the stock market crashed,

and there was talk that the menial jobs formerly reserved for black people should go, instead, to out-of-work whites.[143]

As the economic situation deteriorated Wilk understood that he might not be able to go directly to medical school, as his father would have wished, but he wasn't alarmed.[144]

He would have to go to work for a while, that was all, until he could save enough money for medical school. He could teach mathematics, a subject in which he was quickly becoming an expert.

And anyway, he felt as though he had shed the cloak of ignorance. He was a student, a good one, smart enough to get high marks, good enough to write away to Prairie View and get accepted immediately.[145]

At Prairie View, Mrs. Banks helped him find a job waiting tables in the student cafeteria.[146]

During the next two years at the larger college, Wilk continued his intellectual and emotional growth. He concentrated on mathematics and took up German on the side. There was even enough time, occasionally, for conversations with Geneva.

He said nothing personal, of course, because he was still a student and she a teacher, but in subtle ways he expressed his interest. He couldn't tell by her reserved manner whether she reciprocated his feelings or not.[147]

Semi-Major Resolution: Wilk Overcomes Threat

As the winter of 1930-31 tapered into spring, and Wilk's graduation approached, he faced the world with high hopes. He had become fascinated with languages, and a few years spent teaching math would give him time to get deeply into German.

He sent off applications to every black Texas high school he could think of, and sat back to await the replies.[148]

A week passed. He got a rejection, then another. But mostly there was . . . nothing.

He couldn't understand what was wrong.[149]

As graduation approached, Wilk borrowed enough money to rent a cap and gown. His family didn't come, but Geneva did.[150]

The commencement speaker was a woman who was president of another black college in Texas, and Wilk listened, along with 150 other graduating seniors, as she counseled them not to be disheartened by the economic situation.

"It's not dusk," she insisted. "It's dawn."[151]

Afterwards Wilk approached her, as he had approached Dr. Banks ten years earlier in the Diboll church. But now, as he inquired about teaching jobs, he was not nearly so humble.

"What can you do?" she inquired.

"Well," he said proudly, "I can teach math."

She waited for a moment, as though expecting him to continue. When she realized he had finished, a frown settled on her face.

"Our schools need more than that," she snapped. "They're poor. The windows are broken out. The water is cut off. The roof leaks . . . It's not enough to just teach math! What I'm asking is what *else* can you do."

Interlinked Complication: Wilk Faces Ignorance

Wilk was taken aback. The *cum laude* on his new college degree notwithstanding, he had to stammer an admission that, beyond mathematics, he had almost no skills at all.

The woman shifted her attention to another graduate and Wilk, wounded, withdrew.

Not since he had been a 23-year-old grammar school student, memorizing multiplication tables with children, had he been so acutely aware of his ignorance.[152]

VERSE FOUR

Semi-Major Complication: Wilk Faces Ignorance

After graduation in 1933 Wilk Peters hung around the Prairie View campus, hoping that some high school, somewhere, would hire him as a mathematics teacher. But as the depression deepened, no acceptance letter came.[153]

Developmental Focus 1: Wilk Finds Profession

There was no work in town, either, so Wilk volunteered to help file and cross-reference material at the college library.[154]

He liked library work, and thought it was good for him. There was peace there, in that temple-like place, handling the precious books, indexing the valuable knowledge so that it could be found by other hungry minds. The library freed his mind for thought.

He looked at the shelves of books that he'd never read, and he asked himself, again and again, what he knew of the world. The answer was not reassuring.[155]

As he worked, the chief librarian watched him and noted the reverence with which he handled each volume. She discussed him with Mrs. Govina Banks, the wife of the college president.[156]

Mrs. Banks thought back to the old days at Texas College, when she had been in charge of the library there. She remembered the ignorant young laborer who had gazed with such wonder at her mere 6,000 volumes. Obviously, a college degree had not changed him.

She approached Wilk.

Had he ever thought, she inquired, of becoming a librarian?[157]

Wilk stared at her in shock. The idea was so perfect . . .

and he'd never even thought of it, so firmly had he fixed his mind on his father's edict to become a doctor.[158]

But "becoming a doctor," Wilk knew, had been no more than a symbol in his father's mind. The doctor was the persona of the educated man.

It wasn't an M.D. that his father had really wanted for him, it was *knowledge*. And what was a librarian after all but a custodian of knowledge? Mrs. Banks was right; his father would have approved.

Developmental Focus 2: Wilk Discovers World

The decision made, Wilk's floundering ended.[159] At Mrs. Banks's urging he applied for a scholarship to the Hampton Institute's college of library science in Virginia, and was accepted. Then he proposed marriage to Geneva Crouch, and she accepted him too.[160]

It was a wonderful summer, almost as though life were beginning anew.[161]

That autumn Wilk, who at 33 had never been beyond the borders of Texas, left his bride, hitched a ride to Kentucky and traveled the rest of the way to school in Virginia by train.[162]

He made the trip wide-eyed, his overflowing brain absorbing new sights, sounds and cultures faster than he could process them. He felt himself becoming wiser with each mile.[163]

For years he had fantasized about traveling, but the idea had seemed frivolous and he'd repressed it. But by the time his trip to Virginia ended he understood that travel wasn't frivolous at all—it was another way of beating back the ignorance.

Finally, in Virginia, he stood one cold day on a beach, looking out over the famous Atlantic Ocean. Standing there, the wind in his face and the crashing of the waves in his ears, he found himself trying to visualize the exotic places that lay on the other shore.

Suddenly, he was consumed by the lust to see them all.[164]

Developmental Focus 3: Wilk Studies World

It was an awakening, and though Wilk would return to Texas College the following spring, there to serve as librarian for four years, he would never be the same.

Back in Texas, as soon as his finances would allow he purchased an automobile, and that spring he and his wife drove to New York and spent the summer studying at Columbia. Afterwards they drove to Quebec.

It was like being in fairyland. Wilk was surrounded by foreigners speaking strange sounds . . . *and he understood them*.

On the way back to Texas he thought about the many kinds of peoples in the world, and all the different languages, and how the people were barred from talking with one another.

The language barrier, he decided, was a kind of ignorance . . . an impediment to knowledge.[165]

He was chagrined that he could speak only French . . . French, and a little German. He would have to do something about that.

There wasn't much time or energy for the new dream, though. At Texas College, and later at Langston University in Oklahoma, Wilk was brought face-to-face with hundreds of young black people, ignorant as he had been ignorant, desperate to learn.

He was all but consumed in the task of teaching them to thread their way through the encyclopedias, the histories, the periodicals.

But at night there was always some time, if only a few minutes, to study German.

In 1944 Wilk received an invitation to join the staff of the Cleveland Public Library, which at the time was widely considered to be among the top three city library systems in the country. He jumped at the chance.

Mrs. Banks had indeed been right. Wilk's profession was perfectly matched to his dream of learning. Everything he did in library science brought him into contact with more information, and every job he had taught him something new.[166]

In Cleveland, for instance, he was one of several people who were required to read the new books that came in and report on each one's approach and its value to the library.

Because the other book review librarians worked an earlier shift, Wilk had to read whatever they left . . . dull stuff. And, because it was the mid-1940s, a lot of that dull stuff was contained in arcane, analytical tomes about Russia and communism.[167]

It fascinated Wilk that the Russian people, as far as he could determine, were not much different from Americans. They apparently had the same aspirations, the same dreams, the same need to understand and cope with the world around them. But for the Russians it had somehow gone tragically wrong.

Wilk wished he could speak Russian . . .[168]

Well, why not?

And so Russian became language number three. It allowed him to read books by Russian Jews and, as the son of a black American serf, Wilk identified with their travails.

It would be wonderful, he thought, to visit Russia. He couldn't of course . . . he had neither the money nor the time.

In 1948 Wilk moved on to the Tuskegee Institute, where he landed a good job as an assistant reference librarian. As usual it was hard work and long hours, but also as usual there were many new things to learn.

In addition to languages, he now sought the humble skills he lacked.[169]

He became fascinated, for instance, with small engines. He knew from his farming and gardening experiences that plants, when intelligently cared for, rewarded the gardener far beyond the measure of his effort. Might not small engines respond the same way?[170]

He ordered an engine repair manual and, when he wasn't working or studying languages, he tinkered with his lawnmower. When he had it running perfectly, he started working on his neighbors'.[171]

He also found interesting and profitable relationships with people. One of his coworkers was a native of Haiti, and when the man went home for a visit he invited Wilk and Geneva to come along. They leaped at the chance.

It was Wilk's first truly foreign country, and he was repelled by the poverty . . . but fascinated by the people. The common folk spoke a mysterious language called Creole, but the professionals could all speak French.

They treated Wilk like royalty,[172] and his ability to converse with them made him feel like a citizen of the world. The visit was far too short, and coming back felt like a return to prison.[173]

Wilk turned fifty at Tuskegee. The students, he couldn't help but notice, called him "sir" with increasing frequency.[174]

He shrugged it off. Certainly he didn't *feel* any older and he still had plenty of . . . of . . . of whatever it was that made young men chase dreams.[175]

He sat in the Tuskegee Library, helping students, filing books, organizing material, contributing, working . . .

God, but he wanted to go to Germany.[176]

Or Australia. Australia would do nicely.

Anywhere.

The months passed, one after another, but the yearning didn't go away.

Then one day he got a letter from a friend he'd made long ago in Oklahoma, a man who was now chairman of the English department at Morgan State College in Baltimore. Morgan was expanding into library sciences, and needed a good teacher. Was Wilk interested?

For the first time in his life, Wilk hesitated.[177] After all, he explained via return mail, Tuskegee had a good retirement plan—a better plan than Morgan State.

Wilk's friend in Baltimore thought about it, thought about Wilk, and pondered what he knew about what made Wilk tick. Finally he wrote back.

Morgan State, he pointed out, with the brilliance of a psychological matador going in over the horns with a sharp sword . . . Morgan teachers worked on a nine-month contract, with summers off.

If Wilk took the job he would have time to do, well, to do . . . whatever he wanted.

Wilk stared at the letter. The idea was pure nitroglycerin.

Whatever . . . he . . . wanted.

Whatever . . . or *wherever*!

France.

Germany.

Australia.

The moon.[178]

He forced himself to think logically.

France would be first. In fact, he had a little savings . . . why not go to France the summer *before* moving to Baltimore? Yes. Of course. Adrenaline pumped through his brain. That was a wonderful idea.

Life would never be the same.

At Morgan State, Wilk Peters became the ageless, friendly librarian who seemed to have a personal grudge against ignorance.

He was the one who was always helping out the foreign students . . . the absent-minded fellow who was always ready to assist an American student with a French translation, or to help with an essay that had to be written in German, or to decipher the meaning of an obscure Russian, Italian or Spanish phrase . . . the man who studied languages at night and disappeared every summer.

Semi-Major Resolution: Wilk Enlarges Mind

He traveled inexpensively, on reduced-rate steamships and bargain airlines, tramping through kingdoms his father had never heard of, eating local food, staying in student dormitories or private homes, studying, observing, absorbing, learning.

In the summertime Wilk was a student,[179] not a teacher. He spent three months at the University of Barcelona, studying Spanish, geography, music, literature and art. At the Sorbonne in Paris he studied French and French civilization. He studied in Quebec, in Berlin, in Vienna. As he grew more proficient, he began studying more on his own.

Each autumn he returned to Morgan State, bearing gifts of the mind . . . tales from Denmark, Switzerland, Portugal, Norway, England, Ireland . . . so many countries that, when he was asked to list them by a fascinated student or a campus newspaper reporter, he couldn't name them all from memory. Finally, he started keeping a list.

In the summer he traveled and studied, in the winter he taught library sciences. In 1961 Wilk was appointed the college's official advisor for foreign students.

The years passed.

And then, on the 30th of June in 1966, the timeclock ran out and the professional résumé ended. At 66, Wilk applied for his pension.

He was retired.

Interlinked Complication: Wilk Faces Death

In the terms of a youth-oriented culture he was finished, washed-up, farmed-out and pumped-dry, and it was all over. [180]

The world, as usual, was wrong.[181]

Wilk Peters emptied his desk into a cardboard box and drove home . . . gleeful as a teenager on the first day of summer vacation.

VERSE FIVE

Semi-Major Complication: Wilk Faces Death
(A restatement of the major complication)

At the innocent age of 42 William Shakespeare proclaimed that all the world's a stage. But by the time Wilk Peters retired he was 66, 24 years wiser than a man of 42, and he knew better.

The world wasn't a stage at all.

It was a campus.

Developmental Focus 1: Wilk Pursues Life

And the idea that 66 was old was a wives' tale, a fraud perpetuated by the young. Wilk felt fine; never better. And he was free! [182]

As a free man he could choose what to do with his life. He could study more languages. He could travel in the winter, when the fares were low. He could go to bed when he liked and get up when he liked.

So, on the morning after his retirement, he got up at 7 a.m., dressed, ate breakfast, sat down at his desk and began to study. When he needed to rest his mind, he went downstairs and tinkered with the lawnmower.

Wilk took special pleasure in caring for the 1955 Chevy he'd purchased new—and which now, finally, he had time to maintain properly.[183]

By his retirement in 1966 there were still plenty of 1955 Chevys running around, most of them rusted-out hulks that were followed wherever they went by billowing clouds of smoke. But not Wilk's.

In Wilk's view, 1955 was a vintage year for Chevy's, and his was a standard-transmission model with no extras to conk out.[184] He had kept it in a garage and cared for it intelligently, and it had no rust.

The old car was much like the old man,[185] in many respects, and he drove it with pride. Every winter, before he went overseas, he put it up on blocks.

Spanish . . . now there was another thing, as elegant in its own way as the Chevy . . . a mechanism of beautiful, feminine vowels and romantically-twirled R's. If he knew Spanish well enough he could travel independently in Latin America, spending little, learning much.[186]

When he wasn't working on the Chevy, tending his garden (or someone else's), when he wasn't fixing a lawnmower, he was at his desk studying—or was listening intently to foreign broadcasts on his short-wave radio.[187]

As the retirement years passed, Wilk's front lawn received lavish care and it grew lush and thick, without a weed in it.

Flowers bloomed, the holly grew, and the hedges that surrounded the little yard took on topiary shapes, green bowls and hoops and breaking ocean waves. While Geneva stood by, proudly, the Mayor of Baltimore awarded Wilk the "Order of the Red Rose" as part of the city's beautification program.[188]

The Chevy ran, if anything, better than ever before. That was true of Wilk, too. His mind stayed sharp and his body, while somewhat slower to respond, remained sound.

In the winter he studied at the University of Madrid, in Tenerife, in Switzerland, in Puerto Rico, in Peru, and he traveled throughout South America and Europe. Sometimes Geneva went with him, and sometimes she preferred to stay home.

For the first time in Wilk's life he felt truly satisfied, a student of the world, just what he'd always wanted to be. Year by year, he could see the hated ignorance retreat.

When he wasn't traveling and studying, when there were no more weeds in his yard and when his neighbors' lawnmowers were all running perfectly, he did volunteer work for the Girl Scouts, the Red Cross, the United Fund and other charities.

Several days a week he worked as an unpaid multilin-

gual receptionist at the Spanish Apostolate in the 200
block of East 25th Street. It made him feel good to help
others.[189]

Developmental Focus 2: Death Approaches Wilk

They were wonderful years, the best of his life, but
sometimes he heard an unsettling reminder of passing
time. Sometimes now he thought the teenagers looked at
him strangely, even speculatively, and he overheard one
say to another something about . . . about that "pitiful old
man and that pitiful old car . . ."

The words didn't make sense to Wilk. He was fine. He
was young . . . younger than they,[190] and not nearly so
ignorant. He felt fine, perfect, and the car started every
time without an instant's hesitation.[191]

The year he turned 70 he got a letter from the Gerontology Research Center at City Hospitals. The GRC, the
letter head explained, was an arm of the National Institutes
of Health located at City Hospitals in Baltimore.

The scientists at the center were looking for healthy old
men they could study. They were trying to find out, they
explained to Wilk, why old age was a misery for some
people and a pleasure for others.

In terms of basic science they were also trying to determine the biochemical basis of the aging process—something
that might, in theory, be isolated and identified in people
like Wilk.

Wilk agreed to cooperate and spent several days in the
hospital while the scientists examined him in painstaking
detail. He no longer had the physique of a laborer but, for
a man of 70, he was physically perfect. The doctors were
astonished.

Wilk wasn't though; sure, he was in perfect health. He
could have told them that.

There was an awkward moment, however, when the
psychiatrist asked him where he'd been in his lifetime.

Wilk couldn't remember all the places . . . Argentina, Austria, Belgium, Brazil . . . Ghana, Gibraltar, Greece . . . Panama, Paraguay, Peru, Poland . . . and finally Uruguay, Venezuela and the Virgin Islands. There were 56 in all.

His memory?

Well, he admitted to being a little absent-minded, always had been. And sometimes he forgot some perfectly obvious Russian phrase, or some word in one of his other languages . . .

The psychiatrist stared at Wilk.

Six languages and still learning more at age 70?

Obviously, the old man's brain was fine.

The news from the gerontology center was nothing but good, but the doctors' interest in his combination of good health and old age bore an unmistakable message. And, when he was working outside, the stares of passing children sent a cold wind blowing through Wilk's mind.

He was getting old.

No, he wasn't.

He couldn't be.

He felt just like he always had. He was just as bright, just as curious, just as filled with the lust to learn. And yet what it all meant was that he was going to . . .[192]

He didn't like the word "die." "Passed," was far preferable. But "passed . . ."

Wilk had always gone to church, and hoped that there was an afterlife. He hoped, but it didn't seem very likely. Still, the concept of "God" was helpful here. At 70, anytime . . .[193]

The words that came were, "At 70, the man upstairs might pull your ticket anytime."

And he left it at that, in favor of Spanish, German . . . Italian.[194]

Italian was a new love. Italian was springtime and romantic youth, the youth the old man felt in his bones when he was supposed to be feeling the icy presence of death.[195]

Year followed year, and the Chevy grew older. The

people at the Motor Vehicle Administration told him he could buy historic tags for it, if he liked. It was an antique.

An antique! That was fascinating.

Wilk looked at the car and yes, it was old, but it was well cared for. It'd carry him many a mile yet.

Sometimes, in his late 70s, Wilk's memory started to slip.

His wife Geneva thought he was getting a little deaf, but he denied it. He could hear the roar of a climbing airplane, hear the sounds of Peruvian children, hear the perfectly-timed engine of the antique Chevy.

But the teenagers, now, began to seriously concern Wilk.

They seemed like a new group of people, alien almost, heads full of judgment but empty of wisdom. He saw them pointing at him and the old car, and heard their laughter. It made him uneasy.

He installed heavier locks on all the doors.

Finally one year the doctors at the gerontology center found a break in the armor of health. Wilk had diabetes, and it was serious enough to treat. It could be controlled, but he had to be careful about what he ate.

It was a small thing, but sobering.

If he had to eat special food, that severely circumscribed his ability to live off the land, restricted him to relatively civilized countries.[196] Still, there were plenty of modernized countries to choose from, and there was no use worrying about it.[197]

A joint condition, which he'd had since he was a young man, flared up.

Developmental Focus 3: Wilk Looks Forward

It was ironic. Each day he knew still more about Russian and small engines, more about Germany, Uruguay, Senegal . . . real knowledge sometimes seemed almost within his grasp . . .

But each day that he grew less ignorant he also grew weaker. With advancing age he was increasingly vulnerable to influenza, common colds, and dietary imbalances.

He turned 80, 81, 82 . . . He lived on, as did his Geneva, in the little house on The Alameda.

It was too late now, in 1982, for the dreamed-of trip around the world, too late to safely explore disease-ridden India.

But it was not yet over. It was not too late for . . . where? It was a big decision.

Italy.

So 1982 was the year he took out the Italian books, and started studying.

Learning was definitely more difficult now . . . the words kept slipping away, getting wiped off the blackboard before they could be committed to long-term memory. He sat at his desk, forcing his mind to concentrate, to digest.

There was a break in the routine when one day a letter arrived from Prairie View A & M College in Texas, his alma mater. The college leadership wanted Wilk to be the convocation speaker during homecoming in November.[198]

It was a singular honor, and Wilk laid aside his Italian books to write his speech. He wanted to do it justice.

It was difficult going. He knew many languages, but they were just words, all equally useless when it came time to speak from the heart.

You had to keep on keeping on, that was all.[199]

But how could he tell that to an audience of young students who would never know what it was like to walk behind a mule, to sit in the back of the bus? He thought of the teenagers, who knew too little to comprehend their own ignorance.

Wilk still didn't feel old, not even at 82, but writing the speech dredged up memories and made him think of all the years of learning that came after graduation. And he found, as he searched for honest words, an anger he hadn't known was there.

He was tired, sick and tired, of the complaining he heard around him.[200]

Finally, in November, he stood before the audience.

He told them his story and then, searching for a way to make the lesson real, he told them a parable about a black couple. The couple lost everything they had because of drinking and poor management, but they complained all the time that "whitey" was to blame.

Racism is a fact, he said.

But so is courage.

And then, borrowing the words of James Ephraim McGirt, he read them an old poem:

> *Success is a light upon the farther shore,*
>   *That shines in dazzling splendor to the eye,*
> *The waters leap, the surging billows roar,*
>   *And he who seeks the prize must leap and try.*
>
> *A mighty host stand trembling on the brink,*
>   *With anxious eyes they yearn to reach the goal.*
> *I see them leap, and, ah! I see them sink—*
>   *As gazing on dread horror fills my soul.*
>
> *Yet to despair I can but droop and die,*
>   *'Tis better far to try the lashing deep.*
> *I much prefer beneath the surge to lie,*
>   *Than death to find me on this bank asleep.*

After the clapping and the handshaking was over, Old Man Peters went home to Baltimore, to his red brick rowhouse with steel mesh on the windows, behind the double-locked doors, and he sent off letters inquiring about a small apartment in Rome. When they were written he opened his Italian book.[201]

Major Resolution: Wilk Defeats Death

Late into the autumn he sat at his desk, studying the language of Dante, absorbing the words with the undiminished intensity of a desperate black boy, born in the year 1900, angrily beating back the ignorance.

Each day Wilk forced a few more words into his mind, adding them to the tens of thousands already there, accumulated through a life of study. Each day the new words fitted in with the old, and he felt a little more comfortable with Italian, and with the world.

The man upstairs might have pulled Wilk's card at any time, but He stayed His hand.

On December 1, the Chevy safely up on blocks, Old Man Peters kissed his wife goodbye and flew to Rome.

Annotations: The Ballad of Old Man Peters

1. Originally published as a five-part series in *The Evening Sun* beginning January 31, 1983. Published in condensed form in *Reader's Digest* in January 1984.
2. In the first sentence we have Old Man Peters fighting for more knowledge. From the very beginning the reader gets the perception that the conflict in this story is man against ignorance.
3. This is a story about a man who faces the end of his life secure in the knowledge that he has fought the good fight.
4. Here we say he is a brave man, and we also imply that he's brave because the circumstances of his life require courage.
5. This tells the reader something about Old Man Peters. He is wise as well as brave.
6. Wilk is embattled. It will turn out, later, that he has always been embattled. Note that the image of locks is a classic one.
7. This image strengthens the contrast between ignorance and intelligence, and sets up the focuses below in which Wilk will appear as a poor teenager himself. One of the strengths of this story is what it says about poor teenagers, and what

they can do if they can find, in themselves, the courage of an Old Man Peters.

8. This is a classic major flashback, carrying the reader back from the complication to the story's beginning. From this point on, the narrative is chronological.

9. Here we hint that what Old Man Peters seeks is breadth.

10. But this, we are saying, is a myth. Many would have said he was finished seventy years ago . . . but, thanks to his strength of character, he wasn't.

11. Here again we have a sense of urgency. The reader assumes it's because Wilk has much to do before he sleeps, which is true enough. But, as will be discovered later, this urgency is one of the protagonist's strongest character traits.

12. Here we get the first specific information on the means by which our character gropes to understand the world.

13. The perspective here, of age and wisdom, is important. So it gets brought up several times. Repeatedly evoking an image is much more effective than bringing it up—writing a paragraph on it, and then, having dealt with it, forgetting it.

    Though an outline is constructed with one focus on top of another, the creation of narrative from that outline is essentially a weaving process. As in life, important images (which recall the "threads" of the story) appear, disappear, and reappear later.

14. By quoting actuaries, the narrative emphasizes the coldness of death and, by contrast, highlights the warmth of the "black male." This works because, for the reader, Wilk has already ceased to become a statistic. He is a human being.

15. And the reader is reminded that it is a big world, far bigger than the little house with its locks. We have a major transition with flashback coming, and it pays to foreshadow such things. This minimizes the shock and minimizes the reader's natural instinct to put the story down rather than reorienting himself.

16. Fighting on, heroically, in the fading light.

17. This foreshadows the concept of "library," which will become very important later in the narrative. But more important it brings in the question of memory, and looking back . . .

    The coming transition is a lulu, and I wanted the reader to be as prepared as possible to make it.

18. Fighting, stubbornly, keeping his eye forever on a bright dream of the future . . .

19. The preceding five words begins our transition. "But" is a transition word in itself. The fact that he needs no notes tells us that what the reader is about to see is important. It also hints, since old people never have trouble remembering the past, that we are going into a major flashback.

20. . . . .we are going *way* back . . .

21. There. The key word is uttered, the lock begins to open.

22. In this paragraph the narrative tells the reader what to expect. This allows him to approach what's coming with a prepared mind. It serves the same function as a National Park Service sign that says "Scenic Views Next Five Miles."

23. We flash back here, with a static verb, to minimize the blow.

24. Place transition.

25. Quickly, before the reader gets lost, the scene becomes real. The old scene, in the house in Baltimore, fades and is replaced by the beginnings of a new one. But the old scene, with its dangers, dreams and locks, will find analogies in the new one. We are in a different movement, but the symphony is the same.

26. Cotton and Southern blacks have a pre-formed connection in the reader's mind, and in this story we want to use that.

27. Danger! Wilk is black.

28. As the previous Baltimore scene, with its angry, roving teenagers, is ruled by prejudice against the aged.

29. Opening action. As in: "Once, long, long ago, in a galaxy far away . . ."

30. Wilk's first image was of work in the fields; we say this concretely to emphasize it.

31. His siblings, being less important, get introduced with a static verb.

32. Restlessly searching for happiness.

33. There dreams were always betrayed. The important thing here is that the narrative *shows* these footnoted messages, as opposed to just telling them.

34. He was, in short, a serf.

35. But this time, since I want to drive this image home with a large hammer, so that it can't be missed, I *do* state it . . . but only after having shown it.

    The reason it's so important, of course, is that this is the overall complication of the piece. Serfdom is the general nature of the enemy. The narrative will get increasingly specific about this later.

36. The solution, as first visualized by Wilk. School brings him the following images.

37. Note that the panorama created in the last few paragraphs accomplishes a number of purposes. Like the truck in the opening focus, it reminds us that there's a larger world. And it tells us that Wilk, even at this age, finds that to be of overwhelming importance.

38. A very weak word. Primary emotions should be shown, if possible.

39 . . . . so I back up that weak word, "liked," with a very active image of a word "sliding along the tongue."

40. The dream of a larger world meets language, which will become Wilk's route of access.

41. Lust is *basic*.

42. He wants to escape the life fate has dumped him into.

43. This is mentioned because, while they can't give their son Wilk very much, this perception will prove to be a gift of immeasurable value.

44. This is one of the few ways that a writer can express himself in a story. I personally believe this to be true, which is probably why the Wilk Peters story attracted me.

45. A perception, arrived at in ignorance, that will serve as a minor complication below. Wilk will have to reevaluate this ambition later, at great emotional expense, and it will make him realize his father's ignorance.

46. But, mistaken or not, the ambition did what father John had hoped it would do.

47. Which will turn out not to be glowering teenagers, or red-faced KKK-ers, but something far more formidable: ignorance.

48. I'm working hard here to re-create, in some detail, a scene that Wilk only dimly remembers. So I have to stick with universal actions, like daydreaming, which I can be certain most of the other students did. It is a supposition that his classmates daydreamed, but it's simple to defend.

49. Note the strong verbs—matadors "challenge" and boatmen "pole"—and how they force the narrative to center on images.

50. When you need an example, make it apply widely to your story. I could as well have used the South American rhinoceros beetle, but it would have had a different implication. Here I have Wilk struggling in his small little world, and the South American rhinoceros beetle would have evoked the "big world" image—just the opposite of what I wanted here.

The point is that a thread, once adequately established, will leap to the reader's mind with a single word. If you don't want the reader's mind to leap, *don't use that word!*

51. Remember how he wasn't afraid of the glowering teenagers, above . . . but he was prudent.

52. This is actually a transition that moves the reader further through time. Notice that we proceed in fits and starts. We move to a new time and then stop to tell a story of what happened during that time. Then we move on.

53. Having painted Wilk and his family as desperately poor, the narrative now has to say that life wasn't all bad. The reason is that things are going to get *really* bad later, so the reader has to learn to make distinctions between levels of poverty.

54. Here the narrative sets up love and togetherness as the strength of the family. This, of course, immediately becomes something that can be lost and thus a complication is set up. Will Wilk's family lose what little it has?

55. Aside from the doubtful way I have introduced this solution to Wilk's problem (by characterizing it as an ''innocent hope''), it nevertheless functions as a resolution. If Wilk becomes a physician, his money, ignorance and status problems should be solved.

But in the next paragraph we are going to introduce a new complication that will come between Wilk and his dream of becoming a physician.

This is typical of the saga form, in which an episode often ends with the promise of a resolution . . . a promise immediately broken by the rise of a new complication that prevents the resolution from taking place.

Then the story ends, leaving the protagonist standing in the rubble of his hopes.

This is designed to leave a question hanging in the reader's mind, so that he'll come back to the saga in tomorrow's newspaper.

56. This introduces the secondary complication.

57. Note that following the introduction of the new complication (the father's illness), the narrative deals with the whole family. The most vivid part of the complication will come when the narrative narrows, at the end, to Wilk and his shattered dream.

58. Now there is *real* poverty.

59. Now the narrative narrows to Wilk. Note that it does so with an action verb.

60. The dream is gone.
61. Notice how this plays on the several earlier images of the widening world, and France, and Mexico, and the boatmen of Venice.
62. But Wilk won't relinquish the one gift his father gave him.
63. Saga episodes traditionally begin with a summing up of previous action at the beginning of each focus, so that the reader may be subtly reoriented toward what's coming. This is especially important when they are to be published, as this story was, over a period of several days.

    Even the reader who read yesterday's episode will have forgotten the thread of the story. Ideally, in a situation such as a newspaper series, a summary action lead of this type will allow the first-time reader to pick up the narrative in mid-story.
64. This was hinted at in the first episode, but it's spelled out here because it will be very important to the action of this episode.
65. Like any boy under such circumstances, he misses his father desperately. In his need he finds his father still lives on in his mind.
66. Note how this echoes the use of the boll weevil as an example of an insect in episode 1 above.
67. Whap, bang, without foreshadowing, a brick wall for the reader. Little sister? The reader knew he had one, but until now she wasn't important. Suddenly, the story takes a new turn.

    Foreshadowing was not necessary here because we stay inside Wilk's psyche, even though we're talking about his sister. The brick wall effect is workable in this instance because that's precisely how it strikes Wilk, too.
68. Note how Wilk's viewpoint is only partly concerned with his sister. He's also concerned with his own fate.
69. Even doctors are plagued by ignorance.
70. This is the nadir of their existence.

    Or, on second thought, dear reader, read on. Things can always get worse.
71. This graf makes the father sound good. It needs to, since the reader needs to know why Wilk's mother, in her desperation, jumped at the chance.
72. But Wilk knew that all was not well. Therefore, so does the reader.
73. The verbs here are very strong because they need to drive home the hard labor in the turpentine forests.

74. This reflects the preacher's attitude.
75. In cinema this effect might be accomplished by a picture of Wilk working in the turpentine forests as a calendar, super-imposed over the picture, flipped from year to year. It is a time transition to the next focus.
76. Note how this echoes, and draws strength from, the earlier scene in which he stood at his father's grave.
77. Still another time transition.
78. The stepfather hadn't been brought up for a bit and, since he is never much of a three-dimensional character, his existence must be reinforced.
79. This is a pretty broad view for a man so young and with experiences so narrow. It foreshadows something about Wilk and tells the reader that the boy's dream, however distorted, still lives.
80. Note the double meaning here. These sorts of things, Freud-ian psychiatrists believe, have real impact on the subcon-scious.
81. Firsts are often dramatically important. In this case, the fact that it was the first time in his life makes him seem especially vulnerable.
82. The age of adulthood for black men in those days. But was he an adult? Or was he a child, cast among wolves? That question will be answered immediately.
83. It isn't really dead, though, just moribund. The purpose here, though, is to add to the boy's loneliness. He no longer seems to have even the one thing his father gave him.
84. This is the first appearance of a theme that will develop, as the story proceeds, into the "keep on keepin' on" of his life philosophy.
85. It was a place where minds don't count. This is sinister for Wilk, who wants terribly to have a mind that counts.
86. It was a place without a past or a future, a place where nothing mattered and everything summed up to zero. Wilk is truly lost in the intellectual wilderness.
87. But it's all in the eye of the beholder. The active mind, this shows, is capable of finding newness anywhere.
88. Note the use of concrete and often-active detail to build atmosphere.
89. He thinks he's lost the dream, but he's quick to notice the realities of the mind. This foreshadows that the dream is not really gone, after all.
90. The reader understands the intellectual squalor that this tiny religious college must represent. That contrasts sharply with

Wilk's vision of it. This is the strength of the boy's character: His dreams are everlasting, his hope is eternal.

91. This says it wasn't easy.

92. But Wilk automatically chooses to see the possibility of success and discount the failure of others. This is innocence and stupidity, of course . . . but those are the underpinnings of his courage. It doesn't occur to him yet that he doesn't have a prayer.

     Note that this is implied merely from point of view. That is, the narrative follows Wilk's thought processes and examines the possibilities of achievement before coming around to the likelihood of failure.

93. Aha! It wasn't dead at all!

94. Now, as it occurs to him, we face the failure.

95. He asks the *why* questions right away. This, also, is a strength of his character.

96. This graf illustrates how others, more mature and rational than Wilk, looked at the problem.

97. This is where Wilk recognizes something that has been foreshadowed earlier—he's special. But the mechanism of his specialness isn't tangible; it's his adamant refusal to recognize the odds against him.

98. The big world he craves is characterized, now, by people who *know* things. Wilk's dream is now beginning to refocus itself; he wants to be a doctor still, but this is the first step in realizing that "being a physician" was only his father's symbol for *knowing something*.

99. Though foreshadowed by his tendency to cling to his dream despite his father's death, this is the first time Wilk looks directly at the river of life and consciously resolves to swim against the current.

100. This shows he was not selfish, which otherwise might become a question in his mind. He is, after all, struggling to leave his class. The reader automatically asks the question whether he will forget his family as well. This tells them he won't.

101. Money, of course, is fundamental to Wilk's dilemma. Notice how the act of separating it into three stacks intensifies the starkness of his poverty.

     This is not something, incidentally, that the writer pulls out of thin air. This stacking of money represented Wilk's resolution to *make it work* and, as such, symbolized an incredibly dramatic turning point in Wilk's life. He remembered it with crystal clarity, and in infinite detail.

The general point is that people tend to remember what was important. Certain South American hunting and gathering tribes, who eke a living out of a hostile environment, have dozens of words to describe the distinctly different sensations of hunger. That tells the writer, even if he didn't know already, that hunger is a theme in their lives.

Anytime you think you have a dramatic turning point of a story, but the subject can't remember enough details for you to create a scene, then . . . you are dead wrong. The scene should not be written, and you have misanalyzed the story.

102. This is the first time in the story that the dream has been expressed in terms of hard reality.

103. This is patently obvious, of course. The reader does not need the writer to tell him this. But what I'm *showing* is something quite different. I'm dramatizing the slowness with which pennies collect.

104. New status brings new worries.

105. This further dramatizes the importance of the dream.

106. Time transition.

107. Note how time transitions are often followed by a summary of the new psychological situation.

108. Our hero has, up to this point, had his life changed many times by outside circumstances and tragedy. But this time he has changed as a result of his own mental actions—his resolve to go to school. It is, as a result, an important and dramatic turning point in the story.

That's why it's appropriate to go on at some length about music, which will not play a large role in the story otherwise.

109. Already his dream has brought him a new life, and he's very conservative with it. Notice how his conservatism reverberates with the images above that he is a prudent man. In this pivotal segment of the story the reader is seeing the first expression of that attribute.

110. In the face of the dream, he can turn his back on interests of the moment. He is willing to focus his ambitions.

111. It's very important on this critical issue to have numbers. I'd have preferred an exact number, but Wilk could remember only that it was "pretty near $300."

112. From Wilk's point of view, this man was a giant.

113. I echoed the music here to get the maximum impact from even the most insignificant image. I would have liked to elaborate a bit on the church in this scene, but Wilk had

little memory of it. His attention, at the time, was focused on the minister.

114. Thus the complication, which was the hanging question of whether or not Wilk could go to college, is resolved. So the question arises: Where is the subsequent complication that will bring the reader back the next day?

The anwer is that it was embedded in the story earlier, in the high failure rate—and reemphasized by the minister's hesitation. Everything rational says Wilk can't make it . . . the town knows it, the minister knows it, and the reader knows it. Wilk, however, is ignorant of his hopelessness.

Will he make it?

That complication is so strong, and so clear, that it doesn't need to be stated explicitly.

115. This noun form, "take-aways," evokes the reader's memory of elementary school and emphasizes Wilk's innocence much better than the word "subtraction" would have.

116. Here we're reemphasizing the hopelessness of Wilk's situation. The bigger the problem, remember, the greater the heroism of the one who overcomes it. Make certain your reader always remembers the magnitude of the complication.

117. The ignobility of Wilk's position, hinted at before, becomes very important here. How many people could absorb such an ego blow and yet still cling, stubbornly, to an impossible dream?

118. Again we have Wilk's stubborn, positive attitude coming through.

119. Notice here that three examples are used. To repeat, one example is a contention, two is an argument and three is truth.

120. Others say there is no future for Wilk, but Wilk sets immediate goals and works stubbornly toward them.

121. This was, in fact, foreshadowed in his fear that someone might steal the money he was saving for college.

122. Having faced the fear, he recognizes that fear itself is his enemy.

123. And in his simple, stubborn way he solves the courage problem with the only strategy he knows he can trust. He resolves to work harder.

124. And now, in reality, his world really *does* begin to expand. He finally begins to reap some rewards.

125. This, being pivotal, justifies some descriptive poetry from Wilk's point of view.

126. Character introduction. Normally characters can't be introduced, without foreshadowing, this late in the story. But the rule is less stringent in the case of sagas.

127. This implies that she sees the value in Wilk (the first one to do so) and that she will step into the action in the future.

128. In a story that covers many decades, the writer must frequently use the "More years passed" time transitions from focus to focus. To keep this from being repetitious, add details that will crystallize the emotional nature of those years.

129. This is an important juncture in the story since it's here, for the first time, that the dream actually begins to support itself. In his search for knowledge, Wilk finds, knowledge will sustain him.

130. Nor, if the writer has anything to say about it, will the reader. This is the "moral" of the Wilk Peters story.

131. He'd already begun to change, but now we're focusing the reader's attention squarely on that fact.

132. The writer mustn't forget, ever, that a good story is one in which the character changes. Therefore, character changes are high points of a story and must be handled with care and thoroughness.

133. I don't want anybody to miss this, so I'm not subtle. The prudent writer often makes major thematic points with a large hammer. Beginners, forgetting that the reader will not examine the story as minutely as he, are often too subtle about such things.

134. This is a major break-point in the character development.

135. Notice how the dream is now shifting back to his childhood fantasies, and how the same type of images are being used.

136. Romance is always a pivotal complication in one's life, and must not be ignored in the profile.

   But from the writer's point of view, in this instance the appearance of the girl is especially important for very pragmatic, unromantic reasons.

   We're just about to resolve this episode's major complication by making it clear that Wilk will, in fact, graduate from college. As we document his success, this can hardly be kept from the reader.

   This, though, will happen some paragraphs before another, interlinking complication can be put in place.

   For a short period of the story, in other words, the only tension available will come via Wilk's yearning for the girl. That's the only open question. Technically, it's a scary situation.

137. This presents a danger. Will she turn his head away from his dream?

138. No, he won't. Not now, at least. But another type of yearning has been introduced to the story.

139. This says he's over the hump and implies a resolution. This is a very fragile part of the story, since the only source of tension now is the unresolved yearnings for the girl.

140. This section has to be very fast, active and rich. There's not much tension in the story, and if the reader's mind wanders he'll put the story down and never come back.

141. I need activity here, and growth is very active. Therefore, the shrinking of the campus is very important here; I spent a lot of time putting this paragraph together.

142. That's the only outstanding complication we've got, now, and I make the most of it.

143. Whew! Finally, we have another complication. All is not going to be roses after all and the ice we've been treading on grows a little thicker and safer.

144. The medical-school dream is dead, Wilk isn't willing to put it down yet, though, because he hasn't yet accepted that it's nothing but a metaphor. Also, it is all he has left of his father.

145. Note how rapidly Wilk, whose self-esteem was so low just a few paragraphs back, is growing complacent and egotistical? Will he be destroyed by hubris?

   So it is that another complication, a minor one, is imposed over the others. In terms of tension, we're out of the woods now.

146. All is relative. This isn't nearly as humble an occupation as shoveling coal.

147. This keeps the tension alive. One never has too much tension.

148. Here's where the hubris complication, carefully planted before, explodes into the story as a real force. Wilk has learned what he can do; now he is about to learn, anew, what he can't.

149. Notice that this is another way of saying he was stunned, only it shows rather than tells. The reason he can't believe is that he desperately doesn't want to lose the hard-won image of himself as being the man who can do anything he decides to do.

150. This is the first specific, active sign that Geneva cares about Wilk. As such, it foreshadows their romance and marriage. The reader reads this with a certain sense of relief, and the tension falls.

151. The reason Wilk remembered this metaphor for a half-century is that it meshed so well with what he, himself, believed.

152. And we end, as we must with each saga episode, with a complication.

153. We begin by stressing the complication.

154. Remember how we foreshadowed the library, earlier? It was sacred, like a church. And a church is a place one goes when hurt, frightened, and in need of comfort.

155. He's still smarting from the comeuppance he got at the end of the previous episode.

    It's important to note here that this complication is rather universal. The student begins junior high, for instance, as a mere freshman. Over the years he becomes a sophomore, and then a junior, and learns to look down on the freshman. Then he is a senior and BMOC . . . and then whammo, he's a freshman in high school and he has to start all over.

    It's no different with Wilk except that his situation is more heroic.

    The point is that the writer should not overlook common and easily understood pivotal points on the grounds that they're universal. They are not clichés; they will assume a different shape with each character.

156. Remember her? She's the woman who watched Wilk so thoughtfully years before. The fact that she was foreshadowed makes it seem natural for her to appear and play a role now, so late in the story.

157. Notice how what occurred in one context before (Wilk's love for books) suddenly appears in a wholly different context now, as a possible answer to Wilk's lack of direction.

158. Now, a college graduate, he finally understands the nature of his father's gift.

159. So does the complication that was keeping the tension up. Here we enter another period of relatively low tension. We still have the girl, of course, but . . .

160. And now we don't even have the girl.

    We are now entering a period in our story when the literary tension is the least powerful.

    Not that we don't have tension; we do. Wilk's hubris gone now, he's still ignorant by his own standards.

    Early in the story that would probably be too academic to sustain reader interest, but at this juncture the writer has something else . . . a very powerful something else . . .

going for him. The reader, by now, loves and admires Wilk. This, combined with the rapid pace of the narrative to this point, will propel us over the next few paragraphs while we exhume our original complication (ignorance), give it a new thrust (language), and place it back in the context that it was in when Wilk was a child.

The lust to *know* has been an integral part of Wilk's character all along, but now it becomes the emotion that powers the story.

161. The reader will read this section with the sense of relief that one has at the ending of the story. Most of the complications are solved, save for the one having to do with Wilk's lust for the world.

But that was a long time back, in the first and second episodes. It behooves us, now, to rekindle that one as quickly as possible.

162. A bit of tension rises here, with the question of what will happen to him when he leaves Texas. But it will die quickly.

163. This begins the process of reviving and rendering immediate the old complication concerning Wilk's desire to know the world.

164. And we have, now, another major complication.

165. Now Wilk defines his own complication. He identifies ignorance of language as a barrier to knowledge. He knows too few languages. Therefore, he's ignorant. Therefore, he must learn languages.

166. But it didn't fulfill his need to travel.

167. But, once again, he will make a silk purse out of a sow's ear.

168. And this complication builds.

169. We are now reviving the complication first presented at his graduation, when he was asked what *else* could he do and he had to answer, "Nothing."

170. We have now begun a period in this story where we're showing how Wilk, still in his heart a black Texas sharecropper, applies his childhood values to new problems.

171. It is characteristic of him that he never does anything in moderation.

172. Compare his image with the image of the poor black Texas serf and you can see how far this story has come.

173. Our final and most important complication is now fully formed.

174. Contrast, again, with his humble beginnings. As a result of

Wilk's efforts, coupled with the passage of time, the world is beginning to change around him.

The complications are really beginning to build again, now, as we near the resolution of the story. Wilk is now beginning to age, and we begin to see a hint of the man who, at age eighty-two, will sit behind locked doors and concentrate his mind on the study of Italian.

Will his values serve him still?

And *that* is turning out to be the story's major complication.

175. He has always refused to accept negative facts. So far, this has allowed him to overcome them. But can he overcome the dragging-down process of age itself?

176. Complication again. For it to have its impact at the end, it must begin coming up now again and again, rhythmically.

Notice also that, at this point, a marked contrast has developed between Wilk's daily life and his dream. His life has now taken on that quiet desperation that characterizes the working person. Can he overcome that, too?

177. He is growing old. He hesitates, now, where once he would have leaped.

178. And with this, he is carried back to the enthusiasm of childhood.

179. See, dear reader. He is aging, but *he is not growing old!*

180. This is the final intermediate complication.

181. At first glance this seems to resolve the complication immediately above. But it does so in only a very general way and leaves unanswered the specific question, so important to Wilk, of how it will all work out.

It also leaves open the question of how Wilk's values will help him cope with age and the specter he's so far totally ignored: death.

182. He looks at the bright side of everything, still. But will that view be borne out?

183. This Chevy is about to become our last major symbol.

184. All that came before was calculated to dovetail in this last episode. Note here how Wilk's attitude toward the car fits into the strategies he's used throughout his life. He is a no-frills man.

185. A vintage model, well cared for.

186. And his optimistic, enthusiastic approach pays him dividends even when there's no specific goal.

187. He remains active.

188. His life remains beautiful and constructive.

189. He is being rewarded for his perseverance—his reward is the highest of all, to help others.
190. Now we're summing up the lessons of Wilk Peters' life.
191. Note the juxtaposition of his health and the car's.
192. Notice how he is attempting to reject age the same way he rejected ignorance.
193. But to refuse to accept the obvious would be, in itself, a form of ignorance. Wilk could not abide that.
194. But he was wise enough not to dwell on it.
195. The resolution is beginning to clarify, now. Wilk's approach to life could keep him healthy in his body and young in his mind, but it couldn't stop the clock from ticking.

    But it could provide the courage to deal with whatever was to come . . . and, in the meantime, to live life as he damned well intended to live it.
196. The world is beginning to close in around Wilk, now.
197. But he wouldn't dwell on what he'd lost. He would, instead, enjoy what was left.
198. This plays a large role in the story because it allows a summation.
199. Notice how, in the ending, images planted throughout the story begin to crystallize. In a sense, it can be said that the purpose of a story is to foreshadow its ending.
200. He comes to understand, in his final years, the reality of his own heroism. But he can't see it as heroism.
201. And we have made the narrative loop. We are now back at the beginning of the story.